OnTime/OnBudget

A Step-by-Step Guide for Managing Any Project

Sunny Baker & Kim Baker

PRENTICE HALL
Englewood Cliffs, New Jersey 07632

Prentice-Hall International (UK) Limited, *London*
Prentice-Hall of Australia Pty. Limited, *Sydney*
Prentice-Hall Canada, Inc., *Toronto*
Prentice-Hall Hispanoamericana, S.A., *Mexico*
Prentice-Hall of India Private Limited, *New Delhi*
Prentice-Hall of Japan, Inc., *Tokyo*
Simon & Schuster Asia Pte. Ltd., *Singapore*
Editora Prentice-Hall do Brasil, Ltda., *Rio de Janeiro*

10 9 8 7 6 5 4 3 2 1

Library of Congress Cataloging-in-Publication Data

Baker, Sunny.
   On time/on budget : a step-by-step guide for managing any project
/ by Sunny Baker & Kim Baker.
     p.   cm.
Includes bibliographical references (p.   ) and index.
ISBN 0-13-633447-4
   1. Time management.   I. Baker, Kim.   II. Title.
HD69.T54B35   1992   92-12298
658.4′04—dc20   CIP

ISBN 0-13-633447-4

PRENTICE HALL
Professional Publishing
Englewood Cliffs, NJ 07632
Simon & Schuster. A Paramount Communications Company

PRINTED IN THE UNITED STATES OF AMERICA

DEDICATION

For those managers and businesspeople who struggle on, day in and day out, without clear goals and with inadequate plans, this book is dedicated to a better way of doing things.

ACKNOWLEDGMENTS

Many thanks to the software companies and management firms, listed in the *Useful Sources* section at the end of the book, for the information and products they provided to make this book complete.

Special thanks to Kim Commerato of Computer Associates, Sally Jacobs of POC-IT Management Services, Lenore Dowling of Scitor Corporation, and Nancy Stevenson of Symantec for their help in providing examples and sample plans illustrating the power of modern computerized project management tools.

To our students, clients, and professional colleagues, we acknowledge what we have learned from you over the years. It is our hope that this book reflects the best of your wisdom and insights.

INTRODUCTION:
The Power of Project Management in Business

Business is facing increasingly complex challenges. These include adapting to new technologies, managing rapidly expanding information sources, controlling escalating salaries, predicting limits on raw materials, assessing environmental impact, meeting stockholder demands, and dealing with pressures to remain cost-effective and competitive in a global economy. The cost reduction programs and management approaches of the past are not enough to meet the challenges. Companies need to employ techniques that streamline operations, reduce risks, and improve overall productivity. Project management techniques are one part of a solution to adapt and prosper.

Organizations of all sizes complete projects to meet their goals—whether opening a new sales office, implementing a training program, coordinating a fund-raising program, developing an advertising campaign for a new product, exhibiting at a trade show, or designing a new management information system. A project is simply a sequence of tasks performed to meet a defined goal and this makes almost every kind of business endeavor a project. And the underlying goal of projects in business is almost always the same: to get the defined work done on time and within budget.

Project management, a discipline rich with procedural tools and proven methods, has evolved for bringing projects in on time and within budget. Yet, many businesspeople have not been exposed to the power of project management techniques. When they do think of project management they envision the intricate charts and schedules for managing complex engineering projects, such as constructing bridges or building space shuttles. But project management is not only a discipline for scientists and engineers—it is a discipline for business.

The discipline of project management has predictable value in getting things done on time and within budget in any organization. These proven tools and techniques are commonly used by engineers and scientists in complex projects with huge budgets, thousands of tasks, and hundreds of people; but the power of project management is not limited to engineering and construction applications.

The techniques and advantages of project management concepts can be applied to any project in business. When managers use these techniques for their everyday responsibilities, they become more productive and successful in meeting business goals and objectives.

So what is it that makes project management different from management of the day-to-day activities in business? Why does the project manager in the satellite project regard the work as a project and other businesspeople think of their tasks as just plain work? Think of the tasks you have recently been responsible for. How many projects have you completed in the last year? The difference between your projects and those managed by project managers is only one of focus and technique. The project managers in engineering consider themselves project managers; businesspeople consider themselves managers of functions or enterprises.

Because of the engineering and scientific orientation of most project management texts and reference works, many businesspeople naively consider project management techniques more complicated than the actual projects—and for good reason. The unending jargon, indecipherable algorithms, labyrinthine planning diagrams, and lack of relevant business examples make project management seem too convoluted for a busy manager to employ in the everyday framework of business and industry. As the relevance of project management is not always apparent to business and academic professionals outside the engineering and scientific disciplines, missed deadlines and overrun budgets are more common than they need to be.

In *On Time/On Budget* we have sought to demystify the secrets behind successful project management and make the practical tools and techniques of the discipline available to the business audience at large. Project management principles should be considered a central component of every manager's education, applicable to all kinds of business projects. The project management approach to planning, scheduling, budgeting, and analysis can help any business improve output and results. Project management as a discipline starts with the basic management functions that most businesspeople are already familiar with: planning, organizing, staffing, directing, and controlling. Project management simply expands the manager's basic toolbox with a set of well-defined procedural methods and techniques specifically oriented to completing a sequence of tasks with a beginning and an end. Since most projects in business involve sequenced tasks—almost every business can benefit from the application of project management principles.

Whether it's training a team of new employees, creating an ad campaign, or reorganizing the corporation—the techniques of project management can be used to improve productivity and assure timely completion. Project management tools also can be used to correct midcourse problems that would otherwise go undetected and undermine the success of the project. Most of the project management techniques best used in business are the same ones applied by engineers to manage complex projects, but in *On Time/On Budget* they are presented so nonengineering managers can easily apply them to everyday projects.

We have attempted to present the project management toolbox for evaluating, managing, and troubleshooting projects of all sizes in a way that is both accessible and pertinent for all businesspeople. *On Time /On Budget* takes managers through real business projects from start to finish using project management charts, techniques, worksheets, and checklists—enabling businesspeople to improve their performance in meeting project goals and objectives almost immediately. Managers are shown how to use the power of project management methods to improve performance in meeting project goals and controlling costs in their own unique business endeavors. To put the power of project management methodology to work immediately, it is only necessary to follow the practical advice and step-by-step guidelines offered in *On Time/On Budget*.

The experience-based recommendations and realistic approaches for getting things done can be applied to a wide range of business endeavors. You'll be taken step by step through the fundamentals of planning, scheduling, tracking, and controlling the costs and resources of any project. The practical, easy-to-use checklists are applicable to the projects that people in sales, marketing, human resources, finance, and general management positions are responsible for—yet they are based on the same general, accepted methods employed by engineering project managers in building skyscrapers and satellites.

The book provides methods for answering the most common questions facing every manager responsible for completing projects:

- How can I best define the tasks that need to be done?
- How much work can be expected of each person on the project?
- How long should it take?
- How can I control cost overruns?
- Where is the project in danger of failure?
- What can be done to ensure satisfactory completion of overlapping tasks?
- Is my budget on track?
- How do I know if we're really on schedule?

Tips for recognizing common project pitfalls are clearly identified. Succinct advice for handling the myriad of project management "crises" that managers face in each stage of a project are provided as well. The book spells out how projects work, and how projects can be monitored and controlled for successful completion.

The principles and core concepts of the project management discipline are thoroughly covered, without clogging the presentation with needless theory, complicated mathematics, or excessive technical jargon. *On Time /On Budget* is targeted specifically to managers, business owners, and professionals new to project management in general, though it is also a thorough introduction to core project management principles for people who intend to go on to managing large-scale, people-intensive projects in government, science, and other industries.

Unlike traditional works on project management, with their unduly complicated charting systems and interminable technical jargon, the techniques provided can be used by *every* manager to enhance productivity, manage people and other resources effectively, and control project costs—skills that every business person must learn and use to be successful and remain competitive in the fast-paced, increasingly complex world of business.

TABLE OF CONTENTS

CHAPTER TWO

DEFINING THE PROJECT: PROVEN TECHNIQUES FOR SETTING CLEAR GOALS

CHAPTER THREE

IDENTIFYING THE WORK TO BE DONE: METHODS FOR DESCRIBING TASKS AND WORKFLOW

PUTTING PROJECT MANAGEMENT TO WORK: A Discipline for Making Things Happen On Time and On Budget

> *Problems are only opportunities in work clothes.*
> —Henry J. Kaiser

Imagine for a moment that you are a project manager at NASA responsible for the development of a new space vehicle that will transport the first astronauts to Mars. As the project manager you are responsible for planning the steps for building the vehicle; coordinating hundreds of people and countless suppliers; managing complex interrelationships between staff, vendors, and the government; establishing and monitoring budgets; and producing myriad reports. The project involves substantial risks in terms of time, technology, and money. Your ability to bring the project in as planned will affect both the reputation and future of NASA's space program. To reduce the risk involved, you are expected to be an expert in the use of special project management techniques and computerized tools to assure that the project gets done on time and within budget.

If you work in business in management or professional capacities you are probably responsible for projects as part of your job, just like a NASA project manager, but you probably don't think of yourself as a project manager. The fact is that people in every department and at every level in every business are responsible for projects. Maybe the projects aren't as large or technical as the NASA undertaking, but the projects are equally critical to the well-being of the enterprise.

If you answer yes to any of the questions that follow, then you are a project manager already:

- Are you responsible for tasks or goals with specific deadlines?
- Is there a budget for the work you must accomplish?
- Do you need to coordinate other people or resources to meet specific objectives?

Consider the personnel manager putting together a new performance evaluation system and the marketing communications specialist completing an advertising campaign. Then, there is the operations manager responsible for purchasing and installing a machine for automating the manufacturing process. How about the marketing manager responsible for introducing a new product to the world? Or what about the vice president of sales responsible for restructuring the sales force or the CEO who must merge a newly acquired company into the corporate structure? These people are all project managers, just like a project manager for the mission to Mars project, but they are seldom regarded as such.

These people, like you, are all responsible for objectives that involve multiple people and coordination of time and resources. The jobs all involve managing budgets. The tasks all have deadlines. All these business people need to reach defined goals, just like the NASA project manager, but few managers refer to their undertakings as projects, and fewer managers employ the discipline of project management. Yet these people are still expected to coordinate and integrate all the tasks to meet their goals, and without the benefit of project management techniques their projects are frequently late and often over budget.

The projects in business range from simple to complex, but regardless of duration or complexity, the project goal always sounds the same—finish the prescribed work *on time* and *within budget*. Yet these two phrases, "on time" and "within budget," cause seasoned managers to shake and sweat. While slowly advancing through the echelons of business, managers are forced to build on project failures and other experience to learn and understand how projects work and what causes late finishes and budget overruns—sometimes with serious career impact if the failures are expensive or frequent. Managers dread the responsibility and the risk. Since many lack exposure to the project management techniques that can help them get things done on time and within budget, they live in perpetual anxiety.

The responsibility that goes along with managing projects doesn't need to be stressful, however. The project management toolbox offers a structured approach for handling projects, one that makes them easier to control. Project management reduces the surprises and makes it possible to bring work in on time and within budget, even when large numbers of people are involved.

PROJECT MANAGEMENT IS A BUSINESS SKILL
FOR THE MODERN WORLD

The way companies are managed today is undergoing enormous change. Organizational hierarchy is under attack, with the command and control model of bureaucracy falling to an organizational form that is more horizontal than vertical. More managers find themselves managing "matrixed" teams, involving multiple departments and even multiple companies. Companies are running "leaner" than ever before, with fewer executives and middle managers. Decision making is being pushed down to the operational levels in organizations, and lower-echelon people are being given more autonomy for meeting specific objectives.

The project management toolbox for business includes manual and computerized processes that are directly applicable to improving performance and efficiency in today's lean, matrixed, objective-driven organizations. Project management techniques offer proven methods for working with these new organizational structures across traditional, functional, and organizational boundaries.

Projects are the building blocks used to meet enterprise objectives. Project management is now recognized as a management philosophy as well as a discipline. Project management offers a conceptual framework that contributes to meeting specific, strategic business goals. In fact, many of the techniques developed earlier for project management have begun to work their way into the general management literature—including team orientations, work breakdown structures, matrixed management, zero-based accounting, and more. These "modern" management concepts have evolved from the project management framework, but managers are just now discovering them as possible solutions to the productivity, organizational, and communications problems common to today's complex and ever-changing businesses.

Project management embodies new methods for restructuring management responsibilities. By adapting techniques for the express purpose of obtaining better control and increasing overall productivity, it is possible to center responsibility for work at the individual level. Thus, in a project-driven environment, work is managed and controlled by the people doing the work, not by a manager or executive two or three levels removed from the tasks. The modern business demands for reducing vertical hierarchy and minimizing the negative effects of autocratic boss-employee relationships are well served in the ability of project management to allow the progress of work to be clearly communicated and evaluated in a variety of diverse organizational structures.

Businesses must find new alternatives inside their organizations for increasing productivity and adapting their organizations to new technologies and competitive demands. Project management as a discipline is one of the richest sources of proven techniques for accomplishing these goals, allowing organizations to reduce the need for a strict hierarchical structure where everyone has a superior and an inferior. This empowers people to focus on specific goals. Project management responsibilities can cross organizational boundaries, and as a result, project management structures can be used to integrate diverse operations across an organization. People in project groups are able to assume responsibility and satisfaction for their own objectives, while continuing to contribute to the larger objectives of the organization as a whole.

THE HISTORICAL PERSPECTIVE ON PROJECT MANAGEMENT

One reason businesspeople lack project management skills, or are unaware of them, is that project management is mistakenly considered part of the engineering and scientific disciplines. Core principles of project management are not always taught in business schools, though project management courses are more common than they once were.

Project management as a discipline is a twentieth-century development. As technology increased in complexity in the twentieth century, techniques were required to keep the proliferation of scientific, military, and engineering projects on schedule and within budget. The first formal application of project management is often attributed to the techniques used to coordinate the Manhattan Project, which led to the development of the atomic bomb. This project was under tight deadlines and involved thousands of disparate resources. Techniques were required for planning, coordinating, and adapting the project plan to meet intense deadline pressures. The discipline of project management evolved to meet the challenge of delivering high-quality results in short time frames. After World War II, project management techniques were refined and adapted for uses in large-scale aerospace, military, and construction projects.

The project management discipline really took off in the 1960s when computer programs for project management were made commercially available. Twenty years ago, project management techniques were largely the concern of department of defense contractors and engineering project managers. Today, the tools of project management have been made accessible and appropriate for all kinds of business endeavors—including law, accounting, marketing, advertising, government, and more. So while it is true that project management techniques were originally developed around engineering, military, and scientific projects, it is not true that project management techniques are applicable only to large-scale projects in these disciplines. And, because many techniques have been tried, refined, and adapted over the last fifty years, businesspeople can now benefit from the failures in project management as well as the successes.

As a skeptic you may ask how massive projects like the pyramids in Egypt or even the Great Wall of China were completed without the aid of modern project management techniques. After all, your work gets done, eventually—and doesn't go over budget too often. Sure, just like the engineers in Egypt with thousands of slaves and unlimited resources at their disposal, it is still possible to get work done today without using proven project management techniques—it is just more difficult and more risky. But why work harder when you don't have to? That's not to say that project management techniques will make managing projects simple. Projects always involve people—and getting people to work together to accomplish defined goals is always complex. The techniques and discipline of project management just make it easier and secure more predictable results.

The successful, expedient completion of projects is required for organizations to survive and grow in the future. Therefore, a knowledge of project management principles is required for managers responsible for the projects to prosper in their careers. Knowing about project management is no longer optional; it is mandatory. The companies that survive the changes through the turn of the century will be those companies that are willing to adapt and adopt new technologies for improving performance, control, and quality, as well as job satisfaction and personal enrichment. Project management techniques should be the first on the list for adopting and adapting to meet these business goals. With the pressures on business to become more competitive, more efficient, and more adaptive, project management must be considered a primary business skill, not the discipline of engineers, but the realm of effective executives, managers, and business people in general.

The discipline of project management has advanced over the years to incorporate increasingly specialized algorithms, charting systems, and reporting procedures, but the core principles of project management are not complex. It is these core principles and techniques, which are covered in this book, that are most beneficial in controlling the majority of business projects. The core principles of project management as presented here can be applied to any project in business—no matter how small or large.

WHAT IS A PROJECT?

Before delving into the reasons project management methodology works to improve productivity and performance, it is important to understand how a project differs from other work. It may be hard to believe that a project for transporting astronauts to Mars has much in common with opening a new sales office in Richmond, but when viewed as projects, both these undertakings have similar attributes. Regardless of their size, both projects share structural similarities.

Project Management Buzzword

☛ **Project**—A project is a unique venture with a beginning and an end, undertaken by people to meet established goals with defined constraints of time, resources, and quality.

A project is usually a one-time undertaking with a well-defined set of desired end results, as opposed to a repetitive activity. In addition, most projects meet the following criteria:

- Involve sequenced activities or tasks that combine to achieve a specified goal
- Have a specific objective to be completed within certain quality or operational specifications.
- Have a defined start and end date

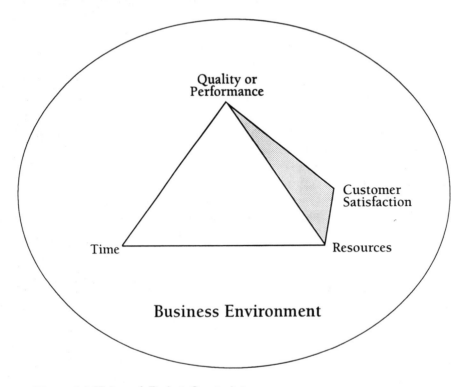

Figure 1-1 Universal Project Constraints

- Use people, money, and/or equipment (collectively called **resources** in project management terminology)
- Have a budget or other resource limitations
- Involve a group of people who temporarily work together to achieve a desired end result

Stated more simply, all projects are constrained or limited by three components: time, resources, and results. And, if a project is completed for a customer, a fourth universal constraint comes into play—customer satisfaction and positive customer relations. (See Figure 1-1.)

Activities that meet these criteria cover a wide range of possibilities and undertakings. So, if you consider the Mars mission and the sales office once again, both endeavors meet the criteria of being treated as projects.

Many business endeavors are projects, though they may not be called projects in most companies. For example, hiring a new marketing manager is a project that involves deadlines, people, money, and time. Developing a newsletter meets all the criteria of a project. Choosing and installing a new telephone system for corporate headquarters is a project for the same reasons. And there are major business projects such as developing a new model automobile, installing a new data processing system, or building an overseas manufacturing facility. The list of projects in business is endless, varying from small to massive and from simple to complex.

Projects and Subprojects

Individual projects are often part of larger projects and must be coordinated as subprojects to meet larger goals. As an example, consider a marketing manager in a computer company responsible for the introduction of a new portable, laptop computer. The superproject is the product's introduction and subprojects include developing the advertisements, coordinating a trade show, and managing the press tour in the United States and Europe. All individual subprojects must be controlled for the larger project, the product introduction, to be successful. If one of the subprojects is late or ineffective, it may affect the overall goal of the product introduction. To make the coordination even more complex, the product introduction itself is only one component in a much larger "sales development plan" that involves many other marketing and sales projects. Thus, projects are typically *interdependent* on the schedules and results of these other projects and activities.

People and Projects

Projects almost always involve new group structures. (See Figure 1-2.) It is rare that the same group of people works over and over again on projects.

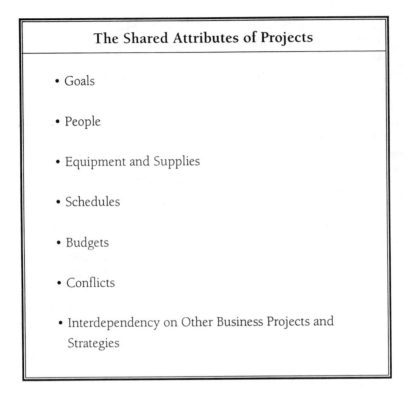

Figure 1-2 The Shared Attributes of All Projects

Projects usually bring a unique group of people together—groups of people who cross organizational, functional, and hierarchical responsibilities to work together to achieve a goal.

Another common project attribute related to dynamic group structures is conflict. Projects almost always incorporate built-in conflicts of priority, use of resources, roles of individuals, and allocation of budgets. For projects to be managed successfully, conflict must be controlled and managed so it does not interfere with the ultimate goals and results of the project.

Unique Project Attributes

Projects also have unique attributes. (See Figure 1-3.) No two projects, even with the same general end results, are ever identical. Project management offers techniques for identifying and managing this uniqueness. People who manage projects successfully learn to become managers of exceptions, because there are always plenty of surprises, even in small projects.

Even though the successful completion and coordination of projects is critical to the success of an organization overall, projects generally operate outside the normal routine of business life. For example, the administrative assistant to the CEO may be responsible for a project coordinating the company's annual United Way fund-raising drive, but this person is also responsible for such day-to-day activities as writing minutes of board meetings, scheduling appointments, screening mail, and attending to countless other recurring tasks. Most businesspeople need to coordinate their day-to-day routines in addition to managing projects. The goals and deadlines of the business routine are general. Routine work is defined within the scope of a department or functional job description. Projects are usually defined as specific end results outside of the routine job functions.

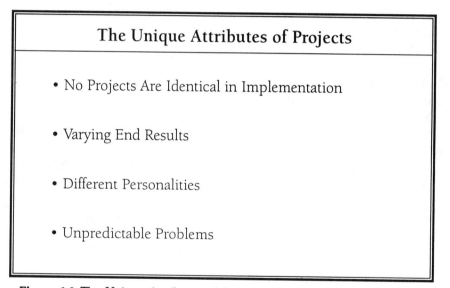

Figure 1-3 The Unique Attributes of Projects

There is one aspect of project management that separates businesspeople managing projects from full-time project managers responsible for major engineering or construction projects. For full-time project managers, the primary focus of the job is managing the project at hand. Thus, everything the full-time project manager does revolves around the planning, coordination, and monitoring of the project—but functional managers in business have responsibilities outside their project goals.

For example, the regional sales manager may be responsible for the project of opening that new sales office in Richmond, but this person is still responsible for contacting new customers, reviewing contracts, answering telephone calls, and answering questions from the salespeople. These activities constitute the daily routine and are separate from project activities. In some ways, this dual responsibility for project and enterprise management makes the employment of project management techniques even more vital to businesspeople, because it can make it easier for them to maintain control of projects with relatively minimum effort and still meet their other organizational and functional responsibilities.

One of the problems in introducing project management techniques into an organization is that the distinction between routine work and projects is not always clear. In order to take advantage of the benefits of project management techniques, projects must be identified as such. It requires a change of orientation to begin looking at work as a series or compilation of projects with defined goals, as opposed to just plain work.

WHY DO YOU NEED
PROJECT MANAGEMENT TECHNIQUES?

The reason for organizing an assignment as a project is to focus the responsibility, authority, and scheduling of the project in order to meet defined goals. Specifically, organizing work as a project allows a responsible person or small group of people to focus on schedules, define quality, identify problems, and make corrections in project work as it proceeds. Project management also provides techniques for making trade-offs between conflicting project goals and enterprise priorities.

Aside from experiencing better control and coordination, project management is often reported to reduce development time, lower costs, and generally produce higher-quality results—measured in better quality or higher profit margins. Other major benefits of project management techniques include the following:

- Clear descriptions of the work to be performed are provided to minimize surprises and conflicts.
- Responsibilities and assignments for specific tasks and activities are more easily identified.
- Tracking of functional responsibilities to ensure that all activities are accounted for, regardless of personnel turnover, is simplified.
- The need for continuous reporting is reduced.
- Time limits for task completion are more easily specified.
- Trade-off analysis for making project decisions is made possible.
- The measurement of accomplishment against plans is enabled.
- Problems are exposed in advance so corrective action may follow.
- Estimating skills are improved for future planning.
- Objectives that cannot be met or will be exceeded are identified early.

Are You Managing Your Projects Effectively?

To determine if you can benefit from the use of project management techniques in your work, answer yes or no to the following questions:

_____   I have identified and named all the current projects I am working on.

_____   All of the projects I am working on are prioritized.

_____   All of my projects have clear, agreed upon goals and objectives.

_____   All of my projects are scheduled in writing.

_____   All of my projects have approved budgets and expenditures are clearly documented.

_____   All of my projects have adequate resources for completion.

_____   All of the people and vendors involved with my projects are appropriately skilled and adequately trained to complete the project work.

_____   Potential conflicts with other projects are easily identified because of clear project plans and open communications.

_____   The potential problems in my projects are identified in advance and actions are consistently taken to eliminate or minimize them.

_____   All the people working with me on projects are enthusiastic and committed to the work.

_____   Other project participants willingly respond to requests related to the projects I am coordinating.

_____   When project disagreements and conflicts arise, effective agreements are reached quickly and with minimum disruption to the work flow.

_____   I am always clear on the current status of projects I am involved with.

_____   Project changes are clearly communicated on a regular basis and always understood by project participants.

_____   My projects are consistently completed on time, within budget, and to specifications.

Give yourself 1 point for each "Yes" answer. If you scored 13-15 points, congratulations! You are already an excellent project manager, though you may discover some useful techniques to become even better by reading this book. If you scored 9-12 points, you are doing okay, but there are definite areas that could be improved in managing and coordinating projects you are working on. If you scored below 9, you are both perceptive and honest about the state of project management in your area of responsibility. Your project management program is typical, so don't despair. If you follow the guidelines in this book, you will be able to complete your projects more easily and with less anxiety.

Figure 1-4 Are You Managing Your Projects Effectively?

Project management provides these advantages over other management techniques because it allows the forecast and authority for attainment of definable goals to be placed on one individual or small group at the operational level. This makes work easier to track and control. The person or group then becomes responsible for coordinating multiple line and horizontal groups to complete the project. This approach does not destroy the vertical, bureaucratic flow of work but simply requires that line organizations talk to one another horizontally so work is accomplished more smoothly throughout the organization. The person responsible for coordinating the project (the project manager) is responsible for assuring that the horizontal work is coordinated and the vertical communication is maintained.

As an example of a typical project in a corporation, consider the specialist in the finance department who is responsible for assuring the smooth implementation of a new sales order system to reduce shipment times to customers and provide better accounting information for financial reports. This person needs to establish a team of people from the sales department, the data processing department, the production department, and the accounting section of the finance department in order to develop and implement an improved system. This person has taken on the responsibility for meeting this objective and as a result is the "project manager," even though this title is not used. This person coordinates the development of the plan and tracks the work to assure that the "project" is completed as specified and must communicate progress to the departments that will be affected by the new sales order system and the project participants. In addition, the line or functional managers this person reports to must be kept informed of the project status. Thus, both horizontal communications and vertical communications must be maintained.

If this person uses project management techniques, including the planning, tracking, and reporting methodologies presented in this book, this horizontal and vertical communication will become easier and tracking the progress against the planned objectives will be relatively easy. (See Figure 1-4.) If project management techniques are not employed, the finance specialist may find that the project suffers from poorly defined performance criteria, unclear and unspecified responsibilities, burdensome and poorly coordinated communications (both internal and external to the department), relatively slow implementation, and a lack of cost and schedule monitoring that makes it virtually impossible to keep things on track. The work becomes frustrating rather than satisfying, and ultimately other departments become frustrated as well, because the status of the new sales order system is never clearly understood.

Project management offers an alternative to this frustration, by clearly defining responsibilities for the project, focusing resources on specific objectives, and providing a structure for communicating within and across organizational boundaries. The result is that project status and problems are clearly understood by everyone involved.

WHAT DOES PROJECT MANAGEMENT ENTAIL?

To manage a project is to manage the design, development, and implementation of people, machines, and capital leading to the creation of something that did not previously exist. Bringing a project to fruition is a creative process with a focus on the "management" of the process.

Project Management Buzzword

☛ Project Management—The combination of systems, techniques, and people required to complete a project within established goals of time, budget, and quality. Project management is also referred to as "program management" in the U.S. Department of Defense, "construction management" in large construction projects, and "product management" in consumer-oriented industries. According to the Project Management Institute (PMI), a professional organization dedicated to promoting and improving project management practices, project management requires coordinating nine areas of expertise: cost, time, scope, quality, communications, human resources, contracts, supplies, and risk management.

In classic descriptions of management, five functions are emphasized as central to the management of any enterprise:

- Planning
- Organizing
- Staffing
- Controlling
- Directing

These five functions are also fundamental components of managing projects. All the commonly used project management disciplines and methods used in business today follow a similar pattern based on these five functions of management: **planning** the work, schedule, and budget; **organizing** and **staffing** a team to implement the work; **controlling** the project through tracking and monitoring progress against the plan; and **directing** people and other resources so the plan is adjusted as necessary and implemented as smoothly as possible. Project management differs from enterprise management in *how* work is planned, organized, controlled, and directed.

Project management as a discipline evolved because of a need to coordinate resources and technology to secure predictable results. The common project management tasks required to do this include establishing objectives, breaking work into well-defined tasks, charting the work sequences, scheduling, budgeting, coordinating a team, reporting, and engaging in ongoing communication. These tasks involve two general types of project management activities: (1) planning and definition activities and (2) implementation and control activities.

Because of these two general types of project activities, people who manage projects effectively, no matter what the size, must know how to both plan effectively and act efficiently. In fact, balancing the interplay between planning and acting may be the most important skill a person must learn in order to be effective at managing projects.

For completing these two types of project management activities, specific types of charting, graphing, and reporting systems have been developed that are the central components of project management that separate it from other management disciplines. These charting, graphing, organizing, and reporting systems form the core of project management. Many of them have names that seem complex and technical, but as you read on, you will find that most of the techniques are not difficult to follow. In fact, when the techniques are appropriately used, the complexity of managing projects is greatly simplified.

The Two Types of Project Management Activities

* Project planning and definition activities
    - Definition of project goals and objectives
    - Definition of work requirements
    - Definition of quantity and quality of work to be performed
    - Definition of resources needed
    - Definition of an organization structure to carry out the work
    - Planning of tasks and sequences to meet project goals
    - Planning of a schedule for timely completion
    - Planning of the budget
* Project implementation and control activities
    - Initiating work
    - Monitoring and tracking progress
    - Comparing actual schedules and budgets to plans
    - Analyzing impact of progress and changes
    - Communicating progress and changes
    - Coordinating activities and people
    - Delegating assignments and providing feedback
    - Making adjustments to the plan as required
    - Completing the project
    - Assessing project results

WHAT ARE THE GOALS OF PROJECT MANAGEMENT?

Most projects in business, whether furnishing a new office or reorganizing an entire corporation, share the same kinds of underlying goals, for example,

- Completing the project on time
- Completing the project within budget and with the resources made available
- Completing the defined work within specifications, at a quality level that is appropriate for the success of the project
- Using assigned resources effectively and efficiently

Successful projects must meet their goals with a minimum of changes and without distributing the main work flow of the organization. Projects must also operate within an existing structure without creating negative political situations that will adversely affect the corporate culture.

The goals of project management methods are to meet the project goals as efficiently as possible by balancing the three constraints of time, resources, and results. Project management techniques also have the objective to make better use of existing resources by getting work to flow both horizontally as well as vertically within the company or organization.

PROJECT LIFE CYCLES
MAKE PROJECT MANAGEMENT POSSIBLE

One thing that makes it possible for project management to meet its goals is the similarity of project work. Even though projects have at least some unique attributes, all projects go through similar stages. Like organic beings, projects have life cycles. All projects start with a conception or idea to do something. This is the **conceptualization phase**. Then, projects are further defined and planned. This is the **planning stage**. During the planning stage, tasks, schedules, and budgets are completed. If the planned project is approved, the project goes ahead. This is the **implementation phase**. During the implementation phase, the project is monitored, controlled, and adjusted to meet the defined goals. Finally, the project is completed and its success assessed. This is the **termination phase**. Figure 1-5 shows how most projects use time and resources through the project life cycle.

Other project management books may refer to the stages with different names or break the phases into more levels, but they all are based on the same basic life-cycle concept. For example, some project management experts break the life cycle into phases of conceptualization, feasibility, preliminary planning, detail planning, execution, and testing. These phases, which can still be summarized in the four phases of conception, planning, implementation, and termination, might make sense for a data processing project or an engineering project. The number of phases you identify for a project depends on its size, complexity, and the preferred terminology in your organization, but ultimately they boil down to the same overall structure.

The diagram shows that projects use time and resources in similar, predictable ways through their life cycles. Most projects start out slowly and

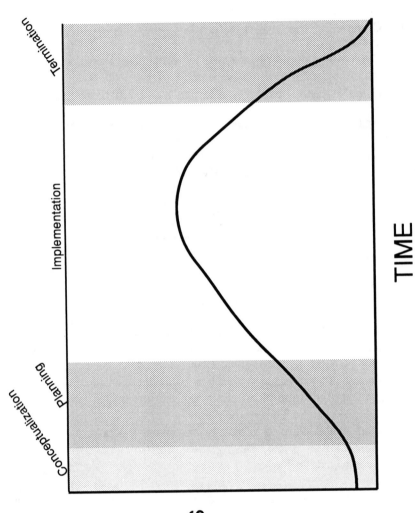

Figure 1-5 The Project Life Cycle Uses Time and Resources in Predicable Ways

progress in activity and the use of resources. Most of the time goes into the implementation of a project. Activity ultimately peaks and begins to decline. Projects then go through a termination phase, which concludes the project. Just like organic beings, some projects try to avoid the termination phase—and they never seem to get done. For a project to be successful, it must meet its final goal of completion and termination.

THE PROJECT MANAGEMENT METHODOLOGY

Though project management uses the traditional management functions, it employs distinct steps in each phase of the project. These steps taken together constitute the project management methodology. The project management steps performed at each phase of the project are summarized in the next chart.

The project management methodology is a structured system for getting work done on time and within budget. Because the stages in projects are similar, it is possible to graph progress at each stage, even though the end results of projects may differ. It is this ability to define, measure, and chart project progress that makes project management methodology possible. In each stage of the project life cycle, there are different sets of techniques and procedures from the project management toolbox that come into play.

Chapters Two through Nine are dedicated to explaining the tools and the steps for each major component of the project management process. And Chapter Ten offers guidelines for choosing a computerized project management program to make project management easier and more effective.

Notice that more chapters are spent on the planning and definition activities, even though these activities account for only a relatively small fraction of the project implementation time. This does not mean that the implementation and control activities are less important—it means that the authors believe that more time spent in planning a project, of any size, will result in a project that is easier to implement and control. And it is the project planning aspects of the project management discipline, including how work is charted and diagrammed, that make project management processes both unique and possible.

THE PROJECT PLAN IS CENTRAL
TO PROJECT MANAGEMENT METHODS

> *When society requires to be rebuilt, there is no use*
> *in attempting to rebuild it on the old plan.*
> —John Stuart Mill,
> *Dissertations and Discussions, 1859*

In project management, the plan is always the baseline for making decisions. It is the plan that is central to the whole project management methodology.

It is the plan that is approved so work can begin. It is the plan that is adjusted and modified as work on the project continues and new information is received. It is the plan that enables managers to make decisions about changing priorities and resource requirements. It is the plan that is used as the common denominator in all communications about the project. Thus, without a properly constructed plan, the rest of the project management toolbox is virtually useless.

Project Management Steps

	Chapter in This Book
Project Conceptualization Phase	
• Evaluate Feasibility of the Project Idea	Two
• Select Best Projects for Implementation	Two
• Establish Project Goals	Two
Project Planning Phase	
• Define and Chart the Work and Task Sequences	Three
• Establish the Required Resources (People, Equipment)	Four
• Create a Schedule	Five
• Develop a Budget	Six
Project Implementation Phase	
• Initiate Work on the Project and Assess Ongoing Progress	Seven
• Monitor Work and Resources	Seven
• Recognize Problems and Make Mid-course Corrections	Eight
Project Termination Phase	
• Complete the Project and Evaluate the Results	Nine
• Draft the Final Report on the Project	Nine

In project management a plan consists of the following elements:

- Clear definition and objectives for the project and consensus to proceed
- A description of the tasks that need to be completed, which can be charted and graphed in various ways depending on the project technique that is appropriate for the project at hand
- Identification of the skills, people, and other resources required to complete the project
- An operational and reporting structure for implementing the project
- A schedule which may be simple or complex, depending on the project
- A budget that forecasts costs and enables ongoing tracking of expenditures

The project plan is fluid and malleable, not a fixed prescription for work to be done. The philosophy of the project management discipline acknowledges that there is more uncertainty at the beginning of a project than there is after the project is near completion. Because the future cannot be seen in advance, project planning involves a certain amount of guesswork. As the project is implemented, there is less guesswork involved because less of the project remains in the future. Project uncertainty always decreases as the project progresses. Still, the closer the original plan is to the actual implementation of the project, the easier the project will be to manage. Thus, plans in project management serve two primary purposes:

1. To minimize as much guesswork and uncertainty as possible at the beginning of the project
2. To form a baseline for making and communicating changes as status information is gathered during the implementation of the project

The development, charting, and maintenance of the project plan are primary responsibilities of the project manager. Most project management techniques focus on ways to chart the plan, communicate the plan, report on the plan, and modify it. It is these plan-centered processes, coupled with people management and motivational skills, that the effective project manager must master in order to succeed in bringing projects in on time and within budget.

THE ROLE OF THE PROJECT MANAGER

Though actual responsibility for securing the success of a project may fall on a group or team of people, for the purposes of this book we will refer to the project manager as a single person responsible for the outcomes of the project. As important as the plan is to the success of project management methods, it is the skill of the project manager that guides the project through its phases. The project manager is a participant in the project, a facilitator of tasks, and most important, a leader.

As the person responsible for developing and maintaining the plan, the project manager is the person who brings the project definition and control elements together efficiently. Even though your job title may not be "project manager" it is important to the success of project management that your responsibility as a project manager be clearly identified and understood.

The common characteristics of successful project managers include:

- Dedication to the project goals
- Clear responsibility for the project, by virtue of assignment or role
- Appropriate level of contact with the people necessary to get the project work completed
- Ability to coordinate, motivate, and mentor people
- Effective written and verbal communication skills
- Ability to delegate and monitor work
- Technical and administrative skills related to the project
- Sensitivity to people and ability to negotiate
- Above all, dependability

Project managers must understand the principles of project management and have the requisite communication and organizational skills to keep things on track without becoming overly autocratic. A project manager who views the responsibility for the project as one of guiding, facilitating, negotiating, and coordinating will do better than will one who views the project responsibility as one of ordering, dictating, and coercing.

The Attributes of a Project Manager

A colleague once told us that to be a successful project manager you must have:

- The intelligence of Einstein
- The patience of two saints
- The integrity of a Supreme Court judge
- The negotiating skills of a Mongolian horse trader
- The savvy of James Bond
- The charisma of Sir Ralph Richardson
- The communication skills of Tom Peters
- The planning skills of General Schwartzkopf
- The personal drive of Donald Trump
- The skin of an armadillo
- The ego of Mother Teresa

Though this isn't far from the truth, we have yet to find a perfect match.

As discussed earlier, project managers in business usually have functional responsibilities in addition to managing specific projects. Businesspeople who manage projects must also have the ability to prioritize project work and integrate it with the day-to-day functional responsibilities. In project-oriented organizations, workers become managers, managers become workers, and everyone benefits by sharing responsibility and achievement in meeting the goals of the enterprise. As a businessperson you will be involved in many projects—some as a project manager, some as a participant. Ultimately, the organization is more complex in project-oriented businesses, but the breakdown of absolute line responsibility can result in improved morale and increased productivity because people become responsible for planning and coordinating their own work.

THE THINGS PROJECT MANAGEMENT CAN'T DO

As useful as project management techniques are in helping to achieve specific goals, project management has its limitations. The old adage "Rome wasn't built in a day" is an important point of view when assessing the potential of project management. No project management system can make impossible things happen—and no matter how good you get at using the charting, monitoring, and tracking techniques in project management as we present them here, you still won't be able to build Rome in a day. In the same vein, if your company needs a new advertisement placed in a magazine in three days, and you know there is no way the project can be completed in less than a week, no project management technique in the world can help you. The impossible remains impossible. However, project management techniques will help you expose the impossible before you commit to a project doomed to failure.

Project management techniques can help identify problems with schedules too, but project management can't change the deadlines. That is something you must do through negotiation and communication. Project management techniques can help you make a case for securing more resources, but the tools won't help you locate the right people or vendors. That you must do through your own network and experience.

Project management can't help you change the skills of the people working on your project either. If your team is not properly trained, the only thing project management will help you do is expose this fact early in the project cycle, when it is easiest to correct the problem. And project management techniques can't solve political problems or predict environmental changes that will affect the viability of a project. Project management can allow you to see problems early and identify roadblocks to completion, but other organizational and communication skills come into play to solve the political issues.

Remember that projects, even when properly charted and planned, are still characterized by inevitable conflicts. There may be resource conflicts, financial conflicts, priority conflicts, personality conflicts, and political conflicts. People who manage projects must learn techniques to manage the conflicts, as well as the tasks and resources. In addition to the planning, charting, and monitoring tools, project management has a set of people-oriented tools for resolving the conflicts. However, none of the tools and the techniques works if the people involved are not willing to participate or are not properly trained.

Project management cannot make people work together or make people work smarter. The techniques only identify the problems and offer suggestions for improving undesirable situations.

What project management will do is provide a system for planning, documenting, organizing, and communicating. The project management methodology empowers the people to make better decisions as the project progresses, but ultimately it is the people who will make things happen and make things work, not the methodology.

THE SUCCESS FACTORS IN PROJECT MANAGEMENT

Based on what project management can and can't do, it is important to realize that in order for project management to succeed, the following components must be in place:

- Appropriately skilled project manager or project management team
- Clear authority for the project manager to implement the project
- Commitment to the project management methodology
- A skilled project team that is agreed on the goals of the project
- A complete project plan that is understood by all participants
- Objectives that contribute to the larger goals of the organization
- Willingness of the team to change and adapt as the project proceeds
- Tracking and monitoring methods that allow for regular communication on status and results and minimize the need for excessive meetings and reports
- Adaptation of the methods to the requirements of the project

Basically, this list of success factors translates into two things: understanding project management methods and using them consistently. Project management also requires commitment from the organization to use the tools. If your boss thinks you are wasting your time doing planning, then project management will never be properly implemented. Unfortunately, its the organization that loses if this is the case, not project management.

Project management demands that you use the entire system to be effective, as well. If you adopt the planning portion of project management and then don't follow through with the reporting and monitoring activities, you haven't really implemented project management. The success of project management is based on a whole system that takes projects from conception to termination. When people say things like, "We've tried project management, but it was a waste of time," they are usually blaming the project management system for the failure of their projects. They say things like, "Well, we developed a plan and it didn't work that way."

Developing the plan is not project management. Critical path method (CPM) and program evaluation and review technique (PERT) charts are not project management. Developing the plan or chart is only one step. Before you blame the methods, try the whole system. Be committed to it. Project management is not perfect, and new techniques are constantly being added to the toolbox, but the basic methods are sound and they do work. However, you can't just pull out one of the steps or techniques and say, "Gee, I really like that chart. I will use that on my next project, but I don't have time for updating it, so I'll just keep doing that the way I always have." All you will end up with is a nice chart, not a well-managed project.

SMALL AND LARGE PROJECTS CAN BENEFIT FROM PROJECT MANAGEMENT TECHNIQUES

There are times when people must streamline project management techniques to make them appropriate for the project at hand. Most of the project management methods presented in this book can be applied to any goal-oriented situation in business. However, the level of planning required for a large project is not appropriate for a small project. For this reason, the project management techniques are categorized in this book into those for small projects and those for larger projects. The overall steps and phases for small projects are the same, they are just streamlined.

Small projects can be categorized with the following general parameters:

- Five or fewer participants
- Deadline in two months or less
- Budget less than $100,000 (not including salaries)
- Fewer than fifty total tasks or activities

Large projects are characterized by bigger groups of people, larger budgets, and/or longer time lines. Large projects in business are three to twelve months in length, though some may be longer. Typically these projects involve matrix organizations (more on this in Chapter Four). The size and task complexity of these projects require different charting and coordination techniques than small projects.

Of course, there are projects that fall somewhere in between large and small. Medium-sized projects should be managed like large projects, but the reports and tracking can be simplified when appropriate because of the shorter duration of the project.

There are also projects called **megaprojects.** These projects involve vast numbers of people and multiple organizations. Their budgets are astronomical, and they may take years, sometimes as much as a decade or more, to complete. The mission to Mars project we discussed earlier is a megaproject. Though the underlying principles for managing these projects are the same as those for lesser ventures, megaprojects require a full-time project management staff and employ sophisticated computerized project information systems to assist the project team in planning and tracking work, costs, and resources. These projects require special extensions of the basic project management tools—just because of size and complexity. The special techniques for managing megaprojects are not covered in this book. If you will be involved in megaprojects, the principles of project management as presented here can be used as an introduction to the planning and control concepts. Then, more advanced texts on the management of megaprojects can be consulted to learn the specifics for planning and executing these monstrous endeavors.

Regardless of size, every project worth doing is important. All projects deserve (and require) the careful planning, control, and monitoring of the project management discipline. Small projects are not necessarily less important or less risky than larger projects. Small projects may be less complex to chart and track, but they may still be critical to the success of an enterprise. For example, the completion of the annual report for a corporation may be categorized as a small project, but it is still vital to the functioning of the enterprise and highly visible to the outside world. The size of a project has little to do with the priority of a project either. The priority, importance, and risk associated with a project are separate criteria that should be viewed independently from the size of a project.

A job not worth doing is not worth doing well.
                                                              Jerry Pournelle,
                                                          Pournelle's Fifth Law

---

COMPUTERIZED PROJECT MANAGEMENT TECHNIQUES

Adaptations of the project management methodology appropriate for projects of different size, priority, risk, and complexity will be discussed in the following chapters. However, all project management systems depend on developing detailed work plans, schedules, budgets, and tracking reports. Producing these reports, plans, and forms can become tedious, even for small projects—and this is another reason why project management techniques are not as widely used as they should be. People get the mistaken impression that the methods take longer than the project. This is not true if the methods are used correctly, but when done manually, the process can seem burdensome to the uninitiated.

This book provides many templates that make the plans and reports easier to produce manually. These templates are most useful for small- to medium-sized projects. As projects get more complex and more sophisticated, the project plans and reports suggested in the book can become awkward to complete without help. As projects get larger, it is more difficult and time consuming to chart and graph the tasks, schedules, and budgets without the assistance of computer programs specifically designed for this purpose.

To overcome this resistance to project management techniques, the use of computerized project management programs is strongly recommended, even for small projects, to assist in planning and implementing projects. In fact, many of the modern project control techniques for large projects are almost impossible without the use of computerized project management programs to help produce the reports and charts.

These programs, which are discussed in detail in Chapter Ten, range from simple to complex, just as the projects they help control. Underneath these programs are the same structured methodology and core principles as described in the book. Without computerization, project management techniques are not consistently implemented, because people often don't have time for keeping things up to date. In reality, using the techniques manually still saves time and money because the projects are ultimately better managed. But computerized project management programs help reduce the resistance to the documentation requirements of project management altogether and eliminate the excuses for not using the techniques.

In spite of the power of the computer, in this book the manual steps for project management will be explained first, before introducing the computerized options. In this way, you will be able to choose a program that is appropriate for your project management requirements and will understand what the computer is doing for you. Without an underlying comprehension of the project management techniques and principles, computerized project management programs can be easily misused or misinterpreted.

It is also important to be aware that the most important aspects of project management—the human requirements—cannot be computerized. These components involve decision making, human intuition, and communication. Computerized project management programs are useful for streamlining the charting, reporting, and documentation of a project and can also aid in "what-if" analysis that allows the project manager to view the results of various scheduling, resource, and budgeting decisions in terms of project completion dates and costs. But computerized project management programs are only an aid. It is still incumbent on the project manager to master human skills to achieve the goals of the project management process.

Worksheet for Listing Current and Planned Projects

Completed by _Ingrid, Vice President of Sales_

Date _January 17_

Projects in Progress

PROJECT NAME	PROJECT PLAN YES OR NO?	SIZE OF PROJECT S/M/L	PROJECT MANAGER	DATE STARTED	TARGET COMPLETE DATE
Boston Tradeshow	Yes	Medium	Joe	Dec	August
New Product Introduction	No	Large	George	June	August
Sales Training Program	No	Medium	Sarah	Nov	May
New Distributor Conference	Yes	Small	Dave	Jan	March

Projects Planned

PROJECT NAME	PROJECT PLAN YES OR NO?	SIZE OF PROJECT S/M/L	PROJECT MANAGER	DATE STARTED	TARGET COMPLETE DATE
San Francisco Office	No	Large	Roger		July or Aug.
Customer Newsletter	No	Small	None		September
Chicago Tradeshow	No	Medium	Joe		September
New Ads	Yes	Large	Gail		March

Figure 1-6 Worksheet for Listing Current and Planned Projects

GET STARTED BY LISTING PROJECTS
YOU ARE INVOLVED IN

Now that you have a better idea about projects and the potential project management offers, before you read the rest of the book you should develop a list of the small, medium, and large projects you are working on now or are thinking about completing in the future. A worksheet has been provided to help you do this. Then, as you read the book, you will be able to match the processes and techniques to the projects you are working on.

Remember, much of the work you are currently responsible for can be categorized as projects, but you may not have thought of your responsibilities that way before. List all of the projects you are involved in and responsible for, not just the major ones. This will give you a better chance to control and prioritize your work using project management techniques. If you list only a few of the projects, you run the risk of overcommitting yourself and your enterprise. This results in a few jobs that get done well and others that get little attention. For consistent, reliable results, all your projects should be managed, not just a few of them.

To illustrate the concepts in the rest of the book, the projects of the Western Regional Sales Division of a hypothetical company called TechMore, Inc., are used to illustrate the steps, methods, and techniques of project management. The company is a six-year-old corporation that manufactures office and computer equipment. The company is located in Santa Fe, New Mexico. The company has been successful to this point in building quality products at a relatively low price and as a result is expanding rapidly.

As the first example from the hypothetical TechMore, Inc., a list of projects produced by the Western Regional Sales Division is provided here to demonstrate a suggested format for listing the projects being worked on and proposed in an organization. (See Figure 1-6.) A blank copy of this worksheet, and all the main worksheets shown in other chapters as examples, are provided at the end of the book for use in your own project management undertakings.

The potential of project management in helping complete projects with better results has been explained in this chapter. The steps in implementing the project management methodology are covered in the following chapters. With your own project list in hand, read on and you'll see how you can realize the potential of project management in your own work.

Chapter Two

DEFINING THE PROJECT:
Proven Techniques
for Setting Clear Goals

The first step in managing any project is to define clearly the end result that needs to be accomplished. Though this sounds obvious, the success of project management depends on the skill of the manager and project team in gaining consensus on the goals and scope of the project. The project manager must also be cognizant of the politics and other organizational factors that will affect the definition and ultimate success of the project. In this chapter, the methods for choosing appropriate projects and then reaching consensus on the goals and objectives for those projects are covered.

Project selection and goal setting constitute the project conceptualization phase of the project management methodology, also called the project definition or project initiation phases by some project management practitioners.

SELECTING THE PROJECTS IS THE FIRST STEP

Project selection is the first of many decisions in the project management process. All projects start out as ideas or concepts, and there are always more ideas in a business than there are time and resources to implement them. Not all conceptual ideas are good ideas for projects, however. Some ideas turn out to be inappropriate or infeasible. Others don't have enough priority to take up valuable time and resources. Still others are better shelved for use at a later date, when the timing is more appropriate.

To determine the projects to act on, a manager needs to evaluate the project goals, set priorities, establish the timing for projects, and weed out projects that are inappropriate or less critical to the success of the enterprise.

Sometimes as the person responsible for a project, you will be brought in after the selection phase. For example, you might be assigned a project by your boss or you might be chosen as the project manager after other people have been considered. For other projects, you will need to make the project selection on your own or as part of a project team.

The Project Selection Process

1. List all current projects or project ideas.

2. Establish the need or opportunity for each project.

3. Establish rough delivery dates and budgets for each project.

4. Establish feasibility for each of the projects.

5. Establish the risk associated with the project.

6. Review the project list and objectives with line management and other members of the potential project team to gain consensus on the goals.

7. Eliminate projects that are inappropriate or infeasible.

8. Prioritize the remaining projects for planning and implementation.

9. Select the projects that will be acted on now.

Whether making project selections for a major corporation or as an individual, the basic steps in the project selection process are as follows:

Selection Step 1. List all current projects and project ideas.

Using a worksheet like the one provided in Chapter One, list all the projects currently being implemented and all project ideas for the future. (See Figure 2.1.) If the list is complete, most people will find that there are more projects being worked on than they had considered. If nothing else, this process of listing projects exposes the volume of work and the number of activities being performed in an organization.

If projects are being selected for a large organization or group of people, each person or department should list its projects separately. Then, the lists can be integrated and completed in a group meeting. The meeting also can be used to establish project priorities for the larger enterprise.

For the next steps in the selection process, more information on each project must be gathered. To help in this process, a project selection worksheet, like the one shown, can be useful in structuring the process.

Selection Step 2. Establish the need or opportunity for each project.

The concept or idea for many business projects starts with a need. For example, a new product might be proposed because the competition has come out with a better product at a lower cost. The need or imperative for the project is immediate competition. A new office might be needed to support the growing number of customers on the West Coast. A new manufacturing machine might be needed because the old one is obsolete and impossible to repair. The salespeople might need a brochure to explain the technical aspects of the products and to improve sales by making better information available to customers.

Sometimes there are legal requirements or needs for a project as well as functional or operational needs. For example, annual reports must be completed within specific deadlines as a legal requirement of the state the company is incorporated in. Completing the corporate income taxes, a major undertaking for large companies, also has legal requirements driving the project.

Some projects may be initiated in response to an opportunity. The opportunity for business projects might depend on marketing, sales, or economic conditions. For example, there might be an opportunity to expand into new markets, to respond to a government bid request, or take advantage of a favorable lending environment as a way of financing a new venture. Thus, the need for the project is to fulfill the opportunity or reduce risk.

Some of these needs or opportunities can be described in terms of the benefits that will be derived from the project—such as reducing costs, increasing profits, enhancing productivity, expanding market share, or whatever.

After the projects are selected, these needs will be expanded and specified to become the goals for the project. At this point in the project, however, the needs can be stated in general terms as we've done here.

Selection Step 3. Establish rough delivery dates and cost estimates for each project.

Some projects will have absolute due dates and time constraints and others will not. For example, if the project is to attend a specific tradeshow, then there is an absolute date when the project must be completed. Other projects have flexible time windows. For example, introducing a new product might have a time window like first quarter of next year, but still be constrained within this window of time. Other projects have relatively flexible schedules for completion—like the opening of a new sales office. There might be a target date for opening the office, but no requirement that the office must be completed by that date to still have value. Still, for practical reasons, you might want to open the new office before next winter's storm season.

At this point in the selection and planning process, the project end dates can be approximated. It's fine to specify a month or quarter as a rough target date at this point. If the end date is mandatory or constrained for some reason, make note of this on the worksheet, however.

Project Selection Worksheet

Completed by Joe, Marketing Communications Mgr.

Date January 4

PROJECT	NEED	TARGET DATE	ROUGH BUDGET	FEASIBILITY SCALE 1-10	RISK H/M/L	PRIORITY
Six Updated Product Brochures						
New Ad Program - Existing products						
PR Agency Program						
Direct Mail Program						
Press Tour						
Ads for New Product						
New Corporate Brochure						
Annual Report						
Customer Conference						
New Product Brochure						
Six Updated Datasheets						
New Logo Design						
Redesign Letterhead						
New Signs with Logo						
Demo Video						
New Tradeshow Booth						
Attend Boston Show						
Attend Chicago Show						
Attend Las Vegas Show						
Company Newsletter						

Figure 2-1 Project Selection Worksheet

A cost estimate for the projects at this point will also be rough and general. The estimate should be based on a target for the cost of the project based on some past experience, if possible. If the project will involve adding personnel or tracking labor costs, don't forget to include these in the estimate. If similar projects have been completed before, use the budgets for these past projects as a general estimate. If the project is something new, do a little research and advance planning to establish a general budget. (Chapter Six has more information on budgeting techniques.)

Selection Step 4. Establish feasibility for each of the projects.

Establishing feasibility for a project involves assessing the organization's ability to implement a project successfully. In large, high-visibility ventures, projects are actually planned out in detail before feasibility is established. In large construction and engineering projects, for example, the feasibility stage is a major undertaking that involves most of the planning processes described in this book. But for smaller business projects, the feasibility stage can be less structured. The more important and complex a project is, the more planning that should go into the project before it is accepted or rejected based on feasibility.

Establishing feasibility centers on assessing the capability of the organization to implement the project. Answers to the following questions are critical to determining project feasibility:

- Are the right resources available?
- Is the expertise available to implement the project?
- Is enough time available to get the project done?
- Will enough money be available to implement the project with the appropriate level of quality?
- Is the timing for this project appropriate?
- Does the project fit into the cultural framework of the organization?
- Does the project fit into the overall goals and objectives of the organization as established by executive management?
- Will the project be cost effective or profitable?
- Are the potential benefits of completing the project worth the resources required to implement it?

Feasibility should be rated on a scale of 0 to 10, with 10 assigned to projects that can be easily accomplished or to projects similar to those completed successfully before. Zero represents a project that is nearly impossible for significant reasons. If a project rates low in feasibility, there are two questions that must be considered before the project is rejected on this basis:

1. Can the project be redefined to make it feasible and still allow it to meet the majority of its objectives?

2. Is the project so important that additional research into the feasibility may be required before making a final determination about the project?

For reasons of priority and survival, some projects that are not currently feasible may need to go through an additional planning process to establish ways to eliminate the feasibility problems. As an example, consider a company whose products have suddenly become obsolete because of a competitor's introduction of lower-cost, more durable products based on a new synthetic material. The company realizes it must develop a new line of products to compete, but based on current resources, expertise, and budgets, the project for developing the new products is rated infeasible. However, the development of a new product line is important to the future of the company and necessary to keep the company competitive. Projects to eliminate the feasibility problems must be planned out and implemented before the new product line project can be completed. This will require creative thinking as well as good project management skills.

Selection Step 5. Establish the risk associated with the project.

Risk and feasibility are related, but must be categorized separately. For example, it may be technically feasible for a sports clothes company to develop a new line of women's fashion clothing, but because the company does not have experience marketing women's clothes, the risk associated with the idea may be high. Sometimes high-risk projects are undertaken to try new ideas or market approaches or to gain expertise in new areas.

- Risk is high when a new technology is being developed.
- Risk is high when large numbers of new people or outside vendors/contractors must be hired to complete a project.
- Risk is high when something has never been tried before.
- Risk is high when unsubstantiated benefits for the project have been claimed by the project sponsors.

High risk alone is not a reason to reject a project, however. Risk is only one factor in project selection, but it is important to acknowledge the level of risk associated with a project at the onset. In this way, appropriate measurement criteria and monitoring methods can be established for assessing the success and failure of the project in each phase.

In most cases, companies should attempt to balance their high-risk projects with low-risk undertakings, to assure overall success as an enterprise. An organization that takes on only high-risk ventures is highly vulnerable. Of course, there are some companies in the form of entrepreneurial ventures that violate the risk rule and prosper by taking on only high-risk projects, but for the majority of businesses, a balance is desirable.

Projects on the list should be rated as low, medium, or high risk as appropriate. This is an extremely subjective rating, so be able to justify why you have assigned a risk level. Don't just assign low risk to a project because it is something you want to do. If the project is worth doing, it should be selected for other reasons, such as its potential in contributing to an organization's objectives or providing new growth opportunities or some other substantive reason.

After completing steps 1 through 6, the completed worksheet based on the projects for the Marketing Communications Department, which is part of the Western Regional Sales Division of the hypothetical TechMore, Inc., looks like the one shown in Figure 2-2.

Selection Step 6. Review the projects with line management and other members of the potential project teams to gain consensus on needs and project priorities.

The process of establishing consensus on projects is a topic worthy of a book of its own. How consensus and agreement on projects are achieved varies with the structure and culture of the organization. At this early stage of project management, consensus is achieved by reviewing the project lists with appropriate people and getting their feedback. This may be handled through informal meetings with your line managers or with a group meeting to discuss the projects on the list. Specific sections on conflict resolution techniques are contained in Chapters Eight and Nine that may be useful if you are having difficulty in getting people to agree to the projects on your list.

Selection Step 7. Eliminate projects that are inappropriate or infeasible.

After projects have been reviewed and general consensus established on project need, goals, and feasibility, the projects that are slated for further planning must be determined. Ultimately, projects are selected for further action because they are predicted to have certain desirable outcomes if implemented successfully. These outcomes are expected to contribute to achievement of enterprise goals.

The primary reasons for eliminating business projects include

- Lack of money, people, skills, time, or other resources
- Goals that are in conflict with the organization or enterprise goals
- Outcomes that will violate existing policies or laws, or otherwise negatively affect the position of an organization
- Inability to act quickly enough, even if the project is otherwise feasible
- Low priority or low need for the project
- Conflict with other projects that are in progress or planned that have a higher priority

Project Selection Worksheet

Completed by **Joe, Marketing Communications Mgr.**

Date **January 4**

PROJECT	NEED	TARGET DATE	ROUGH BUDGET	FEASIBILITY SCALE 1-10	RISK H/M/L	PRIORITY
Six Updated Product Brochures	Update look	August	78,000	6	M	Low
New Ad Program - Existing products	Competition, maintain image	March	200,000	7	L	High
PR Agency Program	Company PR	Jan-Dec	110,000	8	M	Critical
Direct Mail Program	Immed. sales	Feb	96,000	10	M	High
Press Tour	Announcement	August	65,000	7	L	High
Ads for New Product	Promotion,sales	August	111,000	5	M	High
New Corporate Brochure	Update look	June	78,000	5	H	Low
Annual Report	Required by law	June	75,000	9	L	Critical
Customer Conference	Training, PR	May	249,000	3	M	High
New Product Brochure	Distributor sales	August	66,000	8	M	High
Six Updated Datasheets	Update look	August	26,000	10	L	Low
New Logo Design	Improve image	ASAP	11,000	3	H	Low
Redesign Letterhead	Improve image	ASAP	9,500	10	L	Low
New Signs with Logo	Match new logo	ASAP	46,000	4	L	Low
Demo Video	Special offer	Sept	235,000	3	H	Medium
New Tradeshow Booth	Improve image	August	148,000	1	H	Low
Attend Boston Show	Sales, contacts	August	46,000	9	M	Critical
Attend Chicago Show	Sales, contacts	Sept	48,000	9	M	High
Attend Las Vegas Show	Sales, contacts	Nov	52,000	9	M	High
Company Newsletter	Customer contact	August	14,000	10	L	High

Figure 2-2 Complete Project Selection Worksheet

Feasible, appropriate projects on the list that are rejected because of low priority or bad timing may be kept on a list for consideration in the next project selection review.

Project Management Tip

✎ **Avoid the Pet Project Syndrome**—When selecting projects, it's easy for people to rank the projects they want to do higher than the projects that really should get done. There is almost always a "pet" project on everybody's list. These projects are the ones that are personally interesting, promise new career challenges, or hold possibilities for promotion. If these projects are selected objectively and on their own merit, "great." If these projects are selected for personal reasons as opposed to enterprise objectives, "watch out!" These pet projects can dilute a company's resources and negatively affect the achievement of the enterprise. When you implement pet projects, bosses and co-workers may recognize the unnecessary use of your time and resources as well, causing political problems down the road. If you find yourself overly enthusiastic about a project because it is something *you* want to do, let a few other people rate the projects without your input. Their independent ratings will help you maintain your objectivity.

Selection Step 8. Prioritize the remaining projects for planning and implementation.

After the projects worth doing are selected, it will become clear even in the smallest organizations that not every project can be acted on at the same time. Thus, priorities for the projects need to be established. Priorities will relate to the need and goal of the project. Establishing the priority of a project is not as easy at it sounds. Some project management specialists assign numerical rankings to each project. This can certainly be done, but it becomes difficult to rank the smaller projects along with larger ones if this method is used.

Ultimately, as projects compete for resources, the priorities will be refined, but at this stage in project management an alternative to numerical ranking that works well is to assign a specific priority level to each project, instead of a number. (See Figure 2-3.) One way to identify project priority is to assign descriptive priority labels to each project, like *critical priority, high priority, medium priority, low priority*, or *back burner*. An alternative is to assign priority numbers of one to five to accomplish the same thing—with 1 being very low priority and 5 being very high priority.

Because establishing the priorities for projects is usually a political process, it is important to discuss the project priorities with line management and other people involved in the decision process. Again, just because a project is important to you personally does not mean it has the same priority for

Project Priority Levels	
Backburner	Reconsider during the next planning cycle—not important now.
Low	Would be nice to do, but isn't mandatory.
Medium	Necessary, but schedule has some flexibility.
High	Timing and end results are very important to the company or organization.
Critical	Must be done at all costs—*no alternatives*.

Figure 2-3 Project Priority Levels

is important to you personally does not mean it has the same priority for the enterprise as a whole. Be aware of this and try to remain objective as project priorities are assigned.

At this point, after the project selection steps have been completed, the project selection worksheet for the Marketing Communications Department at TechMore, Inc., looks like that shown in Figure 2-4. Note that four projects have been eliminated from the original list of twenty projects because they were infeasible, too risky, or inappropriate at this time.

Project Selection Worksheet

Completed by __Joe, Marketing Communications Mgr.__

Date __January 4__

PROJECT	NEED	TARGET DATE	ROUGH BUDGET	FEASIBILITY SCALE 1-10	RISK H/M/L	PRIORITY
~~Six Updated Product Brochures~~	~~Update look~~	~~August~~	~~78,000~~	~~6~~	~~M~~	~~Low~~
New Ad Program - Existing products	Competition, maintain image	March	200,000	7	L	High
PR Agency Program	Company PR	Jan-Dec	110,000	8	M	Critical
Direct Mail Program	Immed. sales	Feb	96,000	10	M	High
Press Tour	Announcement	August	65,000	7	L	High
Ads for New Product	Promotion,sales	August	111,000	5	M	High
New Corporate Brochure	Update look	June	78,000	5	H	Low
Annual Report	Required by law	June	75,000	9	L	Critical
Customer Conference	Training, PR	May	249,000	3	M	High
New Product Brochure	Distributor sales	August	66,000	8	M	High
Six Updated Datasheets	Update look	August	26,000	10	L	Low
~~New Logo Design~~	~~Improve image~~	~~ASAP~~	~~11,000~~	~~3~~	~~H~~	~~Low~~
Redesign Letterhead	Improve image	ASAP	9,500	10	L	Low
~~New Signs with Logo~~	~~Match new logo~~	~~ASAP~~	~~46,000~~	~~4~~	~~L~~	~~Low~~
Demo Video	Special offer	Sept	235,000	3	H	Medium
~~New Tradeshow Booth~~	~~Improve image~~	~~August~~	~~148,000~~	~~1~~	~~H~~	~~Low~~
Attend Boston Show	Sales, contacts	August	46,000	9	M	Critical
Attend Chicago Show	Sales, contacts	Sept	48,000	9	M	High
Attend Las Vegas Show	Sales, contacts	Nov	52,000	9	M	High
Company Newsletter	Customer contact	August	14,000	10	L	High

Figure 2-4 Project Selection Worksheet After Eliminations

Selection Step 9. Select the projects that will be acted on now.

Evaluate the priority of the remaining projects and then select those projects that can actually be implemented within the resources and time available to the enterprise. All the critical and high-priority projects should be implemented. If adequate time and resources are not available for the high-priority projects, review the priorities and evaluate whether the priorities and schedule limitations are really appropriate and necessary for the success of the undertaking. Projects of lesser priority should be selected for implementation only if resources are (or will be) available.

THE ZERO-BASED BUDGET

The **zero-based budget**, known as the **ZBB**, employs a simple technique that can be used to select the projects capable of being completed within existing resource limitations. And, if your superiors are trying to push you into an impossible situation of being responsible for more projects than there is time, money, or resources, the zero-based budget provides a difficult-to-dispute gauge of project overload.

The ZBB is easy to implement. (See Figure 2-5.) Simply list the projects in priority order on a piece of paper—in pencil, because you may want to reorder the list as you go along. Now, next to each project list out the rough budget for each project. Then, starting at the top with the most important projects and working down the list, add these numbers together as a running total. When you reach the point on the list where you've run out of money, draw a line underneath this project. This is the "zero line." The line indicates the place where your available budget minus project costs equals zero. Based on your budget, all projects above the line are doable. All projects below the line get scrapped, put off until next year, or completed if more resources are made available.

Before you reject the projects below the line, do a little analysis of the ZBB you've produced. Are there several less expensive but nearly as important projects just south of the line? Or, is there a marginally important, but very expensive project, on the "Do" side? If so, consider swapping the less expensive projects for a single expensive one. This restructuring of the priorities may allow you to achieve more enterprise goals for your budget dollars.

You can instantly recognize a ZBB with a problem because you will have drawn the zero line very close to the top of your project list—and many important projects will be left on the scrap side. If you don't have enough projects above the line to meet your enterprise goals, then you need to get more money (or other resources). The ZBB technique can be easily adapted to select projects based on availability of people, equipment, and time as well.

If critical and high-priority projects are really that important to the enterprise, the goals and objectives of the enterprise are at risk if these projects are not completed. Some means needs to be established to accomplish these projects.

Use the Zero-Based Budget to Prioritize and Select Projects

Project List

Project	Cost
1. Six Updated Product Brochures	$78,000
2. New Ad Program	$211,000
3. PR Agency Retainer	$110,000
4. Direct Mail Program	$96,000
5. Press Tour	$65,000
6. Ads for New Product	$111,000
7. New Corp Brochure	$78,000
8. Annual Report	$78,000
9. Customer Conference	$249,000
10. New Product Brochure	$66,000
11. Six Updated Datasheets	$26,000
12. New Logo Design	$11,000
13. Replace Letterhead	$9,500
14. New Signs with Logo	$46,000
16. Demonstration Video	$235,000
17. New Tradeshow Booth	$148,000
18. Attend Boston Show	$46,000
19. Attend Chicago Show	$48,000
20. Attend Las Vegas Show	$52,000
21. New Product Package	$23,000
22. Company Newsletter	$14,000

Make a list of all the project possibilities for the year. List the approximate cost of each project next to it.

Project Priority List

Project	Cost
6. Ads for New Product	$111,000
2. New Ad Program	$211,000
3. PR Agency Retainer	$110,000
4. Direct Mail Program	$96,000
5. Press Tour	$65,000
18. Attend Boston Show	$46,000
19. Attend Chicago Show	$48,000
10. New Product Brochure	$66,000
20. Attend Las Vegas Show	$52,000
21. New Product Package	$23,000
22. Company Newsletter	$14,000
8. Annual Report	$78,000
9. Customer Conference	$249,000
16. Demonstration Video	$235,000
12. New Logo Design	$11,000
11. Six Updated Datasheets	$26,000
1. Six Updated Product Brochures	$78,000
14. New Signs with Logo	$46,000
17. New Tradeshow Booth	$148,000
13. Replace Letterhead	$9,500
7. New Corp Brochure	$78,000

On a fresh piece of paper, copy the list. This time list each project in order of importance, with the most important projects at the top and the least important at the bottom.

Project Priority List

Project	Cost
6. Ads for New Product	$111,000
2. New Ad Program	$211,000
3. PR Agency Retainer	$110,000
4. Direct Mail Program	$96,000
5. Press Tour	$65,000
18. Attend Boston Show	$46,000
19. Attend Chicago Show	$48,000
10. New Product Brochure	$66,000
20. Attend Las Vegas Show	$52,000
21. New Product Package	$23,000
22. Company Newsletter	$14,000
8. Annual Report	$78,000
9. Customer Conference	$249,000 = $1,169,000
16. Demonstration Video	$235,000
12. New Logo Design	$11,000
11. Six Updated Datasheets	$26,000
1. Six Updated Product Brochures	$78,000
14. New Signs with Logo	$46,000
17. New Tradeshow Booth	$148,000
13. Replace Letterhead	$9,500
7. New Corp Brochure	$78,000

Now add up the costs starting at the top and working down. When your entire budget is spent (in this case $1,200,000), draw a line. This is the zero base where the money available equals approximately the money to be spent.

Selected Project List

Project	Cost
1. Ads for New Product	$111,000
2. New Ad Program	$211,000
3. PR Agency Retainer	$110,000
4. Direct Mail Program	$96,000
5. Press Tour	$65,000
6. Attend Boston Show	$46,000
7. Attend Chicago Show	$48,000
8. New Product Brochure	$66,000
9. Attend Las Vegas Show	$52,000
10. New Product Package	$23,000
11. Company Newsletter	$14,000
12. Annual Report	$78,000
13. Customer Conference	$249,000

The projects that fall below the line are dropped for the year unless more money becomes available. This technique can also be used for time and resource availability. Simply substitute days or people for project costs that were used in this example.

Figure 2-5 The Zero-Based Budgeting Process

Prioritized Project List

Completed by **Joe**

Date **Jan 9**

PROJECTS IN ORDER OF PRIORITY	NEED	TARGET DATE	ROUGH BUDGET	FEASIBILITY SCALE 1-10	RISK H/M/L	CURRENT STATUS
Annual Report	Legal	Jun	75,000	9	L	
Ads for New Product	Promotion, Sales	Aug	111,000	5	M	
New Ad Program	Competition	Mar	200,000	7	L	
PR Agency Program	Company PR	Annual	110,000	8	M	
Direct Mail Program	Immed Sales	Feb	96,000	10	M	
Press Tour	Announce	Aug	65,000	7	L	
Boston Show	Sales, Contacts	Aug	46,000	9	M	
Chicago Show	Sales, Contacts	Sept	48,000	9	M	
Las Vegas Show	Sales, Contacts	Nov	52,000	9	M	
Newsletter	Customer Contact	Aug	14,000	10	L	

Figure 2-6 Prioritized Project List

New projects for getting the required people, equipment, and/or funds must be added to the list and given high priority, if the other projects are to be completed. If that is impossible, then it may be possible to modify the scope of the project in some way so the more important aspects of the project can be accomplished.

Unfortunately, it is sometimes the organization's expectations or political situations that cause projects to be ranked at a high priority and not the actual need. A common example of a project prioritized for political reasons is one that everyone knows the boss wants to do, but which really doesn't have a strong imperative for completion. Let's say the boss wants to build a fancy new corporate headquarters to impress the competition—but this will use up funds that could be better spent on developing products or expanding into new markets. Using the ZBB, this problem will be instantly visible. If the boss still demands the new headquarters after reviewing the projects that must be eliminated because of the decision, then it's time to consider your own career options.

A final project selection list like the one shown in Figure 2-6 as an example should be created that summarizes the projects, the target completion dates, and states target dates for completing the project plans for each project. Notice in the example for TechMore, Inc., the projects proposed for the Marketing Communications Department have been weeded down from sixteen feasible, appropriate projects to only ten for immediate consideration. The other projects are put on a "hold" list for future consideration.

The selection process for projects should not be viewed as a one-time event. Selecting projects is an ongoing, cyclic process. Business is constantly changing. As new ideas are created and new objectives formed to meet competitive, financial, and other business pressures, new projects must be evaluated and integrated into the existing project portfolio. In order to survive, businesses must develop ongoing processes for reassessing their projects and their use of resources. This management of change is an important part of the project selection and reevaluation process.

If project reviews are implemented on a regular basis, new projects can be integrated into the portfolio and existing projects can be reevaluated and priorities reassigned if necessary. Each time a new project is considered, it should be evaluated against the current project priority list and accepted or rejected using the same nine steps just discussed.

SAMPLE PROJECTS USED TO ILLUSTRATE PROJECT MANAGEMENT CONCEPTS IN THIS BOOK

Two projects from TechMore, Inc., will be used throughout the book to illustrate the project management process. These projects are the development of a customer newsletter and the opening of a new sales office in San Francisco.

The customer newsletter project is a small undertaking with medium priority. This project has been used because it meets the criteria for a simple project defined in the last chapter. The second project, the opening of a new sales office in San Francisco, is a project that meets the criteria of a medium-to large-sized project. The project is a high-priority project in terms of need and potential benefit to the organization.

These two projects are used because they are familiar types of projects, similar in many ways to the projects managed by a wide range of people in business. Both projects are simple enough to be used as examples in a book of this scope, and at the same time can be used to illustrate most of the basic concepts in the project management discipline. By taking the same projects from start to finish, it will be easier to see how the techniques for a simple and a more complex project are applied through the phases of conception, planning, implementation, and termination.

After Selection, Projects Are Further Defined

Once projects are selected for further planning, the next step in the formal project management is to complete a plan for each project. The individual project planning process begins with the refinement of the project goals. (See Figure 2-7.) Behind the ideas or concepts for projects there are usually specifics that people believe the projects will achieve—these are the goals that become the definition of the project. The goals are the foundation for developing the project plan. The project goal guides the development of each section of the complete project plan, including task definition, charting, resource allocation, devising objectives, scheduling, and budgeting, which will be presented in subsequent chapters. After the project is finished, the success of the project will be measured against the attainment of the project goal(s).

Goals are based on the needs that were established for the project earlier, but goals are different from needs. Needs are the imperative for implementing the project. Goals are the desired end results. The project goals are the end results expected from the implementation of the project. Amazingly, many people responsible for projects cannot specify the goals for the projects they manage.

People can complete all the implementation steps in a project, and never ask if they are performing the right tasks. If you don't know where you are going in the project, how will you know when you get there? The goals for a project are like a map for the project—they establish a direction and a final destination.

For example, a marketing communications person might be responsible for creating a brochure. Even if a brochure is created on time and within budget, on its own it does not accomplish a business goal. It is just a brochure,

Categories of Business Project Goals	
• Strategic	Long-term importance to the enterprise.
• Tactical	An immediate need exists.
• Financial	To improve economic position, reduce costs, or generate more revenue/profit.
• Operational	Improve productivity, quality., efficiency, or effectiveness.

Figure 2-7 Categories of Business Project Goals

and if it was developed without clearly stated goals, it may be nothing more than printed paper with pretty pictures and flowery words. The brochure has to accomplish something, like improving customer response or delivering a specific message to a specific audience or accomplishing some other goal established for the brochure when the project was initiated. The goal will identify the message, distribution, and audience for the brochure, as well as the time-frame and budget for completing it. If the marketing communications person just creates a brochure without nailing down the objectives, the project may be a waste of time and money.

Business goals are either strategic or tactical. Strategic goals are those goals that are part of the enterprise plan, designed to position a company for the future and to take advantage of new opportunities. Tactical goals usually solve specific, immediate problems and needs.

Whether strategic or tactical, business goals for projects fall into two general categories: operational and financial. Operational goals relate to the functional areas in an organization like marketing, personnel, administration, and data processing and include things like improving productivity, entering new markets, building the customer base, streamlining operations, expanding support capabilities, and many more. Financial goals always involve money and include reducing costs, increasing profit, expanding sales, and improving margins.

A business project may have multiple goals. It's not uncommon for a business project to have both an operational goal and a financial goal and also have an underlying, but often unspecified, strategic goal as the central motivation for the project. For example, the goal for creating an advertisement might include the operational goal of increasing awareness in a company's products, have the financial goal of increasing sales, and be motivated by the underlying strategy of expanding into new domestic markets.

After selecting projects for planning, you should already have a broad need or opportunity stated for each project. Now, you must clarify the goals based on these broad needs for the projects so they can be used to guide the project. Many people believe that setting goals is just a matter of stating them. Not so! Setting goals and agreeing on them may be one of the most difficult aspects of project management.

The Six Criteria for Project Goals

1. The goals must be specific.

2. The goals must be realistic.

3. The goals must have a time component.

4. The goals must be measurable.

5. The goals must be agreed upon.

6. Responsibility for achieving the project goals must be identified.

Goal clarification is a process that requires focus and discipline. Goal setting involves time, energy, and communication. You will need to go back and forth with your management, your peers, or others who will be involved in the project to clarify the goals to be achieved.

In setting goals for a project, the project manager must do four things:

1. Focus the planning process and the project team on the end results of the project.
2. Create clarity in the goals so all understand what will be accomplished.
3. Gain consensus and commitment on the goals for the project.
4. Establish the goals as the basis for the project planning process.

Because every project is unique, it is difficult to be clear on the goals right away. The goals for a project must meet six criteria to fulfill the project definition requirements in the project management process.

Project Goal Criterion 1. Goals Must Be Specific

Anyone who reads the goals for your project should be able to understand what you are trying to accomplish. To establish if the goals are specific enough, ask yourself: "If someone else had to take over this project for some reason, would that person be able to achieve the same general end results I have in mind for the project based on the goals I have stated?" If your answer to this question is, "Yes!" then the goals are probably specific enough.

Project Goal Criterion 2. Goals Must Be Realistic

Goals must be attainable using resources available or obtainable by the organization. It doesn't matter how good the idea is or how great a project it might be, if you don't have the time, skills, equipment, or money to do it, the entire effort spent on the project will be wasted.

Consider a company that wanted to hire fifteen new organic chemists and have them trained to develop a new environmental cleanup chemical that needed to be ready for a company next month. It takes more than a month for most people to become adapted to a new company, not to mention that it takes time to find the right people, interview them, and relocate them. You might be able to hire fifteen people in a month, but probably not fifteen organic chemists of the caliber you need to complete the project. Therefore, the goal is unrealistic. If your people complain that the dates are unrealistic or other aspects of the project are unattainable as specified, make the goal realistic, or modify the project requirements, or consider whether the project is really viable and necessary. Something has to give.

Project Goal Criterion 3. Goals Must Have a Time Component

Very simply put, projects without deadlines never get done. Without a time limitation, projects go on and on, lacking priority and focus. Time constrains projects, but it also helps define them. Even if the project has a flexible window, assign a target completion date to the project and be able to justify it. If there is no time imperative for a project, it is likely that the project isn't necessary at all and it's place on the active list should be seriously reconsidered.

Project Goal Criterion 4. Goals Must Be Measurable

This is the hardest one for most people. Some goals are easier to measure than others, but all project goals must be measurable in some way. The measurable end results for projects are referred to as "deliverables." Deliverables are the physical items or measurable services that will be delivered from a project. A "deliverable" is either produced or not, making it easy to measure.

Project Management Buzzword

☞ **Deliverables**—Project deliverables are the physical items or measurable services that are identified as part of the end results of a project. Deliverables can also be specified for individual tasks within a project. Deliverables are always measurable because they can be counted or observed.

Like projects with easily defined physical deliverables, project goals with money and volumes attached are easily measured, but quality and attitude goals are more difficult. For these less tangible goals, you must establish the method of measuring the goal at the onset of the project. For example, if one of your project goals is to increase customer satisfaction, use a questionnaire to ask customers what they think about the product. The questionnaire can be specified as the means of measuring the attainment of the goal. Thus, the goal would be stated as "improve customer satisfaction with the product as measured by a questionnaire to be sent to customers one month after the product is delivered."

Project Goal Criterion 5. Goals Must Be Agreed Upon

If the people responsible for a project do not agree on the goals, then it is unlikely that the goals for the project will be satisfactorily attained. Projects started with conflicting goals often have project participants working to different priorities and end results. Some people may even try to undermine the project for political reasons.

If the project is controversial or complex or involves many departments, gaining consensus on the goals may be a frustrating process to the inexperienced project manager. But through negotiation, compromise, and open communication, goals can be agreed upon—eventually. It is incumbent on the project manager to see that goals are agreed upon by the people who count and that the rest of the project team is aware of these goals before they begin work on the project.

Now, is it to lower the price of corn, or isn't it? It is not much matter which we say, but mind, we must all say the same.
                                            —Lord Melbourne,
                                        At a Cabinet Meeting, 1867

Project Goal Criterion 6. Responsibility for Achieving the Goals Must Be Identified

For goals to be achieved, someone or some group of people must be responsible for the goals. This responsibility starts with the project manager. Even though more than one person will be involved in a project, someone needs to be given the responsibility for coordinating the project and the rest of the project management activities that will guide the project to its desired end results. Sometimes organizations fail to be explicit about who this person is, however, because people are not used to managing the achievement of goals as projects in business. If a person is not specified as responsible for a project, ask who it should be. Someone of authority needs to assign a project manager (or project management team) who is responsible for the goals. A person must be assigned for every project on the organization's list. The responsibility needs to be unambiguous and agreed upon, just like the goals. Before you go off to start work on the project, make sure everyone is clear on who the project manager is.

THE PROCESS OF SETTING PROJECT GOALS

To establish project goals that meet these six criteria, start with the general goals stated in the project selection worksheet. Then, the general goals for the project must be reviewed and specified. This usually involves getting key people together to write and agree on a goal for the project that meets all five criteria. As a way to keep focused on the six criteria for goal setting, a simple worksheet like Figure 2-8 can be used to ask specific questions to help guide the goal-setting process.

Goal setting is an iterative process in most organizations. That means that the discussion of goals goes back and forth until consensus is obtained. Usually the project manager must intervene in the consensus-gathering process to keep the goal focused and realistic by restating goals or offering appropriate compromises. Compromises are often made in goals to accommodate multiple needs for the project in order to maximize the project's effectiveness. It may take more than one meeting or discussion to establish clear goals for a project.

Each party in a goal-setting situation will bring a personal point of view to the process. The political pressure felt in goal-setting meetings or discussions may range from gentle suggestions to dirty power plays. People may use their position, personalities, and relationships to force their points of view. The person responsible for setting the final goals, whether it is the project manager or a managerial person who will ultimately assign the project manager, must have good interpersonal skills, clear authority for establishing the goals, and the ability to negotiate and compromise to help the key players in the goal-setting process to reach consensus.

Identifying key players for goal setting is another challenge. Some projects are high-visibility projects that spark enthusiasm. These high-priority projects often cross organizational boundaries because many people may have an interest in the project and may want to be involved. On other projects, it seems that no one wants to be involved because the project represents additional work. In both cases, the project manager (or other responsible person) must get the

Goal Setting Worksheet

Your Name_____ Date _____

Project Name _____

Initial Goal Statement _____

	Names	Titles
Who should be involved in goal setting?		
Who needs to approve the goals?		
Who should be responsible for achieving the goals?		

Are their any hidden agendas to consider?	
How will attainment of the goals be measured?	
When should the project start and finish for maximum success?	Start: Finish:
Are the goals feasible?	
What are the constraints on the goals?	Time _____ Budget _____ Resources _____

Figure 2-8 Goal Setting Worksheet

right people involved in the goal-setting process, without alienating the people who don't need to be involved at this level—a delicate balance at best and one that depends on the project manager's ability to appraise the potential politics surrounding the project in advance.

Establish the approval process that will be used for deciding on the final goals, as well. Who will sign off on the goals and how will this process be initiated? This will vary greatly from organization to organization. If you don't know, ask. The key is establishing the game rules in advance, so you don't waste time getting project goals accepted by the wrong individuals.

Use informal discussions to discuss or review goals as well as formal meetings. One-on-one discussions will enable a wide number of people to be involved without the political or logistical problems of having them in the same meeting. Meetings help focus the group to resolve conflicts and come to consensus. Both meetings and informal discussions are important.

It is not uncommon to find yourself caught in a power play between two or more senior managers who are unable to agree on the goals for a project. If you aren't regarded as a peer, you may find it difficult for them to resolve the issues in your presence. (Neither person wants to give up ground or power in the eyes of subordinates.) As an alternative to bashing heads, remind these dueling managers that you need to go to another meeting and inform them of the specific deadline for getting the project goals defined. Then, communicate the issues that require resolution, without pointing fingers at either party, and ask them to answer specific questions regarding the goals for the project by a specific date. This, it is hoped, will encourage them to have a private meeting to resolve the conflicts. This way you keep yourself politically neutral and don't have to know the bloody details about the resolution process. The more you avoid participating in the conflicts, the more power you will have to resolve them as an objective, neutral participant.

In addition to primary goals, a project may have secondary goals. Secondary goals are requirements that will be accommodated if possible, but will lack the priority of the primary goals. Establishing secondary goals is often a way to incorporate alternate needs that a particular group has expressed for a project, thus offering a compromise to resolve a political conflict about the goals of a project. The secondary goals should be taken seriously in the other planning processes, but will be eliminated first if trade-offs are necessary to balance the time, money, and other resources needed to complete the project.

Choose the Right Players for Setting Goals

Determining the people who should be involved in setting the goals for projects is both important and fraught with political ramifications that can affect the success of the project. Here are a few guidelines that may prove helpful in selecting the people who should be involved in establishing goals for your projects:

- First, clearly identify the person responsible for making final decisions and resolving conflicts in the goal-setting process. This is usually the project manager, but it may also be a line manager or a senior executive. Someone must have clear authority and responsibility for making the final decisions regarding the project goals or they'll never get approved.
- Get the most senior people possible involved, either to help formulate or review the goals. People are more willing to adopt goals if their bosses or other leaders support them.
- Determine the primary organizations that will be involved and get each organization to participate in developing and reviewing the goals. However, limit the representation in meetings to one or two people from each organization. Too many people and opinions will defocus meetings and dilute the results of the goal-setting process.
- Choose people with the appropriate experience and expertise to participate in the goal-setting process. If the people setting the goals don't understand the requirements of the project, then the goals are likely to be vague or unrealistic or both. If the project requires specific technical skills, make sure these skills are represented in the goal-setting team.
- All the interests in the project should be represented. Even if only one department will be responsible for completing the project, if another department will be affected by the results, make sure this department or group is represented in the goal-setting process—either formally or informally.
- Always communicate the final goals for the project before the rest of the project planning process continues.
- Formally acknowledge people for their ideas and participation, even when their suggestions are not incorporated into the final goals for the project.

SETTING GOALS FOR THE SAMPLE PROJECTS

The process of defining goals for the customer newsletter project can be used to exemplify a typical goal-setting situation for a project. The need specified for this project in the initial selection process was to "establish ongoing communication with existing customers." However, this is too broad and unspecific to be used as a goal for a project. No time frames are specified. You can't measure whether the goal has been accomplished, and there is no formal definition of the content of the newsletter or of the term "ongoing".

Ingrid, the vice president of sales, realized the need for a more specific goal for the project and held a meeting with the five managers who will be involved in the project. First, she asked if everyone agreed that a customer newsletter was a good idea and asked if they agreed on the broad goal as stated. All agreed on the goal because everyone knew there was a problem getting information to customers on a timely basis, and they all felt a newsletter was a good solution.

This insightful vice president asked the group to write their goals for the project independently on a piece of paper. After doing this, she had the individuals read their goals and listed them on the board in the meeting room as each person read them off.

John, the customer support manager, wanted a brief weekly newsletter to explain the technical details of new product releases and to provide work-arounds for known problems. This would help reduce customer calls to his department.

George, the manager of public relations, felt the newsletter should be bimonthly, but wanted the newsletter to reinforce the positive decision customers made in buying the products and felt that it would be a good vehicle for telling customers how others are successfully using the products. In this way, new applications for products would be encouraged, and, it was hoped, more goods would be sold as a result.

Sarah, the sales development manager, wanted a newsletter that was published every quarter and wanted it to include information on pricing and offer special deals to the customers in the region. Her goal was to improve relationships with existing customers by offering them "good deals" on a regular basis.

Joe, the marketing communications manager, wanted the newsletter to enhance the image of the company. He believed it should have full-color pictures and lots of interesting stories about the company and the industry in general, and it should happen once a quarter—because that's all the department had time for in its busy schedule.

After writing the individual goals on the board (see Figure 2-9), the group discovered that there was no consensus about the definition, timing, or purpose of the monthly newsletter—even though all agreed initially that the goal was to "establish ongoing communication with existing customers." They all agreed on the target audience, however, and that was existing customers—though in the discussion they also agreed that the newsletter should be used as a promotional tool at tradeshows and conferences to demonstrate the company's positive and ongoing support of customers.

The lack of consensus about the other aspects of the goals for the newsletter was used by the vice president as an opportunity to explain why the goal-setting process was important—because she wanted to use this goal-setting approach for larger projects in the future and felt it was a good idea to train the group in goal-setting with a relatively small, low-priority project like this one.

Using the worksheet as a guide and the individual goals for the project already presented by the group members, the vice president encouraged the group to discuss each aspect of the proposed newsletter in order to establish

The Initial View of the Newsletter Project Goals		
Initial Goal Statement	➡	Establish ongoing communications with customers.
John, Customer Support Manager	➡	Weekly publication to explain technical details.
George, Manager of Public Relations	➡	Bimonthly publication with customer case studies.
Sarah, Sales Development Manager	➡	Monthly information on pricing and special deals.
Joe, Marketing Communications Manager	➡	Quarterly report to enhance company image with color pictures.

Figure 2-9 The Initial View of the Newsletter Project Goals

a complete, agreed-upon goal for the project. At times the discussion got heated. This conflict was to be expected, and the vice president felt encouraged about the strong feelings because it meant that the people were committed to the project and to the organization.

First, the content of the newsletter had to be established. After reviewing the various needs of the group, it was realized that most of the content objectives of the group could be accomplished in one newsletter. A regular section would be devoted to technical tips—making John happy. Another section would highlight new pricing and special deals—Sarah was satisfied. And every issue a feature article would be written focusing on a customer application or an industry trend—both Joe and George felt good about this.

Next, the frequency and the publication date of the first issue needed to be resolved. The weekly idea was ultimately rejected because it wasn't feasible to produce a weekly newsletter with existing resources and everyone but John felt it was overkill to do so. A newsletter only four or six times a year seemed too infrequent. Finally, it was agreed that a monthly newsletter would be best—and John eventually realized that he could still send out product bulletins separately that met the interim needs to get technical information to customers.

Now, the vice president asked the group when the first issue should be published. After a number of suggestions, the group decided that the first issue would get the most attention if it was published in September, when most people returned from summer vacations and would be more likely to see and read the first issue. In addition, the marketing and sales managers expressed a desire to have the first newsletter available for a major tradeshow in September to distribute as part of the company's promotional materials. Since it was only May, the group felt there was plenty of time to do a good job on the first issue. The first issue would take the longest because the format and design had to be developed. A monthly production schedule would be developed after the first issue was produced. Everyone agreed this would be satisfactory, though Sarah expressed concern about the long wait for the first publication.

Next, a size for the newsletter needed to be established. Based on the content requirements and some general discussion about budget, it was decided that the newsletter should be eight pages long and $8\frac{1}{2}$" × 11", so it could be stored easily in an ordinary file folder or binder. Some in the group still felt it should be longer, but the vice president finally intervened and suggested that an eight-page document would be developed initially to get things started and the size would be reevaluated after a few issues. This seemed to appease the dissenters.

Then the quality issue was brought up. Each member of the group seemed to have a different idea about the final form of the newsletter. Some viewed it as a simple black and white document, reproduced on the copy machine to save time and money. Initially, Joe and George saw it as a high-quality piece with full-color pictures on expensive paper. After a number of alternatives were reviewed, it was clear that what everyone really wanted was something that looked good, but would not take up too much of the advertising budget—the source of funds for the project. Advertising was considered higher priority because it helped develop the new business that the company needed to meet its sales goals.

The quality problem looked impossible to resolve, but finally Joe suggested using a two-color format with a distinctive masthead. Photos could be reproduced in black and white to save money. Thus, the newsletter would look attractive and professional, but would be relatively inexpensive to produce. All agreed this was a good compromise.

Then, someone brought up the issue of responsibility for managing the project. Everyone pointed at someone else, except John, the support manager, who felt the project belonged in his department because he was the one who had the idea in the first place. After listening to the group banter for a while, the vice president realized that the group members would never decide on their own and interjected that the Marketing Communications Department clearly had the most experience producing these kinds of projects and a person from sales and support could be responsible for their own articles each month. After a few grumbles, everyone agreed that this was probably the best approach—and the marketing communications manager found himself responsible for yet another project.

Finally, after reviewing each aspect of the project, the group was able to reach consensus that the goal for the project should be stated as follows:

> *The goal of the project is to produce a customer newsletter on a monthly basis beginning in September that will initially be eight pages in length. The newsletter should measure 8 1/2 × 11" in size and be mailed to existing customers without an envelope. The printed newsletter should present an image of quality through design, but will be limited to two-color printing to control production costs. The purpose of the newsletter will be to maintain contact with existing customers and encourage additional sales, by providing new ideas for applications of the products, useful information in troubleshooting product problems, and special offers and pricing available only to newsletter readers. The newsletter must present a professional appearance and show the company's products and service in a positive light.*

> *The impact of the newsletter will be measured in a survey to be sent to customers after the first issue and yearly thereafter. The project will be the responsibility of the marketing communications manager but will involve designated people from sales and customer support, who will contribute articles and ideas to the newsletter.*

A secondary goal for the project was also established:

> *The newsletter will be distributed as part of the company's promotional materials in direct sales situations, tradeshows, and conferences to demonstrate the company's ongoing support and communication with customers.*

The goal for the newsletter project now met all six criteria of a good project goal:

Criterion 1. It Is Specific

Enough detail is present to create a project plan. At the same time, the goal is not so specific to limit creativity during the implementation phase.

Criterion 2. It Is Realistic

Producing a monthly newsletter is both feasible and appropriate. The use of the budget has been realistically handled.

Criterion 3. It Has a Time Component

The frequency of the newsletter has been specified as monthly. The first issue will be completed in September before the tradeshow.

Criterion 4. It Is Measurable

Many aspects of the goal are measurable, including the monthly delivery, the size of the newsletter, and the content. The quality of the newsletter in meeting its customer objectives will specifically be measured through a survey to be sent to customers who have received the first newsletter. This was specified as part of the goal.

Criterion 5. The Goal Is Agreed Upon

The meeting was used to establish consensus about the goal, and everyone left the meeting satisfied that the project was now appropriate and well-defined, even though some compromises had been made.

Criterion 6. Responsibility for the Goals Is Assigned

The marketing communications manager has been identified as the project manager, though people from sales and support will also be involved in the project.

In establishing the goal statement for the opening of the San Francisco sales office, the process of goal selection was similar, though it involved a different group of people and more executives. Because this project is more complex, more people are involved, and additional meetings and discussions took place before the goals were agreed upon. But because the quality and operational goals for a similar project involving opening the Philadelphia sales office last year had already been established, these goals were used as the starting point for the San Francisco Office project, which made the process somewhat easier. The main modifications involved adjusting the time frames and budget.

After a couple of meetings and a number of discussions with the key players, the vice president of sales assigned Roger, the Western Region sales manager as the project manager. Later, Roger issued a memo that specified that the following goal had been agreed to for opening the San Francisco sales office in a planning meeting with the key executives from sales and administration. The goal was stated as follows:

The goal of the project is to open a sales office and customer meeting facility in San Francisco, using the Philadelphia sales office as a model for decor and size. In addition to office space, the facility will have two training rooms and a separate room for demonstrating products. The office should be leased in a building with the option of expanding the office over the next five years. The office should be opened by August and will be staffed at that time with a district sales manager, three trained salespeople, one technical support specialist, and an administrative assistant. These personnel will be additions to the staff currently serving the Western Region, and will report to the new district sales manager. New territories and quotas will be assigned before the office is opened. There will be a grand opening ceremony inviting customers and prospects in the area to view the new facilities. The office will be announced through public relations activities.

By July of the following year, it is expected that Western Region sales will increase by at least 50 percent because of the new office and staff in San Francisco. In addition, customer satisfaction regarding responsiveness of sales and support in the Western Region will be increased as measured by a survey to be conducted prior to opening the office and six months after the office is opened.

Again, the goals for the project as specified meet all six criteria. They are specific enough to be the basis of a plan. They are realistic because they are based on the success of a similar project. There is a specified time for the project and a target date for opening the office and the goals for the project are clearly measurable. If the office opens on time, one of the goals is met, and if sales in the Western Region increase, another goal is met. If customers report higher satisfaction and the number of complaints about service in the region are reduced, then the third measurable aspect of the goal will be satisfied. Responsibility for opening the office has been clearly assigned to the Western Region sales manager by the vice president of sales.

AFTER THE GOALS ARE ESTABLISHED, THE CONSTRAINTS MUST BE SPECIFIED

All project goals have constraints. This is because no company or enterprise has unlimited time, equipment, money or expertise to use to complete projects. The constraints, coupled with the goals, define the entire scope of a project. The scope of the project will allow the work to be defined so it can be completed within the constraints to accomplish the goals.

Constraints are the limitations that are not usually specified as part of the goals, but that must also be documented and acknowledged before the further planning can ensue. The most common constraints are those of budget and resources.

Project Management Buzzword

☛ **The Statement of Work or SOW**—In many large client-driven or government projects, a written description of the goals, constraints, and assumptions about a project are combined into a document called the Statement of Work or SOW. The SOW is a narrative description of the work to be performed (the goals as we've described them here) plus a brief description of constraints, including overall budgets, rough schedule including start dates and end dates, and any assumptions made about the project, including sources of funding, number of personnel available to the project, and quality of available resources and materials. This SOW is the project description used for initiating the rest of the project planning process.

There are also assumptions behind every project—assumptions about the economic conditions supporting the project and assumptions about the availability of people and equipment to complete the project. In the goal planning worksheet, you probably noticed the sections on constraints and assumptions that were completed for the two sample projects. It is important to document key assumptions, because if something happens that affects the validity of these assumptions as the project progresses, then the project goals and plans must be reevaluated. For example, if a project to expand into new markets is based on the assumption that the economic climate in Eastern Europe will remain stable and all of a sudden a war breaks out between key countries in the region, then the projects based on this assumption of economic stability must be reassessed.

In the newsletter project, the constraints are time and budget. In the sales office project, the constraints are mostly budget related, though there are some specific assumptions made about the availability of skilled people to staff the new office.

It may take several iterations and considerable work to get the goals right for a project, but without properly defined goals and acknowledgment of the constraints that go with them, the rest of the project management toolbox is crippled. Goals written like the examples provide a clear definition of a project—and because of this they take some time to work out. Project management as a discipline assumes that people have specific end results in mind. Project management provides the tools for helping people meet these desired end results—the goals. However, if the goals are vague or unspecific or unrealistic, then project management can't help. People may end up spinning their wheels and accomplishing nothing as a result. The first rule of project management is to never start a project without clear goals!

This chapter has described the process of selecting appropriate projects for a business and defining clear goals for those projects. When the goals you have established for a project meet the six criteria presented here, then the rest of the project management process can proceed. You will move from the project conceptualization phase into the formal project planning phase. The first step in the planning stage is to define the specific work and tasks that need to be accomplished to meet the goals you have established for your project—the topic of the next chapter.

Chapter Three

IDENTIFYING THE WORK TO BE DONE: Methods for Describing Tasks and Work Flow

Once the goals of a project are clearly defined, planning can begin. The first step in the planning stage of the project management process is the description of the actual work that needs to be done to accomplish the goals. The project must be broken down into individual project tasks (also called activities by many project managers) that need to be completed. This list of tasks can be short and simple or detailed and comprehensive—it depends on the size and goals of the project. The underlying principles for defining and sequencing project tasks are the same, regardless of the size of the project or the charting method used.

To make the individual activities in a project easier to track and monitor, the tasks must be organized in some way that makes the work easier to understand and communicate. There are many choices for doing this, including hierarchical charts, network diagrams, or structured lists, which will be described in this chapter. The completed documentation of your tasks is called a work plan. The charting option you choose for your work plan will depend on the size of the project, how the sequence of work is performed in your project, the number of people involved, and your own personal preferences.

The charting of the work plan is what many people think of when they envision the project management methodology. Although important, the charting of project tasks is really only one aspect of the project management process. As you read subsequent chapters, you'll find that the charts and graphs you learn about in this chapter will make the scheduling and budgeting of the project easier, and ultimately provide the basis for tracking the implementation of the project.

THE REQUIREMENTS FOR CONSTRUCTING A WORK PLAN

The project planning process starts by developing a work plan, which identifies the tasks and activities to be performed in order to accomplish the goals and deliverables specified for the project. When resources (people and equipment), costs, and time durations have been assigned to the tasks in the work plan, a complete project plan will be ready to move into the implementation stage. But, for now, lets consider only the work plan portion of the project plan—because this is the basis for everything else in the project plan.

The project manager must accomplish six things when developing the work plan:

- Break the work into manageable "tasks" that can be assigned to appropriate people and resources.
- Define the work as independent elements that can be sequenced, scheduled, and monitored.
- Integrate the work elements into a total system with a beginning and an end.
- Present the sequence of tasks in a form that can be easily communicated to people involved in the project.
- Define the tasks at a level of detail appropriate for the length and complexity of the project.
- Verify that the completion of the tasks will result in the attainment of the project goals.

The development of the work plan is an attempt to eliminate future crisis by preventing required activities from "falling through the cracks." By identifying the tasks and sequencing them, the work plan will answer two primary questions in the project planning process:

1. What will be accomplished?
2. How will it be accomplished?

A work plan that accomplishes the six objectives will typically have two components—the work breakdown structure and the project network diagram (or other sequenced task diagram). Both these components and the associated diagramming techniques are described in detail in this chapter. Ultimately, the work plan will be used to identify a project team, develop a schedule, and establish a budget for the project, but the development of those components of the total project plan is covered in the next three chapters.

DEVELOP A WORK BREAKDOWN STRUCTURE
TO IDENTIFY THE TASKS IN A PROJECT

The first steps in producing a complete work plan is the development of the work breakdown structure (WBS). The WBS is simply a hierarchical listing of the subcomponents of a project that looks like an organizational chart or outline when it's done. In addition to listing the tasks in a project, the work breakdown structure can be used to identify performance criteria, assign responsibilities for tasks, and relate costs and budgets to project components. For now, we will consider only the work component of the WBS. We will look at the work breakdown structure again in other chapters as a way of structuring and monitoring the work assignments and the budget.

Project Management Buzzword

☛ **Work Breakdown Structure or WBS**—A hierarchical approach to defining project work components. The WBS can be represented as a tree diagram, similar to an organizational chart, or listed as an outline. When the WBS is complete, the subprojects, tasks, and subtasks within a project are clearly defined. In addition to defining the work packages (tasks) in a project, the WBS can be used to identify cost components for budgeting and for assigning personnel to specific tasks in the project.

Using the goals and constraints as the guide, the first step in creating a work breakdown structure is to break the project into subprojects or major milestones. Even the simplest project has subprojects—groups of activities that lead to the creation of one major milestone in a project. When all the subprojects are complete, the total project is complete. Subprojects in larger projects are exactly that—projects within a project. In a large project, each of the subprojects will have separate work plans that are integrated by the project manager. Subprojects (also referred to as major milestones) are then divided into tasks and subtasks.

The number of levels used in a work breakdown structure will depend on the size and complexity of the project. In a WBS, each higher level is a summation of the levels below it. The following lists one possibility for defining levels in a WBS for a business project:

WBS Level	Definition
1	Total project
2	Subproject or major milestone
3	Combination of tasks
4	Task
5	Subtask
6	Individual processes or actions

Another WBS that could be used might look like this:

WBS Level	Definition
1	Overall project
2	Division
3	Group
4	Work package (another name for task)

The level of detail and the definitions of the levels represented depends largely on the size of the project. Some projects may have three levels in the WBS; other projects may have ten. The larger the project, the more levels that will be represented in the WBS. Typically, projects have six levels or fewer.

If not enough levels are present, the integration and coordination of activities may be difficult when work on the project begins. If too much detail is present, then unproductive time will be spent in monitoring and tracking work at a too low level of abstraction. The cost for planning and tracking at this level will negate the potential benefits of the project management process—and may alienate people on the project team who feel insulted or threatened by such low-level tracking.

The lowest level of work which you want to monitor should not end up being ridiculous. It is impossible to manage any project down to the minute, though some overly zealous project managers have tried to do this with less than satisfactory results. In most projects, the lowest-level task in a WBS should account for 0.5 to 2 percent of the total budget—in terms of time or money, depending on what is most important to monitor. Thus, for a project that will take a total of thirty days, it would be typical to summarize some of the tasks at the half-day or quarter-day level, though most of them would be specified in number of total days. In a project that will take a year or more to complete, the lowest level of work might be a one-week task—though some one-day tasks of extreme importance and criticality might be specified in the WBS.

There is no magic formula for the level of detail required in a WBS or project plan—so don't establish one standard for all your projects. Even though the Mars mission, the reorganization of a major corporation, and the furnishing of a new office are all projects that share certain principles of organization and management, the formula for detailing one of these projects will have little to do with the others. The only formula is to establish a level of planning appropriate for the work at hand.

The WBS can be organized based on a number of criteria. These include breaking the work down based on the following:

- Functional or technological disciplines, if distinct areas of expertise or technology are involved in completing the project
- Organizational structure if work is clearly divided among various groups or people in an organization
- Systems and subsystems if distinct subcomponents in a project must be developed that are integrated to complete the total project
- Vendor responsibilities if outside vendors or suppliers will be used in the project
- Physical location if various operating facilities will be used to complete a project

Or use a combination approach for different components of the project that require different focus. For example, the first level of the project might be broken down by organization and the second level of the project by subsystems the various organizations are responsible for.

There are some other basic guidelines for creating a work breakdown structure, that are useful as well:

- The work described in a higher level must be the sum of all the work in the next lower level.
- Each element of work in a project should be assigned to one and only one level of effort.
- In large projects, it is usually necessary to describe the scope of work in a narrative form, so people have a clear idea of what is to be accomplished.
- The definitions of work should be usable as communications tools so results can be compared with expectations for the work when the project is implemented.
- Work that will be performed by different people in the project should be clearly distinguished in the WBS. Each task at the subtask or action level should be the work of only one group or person in the same department or functional area.
- The WBS should define measurable deliverables for each work component of the project.
- The WBS should be flexible enough to allow for changes in the scope and goals of the project as the project progresses.

A WBS FOR A SIMPLE PROJECT

To see how a work breakdown structure is created for a simple project, the newsletter project presented in the last chapter provides a simple example. The final result of this project, based on the goals, is the distribution of a printed newsletter to customers in September. This becomes the top level in the work breakdown structure. On examining the newsletter goals, the following

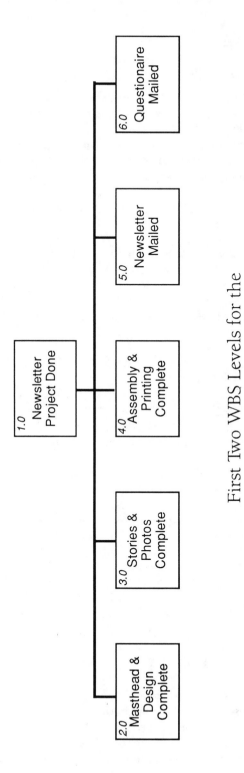

First Two WBS Levels for the
Newsletter Project

Figure 3-1 First Two WBS Levels for the Newsletter Project

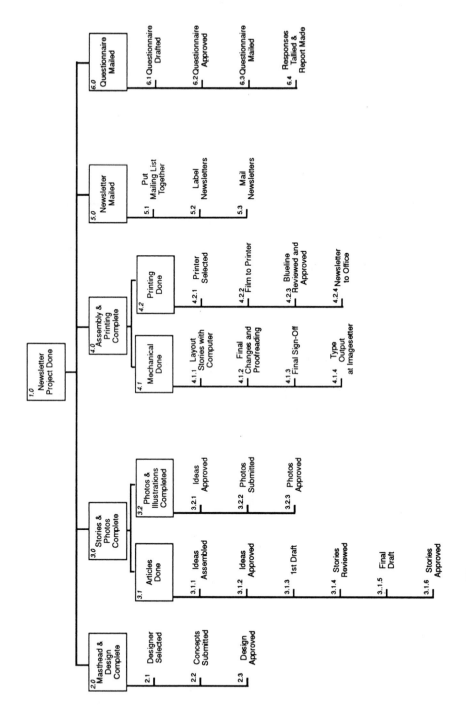

Figure 3-2 The Final Work Breakdown Structure for the Newsletter Project

subprojects (or milestones, if you prefer) need to be completed to finish the newsletter: the design of a format and masthead for the newsletter, the completion of the articles, photos and illustrations, assembling the components into a ready-to-print format, and printing. In addition, there is a subproject to mail the newsletter and one to create and distribute the questionnaire about the newsletter

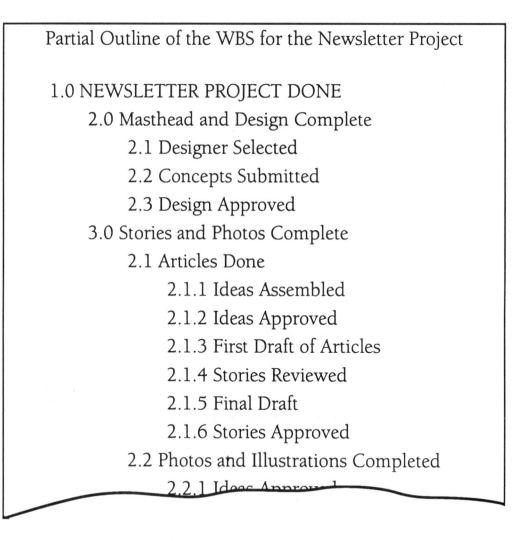

Partial Outline of the WBS for the Newsletter Project

1.0 NEWSLETTER PROJECT DONE
 2.0 Masthead and Design Complete
  2.1 Designer Selected
  2.2 Concepts Submitted
  2.3 Design Approved
 3.0 Stories and Photos Complete
  2.1 Articles Done
   2.1.1 Ideas Assembled
   2.1.2 Ideas Approved
   2.1.3 First Draft of Articles
   2.1.4 Stories Reviewed
   2.1.5 Final Draft
   2.1.6 Stories Approved
  2.2 Photos and Illustrations Completed
   2.2.1 Ideas Approved

Figure 3-3 Partial Outline of the WBS for the Newsletter Project

after the issue has been mailed to customers. These form the second level in the WBS. These first two levels of the WBS are illustrated in Figure 3-1.

Each of these subprojects has specific tasks associated with it as well—the third and fourth levels in the WBS for this project. It would be possible to break each of these tasks down even further, but for a project of this scope, the levels shown for the WBS are adequate. The final WBS for the newsletter project is shown in the diagram.

In developing a WBS it is typical to number each level or otherwise identify each task for reference in further planning activities. Several coding methods can be used for the WBS. One of the most popular in scientific and engineering circles is decimal notation, where levels of the WBS are denoted by decimal points. Other systems use unique numbers or letters for each box shown on the WBS. You can also combine letters and numbers, using identification labels like 1.A.2 or 2.C.3 to identify each WBS box. In Figure 3-2 a simple numbering system has been used to identify each level and task in the WBS.

Using a numbering system and indented paragraphs, many people prefer to represent the WBS for a project as an outline instead of a hierarchical chart (also called a tree diagram). (See Figure 3-3.) Both the outline and the tree diagram represent the same structure and detail. The use of one representation over another is strictly a matter of preference.

A WBS FOR A MORE COMPLEX PROJECT

Creating a WBS for a more complex project involves the same steps as for a simple project like the newsletter. However, developing a WBS for a complex project may involve more people and take a few more iterations to get right because of the number of tasks involved.

As an example of the WBS for a slightly larger project, let's look at the structure of the San Francisco sales office project. (See Figure 3-4.) On examination, it becomes apparent that the project is really three separate projects that must be integrated to meet the overall goals that have been specified for opening the office: the project to find and prepare the facility, the project to hire and train the personnel to staff the office, and the project to publicize the new office to customers and prospects.

A more detailed WBS should be created for each of the subprojects, down to the task level. In a very complex project this may require six or more levels. Ultimately, the tasks in all these subprojects must all be coordinated and sequenced so the office is opened in the first quarter of next year as specified in the goals for the project.

When the WBS for a project is completed, it should be reviewed by the key managers and other people involved in the project. In large projects, project managers for each of the subprojects in a WBS will be assigned, and they will create the WBS for their part of the total project. Then the project manager will integrate these individual work plans into a total project plan. It usually

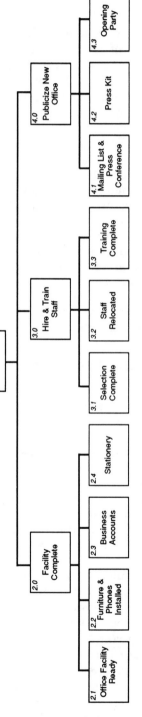

First Three WBS Levels for the San Francisco Sales Office Project

Figure 3-4 First Three WBS Levels for the San Francisco Sales Office Project

70

takes a few meetings to do this, so the various project managers agree on the level of detail and the tasks that must be performed.

USE A NETWORK DIAGRAM TO SEQUENCE THE TASKS IN A PROJECT

Work breakdown structures are a great first step in identifying the work packages or tasks in a project. However, WBS representations cannot show the relationships between various parts of the project. A WBS does not show the sequence of events either—only the hierarchical relationships. Therefore, a WBS cannot be used to create a schedule or coordinate work done by different people or resources, unless all the tasks in a project are sequential—and they rarely are, except in small projects.

Project Management Buzzword

☞ Network—The logical order of tasks that defines the sequence of work in a project. Networks are usually drawn from left to right, with lines drawn between tasks to indicate the precedences between tasks. Arrowheads are often placed on the lines to indicate the direction of the work flow through time.

Network diagrams show the interrelationships between tasks that are not visible in a WBS format. Networks reveal the work flow, not just the work. Though it is possible to create a network diagram without first developing a WBS, there are some limitations to network diagramming that make this undesirable. Network diagrams are awkward for managing budgets and personnel assignments. WBSs are awkward for scheduling. Thus, the use of both a WBS and a network to describe a project offers more efficient planning options.

If a WBS is done first, completing the network for a project is easy, because the tasks used to create the network have already been identified. Since tasks and milestones must be identified for a project anyway in order to create a network, we recommend that a WBS be created first to identify the tasks in a project and the network diagram be created next to show the sequence and relationships between tasks.

Network diagrams simply sequence the work tasks and identify their relationships in time. Networks are not as good as a WBS in demonstrating hierarchical relationships in a project, but they can be used to demonstrate the sequential interrelationships between various tasks in the WBS.

A network diagram, if properly sequenced, will accomplish the following:

- Show the sequence of tasks in completing a project.
- Identify milestones in the project that can be used for monitoring progress and accomplishments.
- Show the interrelationships of tasks in different parts of the WBS hierarchy.
- Establish a vehicle for scheduling tasks (covered in the next chapter).

There are two central concepts that must be understood before a network diagram can be created for a project; the concept of precedence and the concept of concurrent (or parallel) tasks.

Precedence Relationships in a Project Network

Precedence is a way to define the way in which some tasks are sequenced or related to one another. If one task must be completed before the next task can be started, the first task has precedence over the second. For example, in the newsletter project, the articles must first be written before they can be reviewed. In a network diagram, this precedence is illustrated by drawing one task after another. There are other precedences in the project as well. For example, the newsletter must be designed before it can be assembled, and it must be assembled before it is printed.

In some systems of project management, the term "dependency" is used in place of the term "precedence." Some people refer to network diagrams as "dependency diagrams" for this reason. When a task is dependent on another

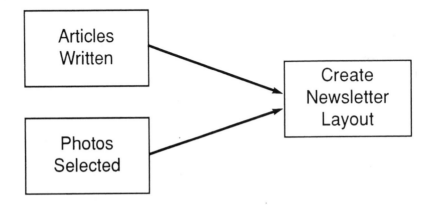

Figure 3-5 Two Concurrent Tasks that Are Precedent to the Same Task

task, it means that it must follow that task. It means the same thing as precedence, but takes the opposite point of view.

Project Management Buzzword

☛   Precedence—When one task must be completed before another task can be started, the first task is said to have precedence over the other.

Though some tasks are dependent on one another, other tasks can be started in parallel with other tasks, and this leads to the other important concept in network diagramming—the concept of concurrent or simultaneous activities. (See Figure 3-5.) Many tasks in projects can be worked on simultaneously or concurrently, as long as resources are available to do this. For example, it is possible to begin writing the newsletter articles before the format and masthead have been designed. However, both completing the articles and designing the format are precedents to assembling the newsletter. In a network diagram, it is possible to identify concurrent activities by drawing them parallel to each other in the same plane.

These notions of precedence and concurrence are important because the relationships between tasks will ultimately establish the basis for scheduling a project, which we will discuss in the next chapter. Adjusting the parallel activities and the precedences alters the time and resources required to complete a project. The goal in developing the network diagram is to maximize the relationship between the tasks by identifying activities that can occur in parallel and to specify the precedences that exist between the activities.

Project Management Buzzword

☛   Concurrent Tasks—Tasks in a project that can be worked on at the same time are called concurrent tasks.

Symbols and Conventions in Network Diagramming

We have found that the simple networking diagramming techniques are best used for most business projects. In every networking method there are specific symbols used in the charts. The system we are using here is based on a simplification of a diagramming technique called **precedence diagramming**. (See Figure 3-6.)

Boxes are used to describe each task. Lines are used to connect the tasks to one another, as we have shown. The tasks are laid out horizontally from left to right to coincide with the time sequence the tasks will be completed in.

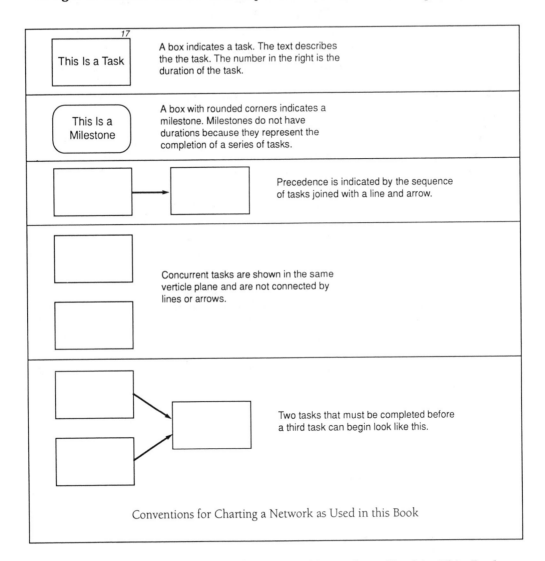

Conventions for Charting a Network as Used in this Book

Figure 3-6 Conventions for Charting a Network as Used in This Book

Groups of tasks that lead to specific deliverables are identified by boxes with rounded corners. These mark the milestones in the chart.

The precedences between tasks and milestones are shown by drawing lines from a task that is precedent on another. Examples of possible precedence relationships are shown in the chart. The basic relationships that must be diagrammed are the following:

- The defined sequences of tasks are represented by placing tasks in horizontal order in the network.
- One task may depend on the completion of multiple tasks or milestones. The precedences for all these tasks must be shown by drawing lines between the tasks.
- A task may start independently of some tasks but still be dependent on others. Lines are only drawn between tasks with dependency. A task without a precedent task or milestone can logically be started at any time because it has no dependent relationships.

THE STEPS IN CREATING A NETWORK DIAGRAM

There are five steps that should be followed to produce a network diagram for any project:

Network Diagram Step 1. List the tasks, using the WBS as a guide.

You have already learned how to create the WBS. For a network, each task should have a unique identifying number or other code. A network diagram will diagram the work units or individual task level in your WBS. Higher WBS levels will be identified as milestones (see Network Diagram Step 3).

Network Diagram Step 2. Establish the interrelationships between the tasks.

To determine the sequences and precedences that need to be diagrammed for the tasks, ask the following questions about each task:

- What tasks must precede this task? That is, what other tasks must be completed before this one can be started?
- What tasks follow this task? Or, what tasks cannot be started until this task is complete?
- What tasks can take place concurrently with this one? Or, more simply, what tasks can be worked on at the same time this one is being completed?

The precedences and relationships should be noted in a simple list. Some of the precedences won't become apparent until Network Diagram Step 4, however, when you actually draw the tasks and link them together.

If you don't identify all of the precedences now, that's fine. Just list them as you discover them to form a record. This list of task numbers and their precedences is particularly useful if you use computerized project management programs.

Network Diagram Step 3. Identify the milestones you want to specify in your network.

Milestones summarize a sequence of tasks or specify a key accomplishment during the project. Milestones are not tasks. Milestones do not take effort—they are just convenient markers for summarizing work that has been performed to that point on the network diagram. The summary levels in the WBS are a good source of milestones for the project. Milestones also have defined precedences and sequences.

Network Diagram Step 4. Layout the tasks and milestones as a network.

Some experienced project managers start from the last task in the project and work backward when charting the project. Many people find it easier to identify preceding tasks than successive ones. However, there are many arguments for starting with the first task and working forward, since this is how the work will actually be done. The outcome is the same—the approach used is a matter of preference.

When you draw out the tasks in a network you are actually trying to predict the future. That is what planning is—a description of work in the future. By sequencing the tasks in a network you are describing the way you want the work to occur in time. Since no one we know is omniscient, planning always has error associated with it. Because of this, you can expect that the actual sequence of events may vary as the actual project starts. You can also expect to miss a few tasks in the process. However, your goal is to diagram the tasks as closely as possible to what you believe should actually happen and to identify as much of the work as possible.

By convention, most network diagrams start with a box labeled "Start Project" and end with a box labeled "Project Finished." All you have to do is fill in the tasks in between.

Network Diagram Step 5. Review the logic of the network.

The network review process is important because it is through adapting sequences and precedences that an optimum sequence of project tasks can be identified. To review the logic of the network, look at each task and each connection and ask yourself the following questions:

- Are the tasks properly sequenced?
- Are all the precedences identified?
- Are there some precedences that aren't really required? Or are there tasks that can be completed concurrently that are incorrectly shown as sequences?
- Are all the tasks necessary?
- Does the completion of the tasks in the network represent the accomplishment of everything necessary to meet the project goals that have been specified?

Project Management Tip

✎ **Number the Tasks in Your Network**—Though we haven't done it in the examples, because we wanted to keep things legible, to make tasks and sequences easier to find in your network, be sure to identify each task and milestone with unique numbers or other identification labels. In computerized project management programs, tasks are always numbered as well as identified by task description. The same method of identification or numbering used in the WBS is usually appropriate though it is common in networks to skip numbers between tasks to allow flexibility in the network when requirements for new tasks or different ones may become apparent later in the project. For example, instead of numbering tasks as 1, 2, 3, and so on, it might be better to number tasks as 10, 20, 30, 40, . . . Then, when you need to add new tasks between task 10 and 20, you can number them 11 or 12 without disturbing the logical numbering sequence of the original tasks. The numbering system should be flexible because projects almost always have changes that need to be represented in the network.

The sequences of tasks you put in your network are not absolute. Experienced project managers often revise and adjust the networks until they are optimized. People often find when they begin mapping precedences, that tasks have been left out of the WBS. Add these new tasks—and make sure to note them in the appropriate place in the WBS. The network and the WBS should always match. In reverse, if you find that some tasks are redundant, remove them.

Be careful not to list tasks in an arbitrary order. Just because you've always done something a certain way does not mean it is the best way to do it. Try to look at the network from a new point of view to find better ways to get the work done. A network diagram provides a great opportunity to do this. Can the tasks be sequenced differently for better use of resources? Can some tasks be "split" into two or more tasks to make the organization of work more flexible? It is usually a good idea to have objective outsiders review the sequences, in addition to the project team, to avoid bias in the

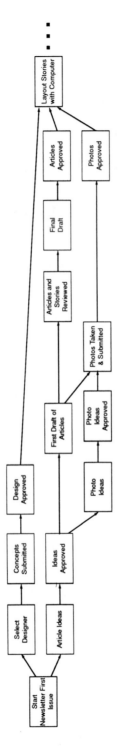

Partial Network Diagram for the Newsletter Project

Figure 3-7 Partial Network Diagram for the Newsletter Project

sequence of the work. Sometimes a person outside the politics of a project can identify a better way to complete the work.

Going back to the newsletter example to see how the five steps come together, we can review part of the network diagram that Joe developed for the newsletter project. (See Figure 3-7.) (We only show part of the network here because of space limitations.) Joe reviewed this network with the other members of the project team and with Ingrid, his boss, before it was finalized and had to make three or four rounds of changes before it was the way everyone wanted it.

Another example of a network diagram, a subset of the tasks for the San Francisco sales office project, is provided in the next chapter when we discuss scheduling. Notice that the tasks are laid out so each of the individual subprojects are shown on different levels. This makes it easier to visualize large projects.

HOW MUCH DETAIL SHOULD YOU REPRESENT IN YOUR NETWORK?

The goals and the constraints for the project, as described in the last chapter, establish the scope for the project. In creating a network, as in creating the WBS, the scope establishes the level of detail for defining the work that must be completed. Thus, the question arises in developing every network as to how many tasks should be included. There are no hard and fast rules, but the experiences of early project management practitioners revealed that after a certain point the marginal return in control offered by more detail is far outweighed by the additional work required to develop and maintain the network. At some point in every plan more detail becomes a negative rather than a positive attribute.

Some giant networks for major construction or engineering projects may have 25,000 or more tasks. It is obviously impossible for any one person to understand all the relationships between these 25,000 individual tasks—and the network diagram would take up an entire wall or more of a large conference room.

One way to reduce detail in networks is to create network diagrams for each major subproject or milestone of a project based on the WBS. These milestones can then be summarized in another diagram. If there are dependencies between the milestones, these can be noted in the milestone network. (See Figure 3-8.) This approach also allows people responsible for specific milestones within a project to be responsible for a detailed network of his or her own subproject. Thus, in a large project, there are plans within plans and projects within projects. A network diagram at the milestone level for the San Francisco sales office project is shown as an example. This milestone network would be good to use in a presentation, but would not be useful for managing the details of the project.

Most people can deal effectively with network diagrams with two hundred tasks or fewer. If your project has more tasks than this, then it is appropriate

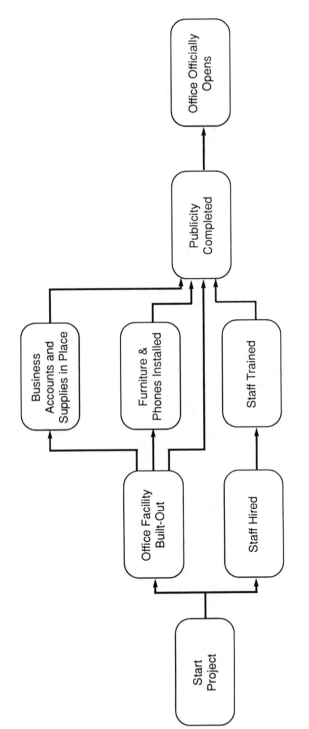

Figure 3-8 Milestone Network of the San Francisco Sales Office Project

to make multiple network diagrams for each of the subprojects and integrate them later. Of course, if you are working on projects of this size, you will definitely want to read Chapter Ten to help you select a computer program to assist you in creating and maintaining your project networks.

It is important that the task complexity represented in a network should be consistent in its abstraction, however. The tasks should all come from the same level in the WBS. For example, it wouldn't be appropriate to have one task defined as "develop the newsletter" connected to a task called "print the mailing labels." The "develop the newsletter" task is really a combination of tasks, where "print the mailing labels" is a singular activity. The level of detail represented in the tasks should be similar. If it's not, the network will give a false impression about the complexity of the project. Milestones should be clearly differentiated from tasks as well by using a different shape or color for milestones.

In every project, regardless of the number of actual tasks that will be monitored, a milestone network or network summaries that display only a subset of the total tasks in a project can be used to make presentations to project participants or management. They also can be used as a tool for communicating major project sequences and goals, without getting bogged down in the work details. As mentioned before, milestones have sequences and precedences, just like the tasks that comprise the individual milestones.

The level of detail communicated to people involved with a project depends on their level of involvement and their level of management authority. The project manager obviously needs access to the total project plan, but an executive or line manager who only has an interest in a project and not direct involvement might only need to see a milestone plan or other summary-level representations.

PERT, CPM, AND PRECEDENCE DIAGRAMMING: THREE MAJOR NETWORK METHODS AND OTHERS YOU MAY ENCOUNTER

There are three major systems of network diagramming and scheduling techniques used in industry today: PERT, short for performance evaluation and review technique, CPM, the acronym for critical path method, and precedence diagramming. The techniques are almost identical in principle: the differences lie in how the projects deal with scheduling uncertainties and in the use of symbols used to represent the relationships between tasks in a network.

Until PERT/CPM were developed, Gantt charts or other bar charts were used to represent and schedule projects. Gantt charts show a graphic representation of work on a time scale. You will learn more about Gantt charts in Chapter Five as a way to represent the project schedule. It's sufficient to say that Gantt charts are really just lists of project tasks and do not show the interrelationships between tasks that are represented in networks.

One of the first pioneering efforts to show these interrelationships was undertaken by the science management team of Morgan R. Walker and James

E. Kelly in the mid-1950s at the E. I. Du Pont Company. Their joint efforts resulted in the Kelly-Walker network technique. However, in later publications of their work, they referred to the method as the critical path method or CPM. Du Pont tested the CPM method in the construction of a major chemical plant and several maintenance projects that were completed by the middle of 1958. It is claimed that Du Pont credited over one million dollars in savings to this technique in the first year it was used.

During the same period of 1957-58, the management scientists of the Special Projects Office of the U.S. Navy along with the firms of Lockheed and Booz, Allen & Hamilton, developed a similar network system called PERT, which stands for program evaluation and review technique. The system was developed to help coordinate more than three thousand people involved in the development of the Polaris missile. The use of PERT is credited with reducing the time required to complete the project by two years.

CPM is often cited as being better for construction type projects. It is often argued that PERT is more appropriate for research-oriented projects. The primary reason for this is because of the different approaches the two systems use for scheduling, not because of the networks, which are largely the same. In CPM, one time estimate is used for creating the schedule; in PERT a more complex system is employed based on three time estimates that are used to determine the most probable time for completion. This more complex time estimating approach is deemed by some as more appropriate for research projects with high degrees of uncertainty and risk. For most business purposes, these differences are irrelevant, and people have begun to call network systems by the name PERT/CPM because of their similarities.

Traditionally, PERT/CPM networks use circles and arrows to describe work in a project. The two systems use the same basic diagramming conventions. The arrows are activities and the circles are events. These two concepts—activity and event—are central to the traditional PERT/CPM diagrams. An activity is a specific project task that requires resources and time to complete. An event is a specific end state for one or more activities that occurs at a specific point in time. An event occurs as a result of completing one or more activities.

AOA and AON

There are two methods of representing activities and events in PERT/CPM networks: activity on arc and activity on node. The use of method is largely a matter of preference. In activity on arc (AOA), the arrows are the activities and the circles (called nodes in PERT/CPM) are the events. In the activity on node (AON) method the activities are the circles and the lines demonstrate the precedences between the activities. Some of the traditional ways of diagramming tasks in a PERT/CPM chart are shown in Figure 3-9.

Simple precedence networks using boxes as we've shown here are really just another version of an AON PERT/CPM network. We've found that most

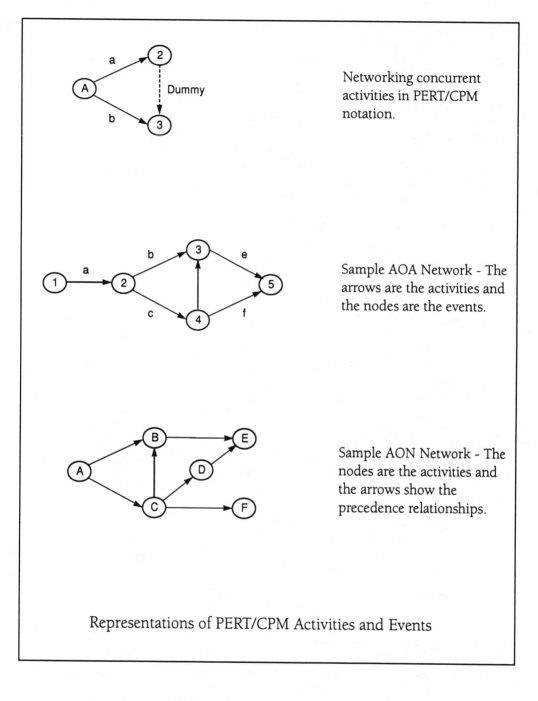

Networking concurrent activities in PERT/CPM notation.

Sample AOA Network - The arrows are the activities and the nodes are the events.

Sample AON Network - The nodes are the activities and the arrows show the precedence relationships.

Representations of PERT/CPM Activities and Events

Figure 3-9 Representations of PERT/CPM Activities and Events

business projects are easier to describe and understand using the boxes than by creating complex number, circle, and arc networks. In fact, most computerized project management programs now offer AON boxes as options to replace the circle/arc format.

We will use the simplified precedence diagramming technique already presented throughout the book to illustrate the project network. However, it is important for an informed project manager to be familiar with some of the other diagramming options in project management. As you get more experience, you may want to experiment with these other diagramming techniques for your networks. As long as the logic and precedence relationships remain in tact, it really doesn't matter whether you use circles, boxes, or any other shape for representing tasks and milestones.

LEAD AND LAG DIAGRAMMING FOR COMPLEX OR TIME-CRITICAL PROJECTS

The box and arrow technique we use in the book is simple to understand and is employed by many modern project management programs to replace the circles and arrows. The basic logic and underlying meaning of the circle and arrow approach of the box and line approach is the same. However, there are some advanced concepts in network and precedence diagramming that are important to consider. Basic network methods employed in PERT/CPM do not allow for specific relationships that are possible in the precedence diagram approach.

Precedence diagrams can be made more detailed to specify complex timing relationships between tasks. (See Figure 3.10.) By overlapping tasks in the diagram and using arrows to represent specific timing, relationships can be shown where tasks must be started at a certain point after another task is started. This is especially important in complex construction projects. For example, using precedence diagramming techniques you can show complex task sequencing requirements, such as

- A task that must not start before a specific task has been in progress for at least two days.
- A task that must be completed at least five days before another can begin.

Project Management Buzzwords

☛ **Lead Time and Lag Time**—The more complex precedence relationships as shown in the diagram are called lead and lag times. Lead relationships as shown in the diagram are called lead and lag times. Lead time is the time required by one task before another task can begin. Lag time exists when a task must start a certain period after another task.

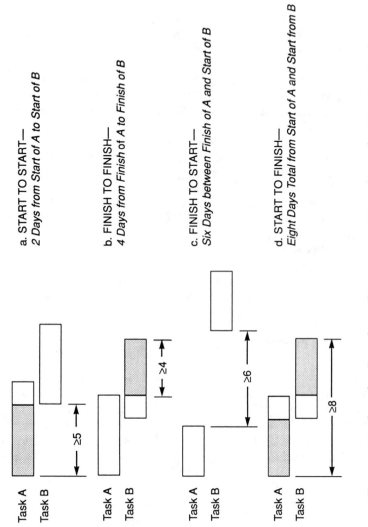

a. START TO START—
2 Days from Start of A to Start of B

b. FINISH TO FINISH—
4 Days from Finish of A to Finish of B

c. FINISH TO START—
Six Days between Finish of A and Start of B

d. START TO FINISH—
Eight Days Total from Start of A and Start from B

Figure 3-10 Complex Precedence Diagramming Conventions for Showing Lead and Lag Times Between Tasks

- A task that must start three days after the first task but that must be finished at the same time as the first task.

For most business projects it is not necessary to define lead and lag times at the subtask level. Simple precedence relationships are adequate for all but the most complex business and construction projects. However, they are mentioned here because the terms are often referred to in computerized project management systems or in other project management literature.

Over the years, and with the advancements in computer software, some of the representational techniques in PERT/CPM and precedence diagramming have been improved or have been modified and expanded, though the simplicity of the original systems has withstood the tests of time and application and no fundamental changes have been made in the original methods.

There are other networking systems you may come across as well, including GERT (graphical evaluation and review technique), which was designed for complex project modeling and employs probability techniques and advanced decision trees as an extension of PERT/CPM. GERT is not widely used in general business projects, but is appropriate in complex manufacturing and research applications.

Some computer systems for project management combine the advantages of the various network methodologies into programs that give project planners the option of representing projects at various levels of detail and complexity, using modified and/or expanded network representations.

WHEN IS A NETWORK A WASTE OF TIME?

The more complex a project is, the greater the value the network diagram is to someone responsible for projects in a business setting. Though there is a cost associated with implementing network management of a project, this cost is relatively low when compared to the potential advantages. Typically, the cost in time and money for implementing a network-based planning system is somewhere between 0.1 and 1 percent of the total project—the percentage becomes smaller as the project becomes larger.

The value of using network diagrams is not universally accepted, however. Wags often argue that taking time to develop a network is a waste of time. And there has been some research that indicates that the use of PERT/CPM or other related methods has no significant affect on the technological performance or final deliverables of projects. In other words, projects that were managed without the use of network systems in these studies seem to get the same amount and quality of work done. However, there was a significantly lower probability of cost and schedule overruns when network systems were used. In a business world concerned with profitability and performance, this in itself seems a good reason to employ the network technique for organizing and scheduling work.

There are some small projects that do not require a network diagram, however, because the tasks are largely sequential. When one task ends, the next task can begin. To list the sequences of project tasks, you can simply work from the WBS and put the tasks in a sequential list. Any boxes on the WBS that summarize tasks can be listed as milestones. (Note that sequential scheduling can be used in larger projects as well, if time is not important in the completion of the project. This is rarely the case in practice.)

Project Task List for the Second Issue of the Newsletter

Because the design for the newsletter is complete and production vendors have already been identified for production, the second and subsequent issues of the newsletter can be monitored using the following sequential list of tasks:

Task Number	Task Description
1.	Assemble story and illustration ideas.
2.	Meeting to approve story ideas.
3.	First draft of stories.
4.	Stories reviewed.
5.	Final draft of stories.
6.	Final draft approved.
7.	Layout stories and illustrations with the computer.
8.	Layout approved.
9.	Final changes and proofreading.
10.	Final sign-off before printing.
11.	Type output on imagesetter at service bureau.
12.	Camera-ready film to printer.
13.	Review "blueline" proof at printer's shop and approve.
14.	Finished newsletter delivered to office.
15.	Distribution of newsletter to customers.

In subsequent chapters, this simplified list of newsletter tasks will be used to illustrate the scheduling and management of a simple project.

Figure 3-11 Project Task List for the Second Issue of the Newsletter

Consider the newsletter project as an example of a project that could be managed sequentially. Though a network diagram should be used to represent the project for producing the first issue of the newsletter, because there are quite a few concurrent activities, a network is not really necessary for future versions of the newsletter because most of the tasks are sequential for producing the monthly issues. The only place where significant overlapping tasks occurred in the first issue was in the design of a format and masthead. Because this same format and masthead will be used again, this subproject won't be needed again. Because of the small number of tasks in the subsequent project of issuing a monthly newsletter, the project can be managed adequately with a simple sequential list of the project tasks.

As the example shows, the monthly newsletter can be easily be documented as a sequential project after creating the initial issue, because it is relatively simple and because a case can be made for ordering the tasks sequentially. A simple sequential task list based on the WBS for the project could be used just as well as a network to manage this simple project. (See Figure 3-11.) However, for a project of more complexity, like the San Francisco sales office project, a network is desirable for scheduling and controlling tasks and resources.

WHO SHOULD COMPLETE THE WORK PLAN?

When you have completed a WBS and a network diagram, you have a complete work plan for your project. Of course, this work plan will likely be performed by more than one person. Therefore, it is important that the people who will be working on your project understand the work plan and agree that it is appropriate.

You have three general alternatives in preparing the work plan (and the other components of the plan for that matter) for your project. Your choice of approach will depend on your organization, your personal experience and expertise, and the complexity of the project.

Alternative 1. Create the work plan yourself and have it reviewed. This is a good approach for small projects that have only a few participants or if you have expertise in a project that makes you especially well qualified to draft the work plan. Also, if you are basing your project on the plan of another project, this approach can work because you will be making adjustments to an existing plan that has worked before.

The downsides of completing a detailed work plan on your own are the following:

- The ability to examine alternative organization and sequencing of the tasks is limited to the skill of one individual.
- It is more difficult to identify errors in the logic of a network or WBS.
- Missing tasks or incomplete activities may not be identified.

- It is often difficult to see your plan objectively when you do it yourself—and even when other people review it, they are not familiar enough with the logic of your plan to offer alternatives.
- In a complex project, it is rare that one person has the expertise and experience to detail all the tasks at the same level with great accuracy.
- People may feel left out, thus creating a negative political environment that affects your ability to manage the project through the next stages.

There are two primary advantages of doing the work plan on your own, however:

1. It is faster. If you are familiar with the steps and logic in a project, you can usually create a WBS and network with little input. It takes less time than asking opinions and having meetings to discuss the options.

2. You can complete a work plan on your own before the final team is identified. Of course, when you do identify other people who will be working on the project, they will need to review your work and offer suggestions for modifying the work sequences and tasks.

In a project with a short deadline, these advantages can be critical to getting a plan done on time, but the disadvantages usually outweigh using this approach.

Alternative 2. Lead a meeting and construct the work plan with the whole project team involved. This approach to planning requires one or more structured meetings and advance preparation by each of the team members. Of course, if you haven't yet identified the key players in the project, this is not practical. Instead, you might identify a team of people who have had similar responsibilities to those on your project to help you create the work plan, even though these people won't necessarily be involved in your project.

The disadvantages of the team approach to work planning are the following:

- It can be time consuming. Meetings take time and a complex project may take multiple meetings to plan out to the task level.
- Unless you hand-pick the participants, different levels of planning expertise will be evident, making it difficult to establish consistency in each component of the plan.
- Conflicts will need to be resolved and compromises in the work plan may be necessary to keep the project team cohesive and focused on the project goals.
- To be successful using this approach, the project manager will need to spend a significant amount of time in preplanning activities to coordinate, structure, and lead the meetings.

The potential benefits of this approach are the following:

- It can create shared responsibility among team members for planning the project.
- Team members will benefit from a better understanding of the work required of others.
- It can identify potential conflicts and inconsistencies early in the project planning cycle, so they can be dealt with before they affect the project outcomes.
- It can be used to create camaraderie among team members who have not worked together before.
- It provides a way to verify and clarify the team's understanding of the project scope and goals.

For completing the work plan for an entire project, this approach works best if there are ten people or fewer on the project team and the total project network involves two hundred tasks or fewer.

Alternative 3. For large projects, you can assign small groups to develop the work plans for individual subprojects. These small groups will develop work plans for their own components of the project. Then, a few selected people from each of the groups will be assigned to integrate the subplans into a project work plan, using a methodology similar to the team approach described earlier.

The disadvantages of this approach are the following:

- The coordination of the various groups can be difficult and time consuming.
- The different groups may define tasks with inconsistent levels of complexity. This can be minimized if the project manager is involved with each of the groups to help assure consistency.
- Each group must have a manager trained in project management techniques. This is not necessarily a disadvantage, but it may be a constraint in some organizations.

For a large or complex project, this approach can have all the advantages of the team approach, and for an extremely large project, it is mandatory. No single project manager can define the work for something large and complex without making mistakes or omissions in the plan.

No matter which of the alternatives you choose to develop the network and work plan, you will need to have the plan approved and reviewed by the appropriate people in your organization. Again, as you bring new people into a project later in implementation, this may necessitate changes, because these new team members may offer better or more appropriate alternatives for completing their assigned tasks and milestones. (As an aside, when you start thinking about changing and modifying a network diagram with hundreds of activities during the life of a project and communicating these changes to multiple people, the rationale behind using computerized project management tools becomes apparent.)

THE WORK PLAN WILL BE USED FOR
PROJECT PLANNING AND IMPLEMENTATION

The work plan will be used to complete the rest of the project plan. In practice, the work plan, the resource assignments, the schedule, and the budget—which are the components of a complete project plan—are all worked on concurrently. The project planning stage, starting with the work plan which we've just covered, dominates over one third of the book—but the actual time required to complete the plan (including work plan, resource assignments, schedule, and budget) may only be a few hours for a very short project. It may take a month or more for a very large project. But it is the quality and thought that goes into a plan that determines its value in the project management process—and that's why it is so important to understand the issues in creating each component of the plan.

As mentioned before, the plan is the heart of the project management process—and the WBS and network are the central components of the plan. Starting with the WBS and network, tasks and milestones can be assigned to individual people. Using the tasks as a starting point, skills required to complete tasks can be matched to people and equipment. Once people and equipment are identified, a schedule can be developed by assigning durations to each of the tasks. Then, using the network precedences to determine the length of time required to complete the project, a schedule can be developed. The length of the project will determine the final costs of the project—so the budget depends on the tasks and task sequences as well.

In the real world, the plan for a large project will go through multiple versions on its way to completion. First, a rough work plan, schedule, and budget will be produced. Then, these will be debated, discussed, enhanced, expanded, and revised until the project plan is complete and approved. If you use a WBS and network to represent your project, the implications of changes during these iterations can be easily seen and the resulting plan will be better constructed and understood as a result.

After the plan is complete, the work plan, including the WBS and the network, will be key components for controlling schedules and modifying work priorities to assure timely completion of the project. Without these tools, the impact of changing tasks and sequencing is not clearly evident—and mistakes can be made because the implications of changes are not easily seen.

This central role of the work plan in the project management process often leads people to the mistaken conclusion that the creation of the work plan is project management. As you've already seen and as you'll learn, project management involves much more than this—but don't be surprised if people identify your project management skills with your ability to create a WBS or a network diagram.

The next three chapters of the book will cover how the rest of the plan is created from the work plan—starting with the identification of people and resources required to complete the project, the subject of the next chapter.

Chapter Four

CHOOSING THE TEAM
AND THE RESOURCES:
Getting Who and What You Need to Get Things Done

The success of a project depends on the people and resources available to complete it. If appropriately skilled people and adequate resources aren't available, no project can be completed on time or on budget. Thus, choosing the project team and identifying the required resources is a critical step in the project planning phase.

Once the scope and tasks of the project are defined, a project manager can identify the people skills and material resources required to complete the project effectively. To do this, you, as a project manager, need to answer three basic questions about the project team and other required resources:

- Who and what are already available for the project?
- What people, materials, equipment, and other resources are needed to complete each task?
- What materials and skills are missing from the current inventory of resources?

This chapter explains how to scope out required skills, assess current resources, and develop a list of people and other resources required to complete the project. It also covers organizational considerations and options for managing the project. In addition, it provides guidelines for filling the gap in people skills and material resources when adequate resources are not readily available.

Seven fundamental resources are required to implement almost any project:

- Money
- Manpower
- Equipment
- Facilities

- Materials and Supplies
- Information
- Technology

To be successful, a project manager must identify the appropriate mix of these resources during the planning phase and then control these resources within the constraints of time, budget, and desired outcomes during the implementation phase of the project.

Strategies for identifying and fulfilling the resource requirements for the project, except money, will be covered in this chapter. The financial aspect of project planning and control is covered in Chapter Six as part of the discussion on establishing and controlling budgets.

CHOOSING THE RIGHT PEOPLE TO GET THE WORK DONE

People are, as they have always been, the common denominator in making projects successful. In a small project or a routine one, choosing the right people to complete the work on a project successfully can be a relatively simple task. However, in a large, complex project, the selection of people to complete various aspects of the project is more difficult, more risky, and potentially time consuming.

In any project, there are three major questions that must be answered regarding the people used to complete the work on a project:

- What skills are required to complete the tasks on the project?
- Where will the people come from to complete the tasks?
- How should the people working on the project be organized?

Each of these questions can be answered with confidence using a structured approach that starts with the project's WBS or network.

The first step in choosing the right people is to define the skills and experience required to complete each task in the WBS or network. (See Figure 4-1.) For each task in the project, answer such questions as:

- Is there a specific technical skill required to complete this task?
- How much experience should the person or people have to complete this task?
- Does a person need to have specific experience doing this task or can general experience be applied? If so, what general experience is required?
- In addition to technical skills, are there any specific interpersonal skills required to complete this task effectively, such as good written or verbal communication skills, diplomacy or negotiating skills, or management ability?

Worksheet for Determining Skills
Required for Project Tasks

Project __Newsletter__   Date __Jan 7__

Completed By __Joe__

TASK	SKILLS REQUIRED	POSSIBILITIES
1. Assemble story ideas	Knowledge of customer issues Knowledge of new sales	Members of technical support and sales development staff - ask Ingrid and Roger
2. Meeting to approve story ideas	Good judgement Understanding of the project goals	Department managers
3. First draft of stories	Writing skills Word processing Good interpersonal skills with staff	Staff writer - perhaps Gail or Julie Members of support or sales staff - perhaps John or Sarah Freelance writer Advertising agency
4. Stories reviewed.	See Task 2.	Same as Task 2.
5. Final draft of stories.	Same as Task 3.	Same as Task 3.
6. Final draft approved.	Same as Task 2.	Same as Task 2 and Project Manager
7. Layout stories and illustrations on the computer.	Desktop publishing skills. Illustration skills. Design background. Familiarity with corporate communication guidelines.	Staff designer - perhaps Steve or Gail Freelance designer Advertising agency

Figure 4-1 Worksheet for Determining Skills Required to Complete Tasks

List the skills next to each WBS level or use a worksheet like the example shown for the newsletter project. After this is done, the hard part begins— identifying where the people will come from.

WHERE WILL THE PEOPLE COME FROM?

In most projects, you have predictable sources for locating team members for your project:

1. Choosing people from your own organization
2. Using people from another line organization or functional area of the company
3. Contracting with outside vendors or consultants
4. Hiring and training new staff (See Figure 4-2.)

Each of these options has advantages and disadvantages, as described in the paragraphs that follow.

Sources for Project Staff

- Assign your own staff or other people from your department.

- Negotiate to use staff from other departments or functional areas.

- Hire consultants or outside vendors.

- Hire and train new staff.

Figure 4-2 Sources for Project Staff

Team Member Source 1. Choosing people from your own organization.

If all the skills exist within your own organization, and the project is the primary responsibility of your organization, then use as many people as possible from your own functional area or department. Obviously it is more likely you will have ready access to the people in your own department than to those in other departments.

There are many projects where it is appropriate to use as many people from your own line organization as possible, but in complex projects that require special skills and involvement with other functional areas, it is usually impossible to staff a project from one functional area. In some projects, it can be political suicide to do so. Your use of people exclusively from only your own department might be considered arrogant or uncooperative or territorial in some projects—especially projects with high visibility and high priority in the company. This negative response by other departments could affect your ability to get support when you run into problems or could affect other projects that involve these other groups.

Even if you don't get people involved working on the project from other departments, for a variety of communication and political reasons you will probably want to have people from outside the department review your results and your plans. Your project is one part of a whole enterprise. Remember, "No department is an island."

Team Member Source 2. Using people from another line organization or functional area of the company.

As projects get larger, they typically involve multiple line organizations or departments within the same company. People from other functional areas in the organization may need to be involved because they have obvious responsibilities in the project. For example, the finance department has responsibility for tracking budgets and the human resources department has direct involvement in hiring people. In other projects you may need to use specific people with technical abilities or experience including engineers, writers, salespeople, or manufacturing personnel.

Of course, the assignment of people from other departments to your project will need to be negotiated with their line managers. Authority to use resources from other departments must also be clearly assigned to the project or obvious conflicts will arise when you try to develop specific priorities and schedules for your project. This authority to use resources from other departments should come from high level managers in the organization who have responsibility for the line organizations involved or through specific agreements with line managers at the same level in the organization.

Thus, in the example we have been using for the newsletter project, the marketing communications department needs to use people in the customer support department and sales department to write articles for the newsletter. The authority to assign schedules and tasks to these people was authorized by the vice president of sales, who is responsible for these departments. If this authority had not been granted by the vice president, then conflict between the marketing communications manager and the customer support manager may have resulted when the marketing communications group tried to assign and schedule the articles.

Team Member Source 3. Contracting with outside vendors or consultants

The use of consultants or other vendors is one of the best options when unique skills are required on a temporary or intermittent basis. For example, a printer must be contracted for printing the newsletter because the company doesn't have the people or equipment to do its own printing. Because printing is a specialized skill that requires extensive experience, technology, and considerable capital outlay, it makes sense to hire outside vendors to do this, rather than developing the capability in house. If the company completed large volumes of printing on a regular basis, it might be cost effective to establish an in-house printing service, but it is unlikely that an in-house facility could offer the same range of quality and services accommodated by hiring specialized printers for each job. The same is true in the San Francisco sales office project when a leasing agent is required. It wouldn't make sense to have a person familiar with San Francisco real estate on the staff full-time just to complete the negotiations on a single office. However, if the company plans on doing a lot of leasing and property management, then a full-time staff person in the corporate offices might make sense.

Team Member Source 4. Hiring and training new staff

If the project is part of an ongoing and long-term commitment, then hiring new employees may be the best solution to meet project staffing requirements—but hiring new people is always the most complicated and risky choice in staffing a project. Hiring and training staff is a project in its own right.

Clear identification of the skills required for these new employees should be the first step in the hiring process. If hiring new staff is a requirement, adequate lead times must be available in the project plan to find these new people. And always remember, new people do not become productive instantaneously, regardless of their past experience—so you need to add time for training and integration.

Even in the most routine jobs, some time is required for learning the procedures in the new company and adapting to the new work environment.

This is true of some consultants as well, who must become familiar with your company's way of doing business before they can get down to work. When you schedule your project, allow for these various training and development requirements. You may even want to identify training activities as specific tasks in your WBS or network.

DEVELOP A SKILLS INVENTORY FOR EXISTING PERSONNEL

Before you can decide whether to use existing staff, hire new people, or use outside vendors in your project, you need to develop a skills inventory of people in your own organization. A skills inventory in a large organization is often maintained by the personnel or human resources department—though this normally lists only the technological skill levels and formal educational background of people in the company. Managerial skills and communications skills are not available in most company skills inventories—and would be suspect even if they were. Skills in communication and management should be assessed after you have experience working with a person.

Developing a skills inventory can be an informal process or part of a formal personnel review system. The end result of completing a skills inventory will be a listing of the technological, management, administrative, and human skills for each staff member in your organization. (See Figure 4-3.) If you have a complete, up-to-date skills inventory, you can easily match the skills required on your project to the people who have those skills.

A simple list for a small project or a database program on a personal computer can be used to maintain the skills inventory. The skills can be assigned codes for easy sorting in a database system. Some of the more sophisticated project management programs allow you to include skills inventories as part of the project data, and the programs even offer suggestions for staffing each task on the project.

A skills inventory is something that must be kept up to date to be useful. It is also something that can be used for many projects—so developing a regular procedure for keeping it up to date is worth the effort. Skills inventories can also help you identify people for your project that you might overlook if you rely on memory or intuition to establish your project team.

If you will be working on many projects, you will want to build and maintain a network of contacts as well as an inventory of your own organization's skills. If you will be producing a lot of different kinds of printed projects, for example, you will want to interview a wide variety of printing companies in your area and become familiar with their pricing structures and quality of work. If you will be using a large number of temporary manufacturing services, you will want to keep a list of temporary

Skills Inventory

Group <u>Western Sales Division</u>   Date <u>January 17</u>

Completed By <u>Ingrid, Vice President of Sales</u>

NAME	EDUCATION	PRIMARY SKILLS	RATING	SECONDARY SKILLS	RATING
Roger, Regional Sales	MBA	Management Large account sales Planning	9 9 7	Product knowledge Team player	5 9
Sarah, Sales Development Manager	MBA	Sales Ideas	7 10	Writing skills	8
John, Technical Support Manager	MS, EE	Product knowledge Programming Customer rapport	10 8 8	Writing skills	7
Joe, Marketing Communications Manager	BA, Comm.	Advertising Public relations	9 9	Market knowledge	6
Gail, Marketing Specialist	BSBA	Desktop publishing Writing Design	8 6 8	Word processing	8
George, Manager of Public Relations	High School	Contacts with editors Negotiating Ideas	7 8 4		
Dave, Sales Support Specialist	BA, Arts	Small account sales Coordination Budgeting	7 9 8	Product knowledge	8

Figure 4-3 Sample Skills Inventory for the Western Regional Sales Division of TechMore, Inc.

agencies that supply these types of services. You can develop your own skills inventories and ratings for these contacts and vendors, just like you would describe your own internal staff. Then, when a project comes up, you are ready with a list of people and vendors who can fill your project's needs.

Skills inventories are useful after the project starts too. What happens if a key staff member assigned to your project quits or gets sick? Pull out your skills inventory to identify potential sources for helping out. If you don't have a network and skills inventory ready, you will waste valuable time trying to find someone who can take over for the lost resource, and the project may suffer delays or other problems as a result.

SELECTING PEOPLE FOR A PROJECT

After you have considered your options and the skills available to you, a list of possible people and vendors for each task on your list can be created. This list should include all the alternatives available to you. In large, complex projects, the alternatives should be ranked in priority order and the strengths and weakness of each choice should be well understood. A worksheet like the one shown already can be useful in identifying people and their strengths and weaknesses for a project team.

If you depend on your skills inventories, you will probably discover that there are almost no perfect matches of people and project requirements on your list. Since no one fits your needs perfectly, the selection process usually involves some trade-offs. Identify people with the closest match of required skills and ask yourself if the skills deficiencies are workable. Can you use two people who complement each others skills on the project? Can you make up for the lack of skills in other ways? The more critical the tasks, the more important the match of skill requirements to people becomes.

Obviously you want the best people possible for your project; but even after making compromises and trade-offs, it is not always appropriate to use your first choice person for every task—especially if another person's skills are adequate. For example, there might be two designers who could be hired to create the newsletter. The first designer is truly exceptional in creativity but is also very expensive. Another designer has experience with adequate creative skills and is much less expensive. Because the newsletter project requires a relatively straightforward design, the use of the first person would not be a good choice, because the project budget would be exceeded. Thus, the most technically qualified person in this case is not a good choice because of the budget constraints on the project.

Project Management Tip

✎ **Don't Forget Training as an Option**—When selecting staff for a project, it may be possible to train or retrain existing staff instead of hiring new people. Existing employees are already familiar with the company policies and culture, a distinct advantage. Existing employees are also known quantities, so you avoid the risk of hiring someone who doesn't fit in. Besides, training people is often cheaper than hiring new staff when all the costs and time are added together. In addition, if you encourage the development of existing staff, the entire organization will benefit from the resultant atmosphere of support and encouragement. If people are given an opportunity to advance, they are much more likely to be consistently productive and loyal. When considering training as an option to meeting skills requirements, the following choices are available:

- **Mentoring relationships with existing experts in the organization.** Mentoring programs are excellent for developing management skills. There are books on mentoring available in the business sections of most well-stocked bookstores.

- **Formal training programs offered by schools or consulting firms.** The programs are best for general technical training or basic skills training. Because these programs can be costly, check their quality before you enroll people.

- **Internal training programs developed by in-house specialists.** These programs are good for company-specific technologies and procedures. Internal training programs may be time-consuming to produce, but if there is continual need for new skills in specific topics, then a project to create these training programs is in order.

INCORPORATING HUMAN FACTORS INTO TEAM PLANNING: PERSONALITY, POLITICS, AND CORPORATE CULTURE

The most technically qualified person for a project may not be the best choice for reasons other than economic ones. Perhaps there are interpersonal problems with other team members or this person is difficult to manage or has a reputation for being late delivering results. Maybe someone who is almost as proficient technically with better personal skills would be a wiser choice. There are times when technical skill wins out over every other factor, however, and that is when a person has a required skill that few other people possess. Then, you just have to learn to work with the difficult personality to get the job done. This is one of the standard challenges project managers must learn to handle with aplomb.

Sometimes after you create your list of staffing choices, you find that the first choice for a team member is not even a possibility. For example, a person you would like to use in the project may not be available because of commitments to other, higher-priority projects. Or, you may ask to use one person from an organization and the manager from the group assigns a different person to your project. Line managers might also "borrow" people from other departments with less desirable skills for your project. Thus, you may not get the experience you want and will have to adjust the schedule to accommodate for the slow learning curve. Project managers often need to make these kinds of concessions to other managers to get people for a project. (See the next chapter for more on adjusting schedules to skill levels and availability.)

Because of the potential conflicts, interaction between project managers and line managers during the project staffing process is critical. The relationship must be tempered with mutual trust. If you say you need a person with a particular skill for your project and the line manager assigns a person to you, then you usually must accept this person's judgement, unless you can make a good case for someone you have more direct experience with. If you find out later that the assigned person lacks the required skills, you can negotiate or look at other alternatives.

The Problem of Imposed Teams

You won't always have the advantage of being able to choose a team for your project—the team may be imposed on you by other managers or is the result of the structure of your own organization. Sometimes people are selected because they are available and not because of their skills or talent. Imposed teams are common in every business for a variety of practical and not-so-practical reasons. The ideal approach to choosing a team is to define the skills required to complete the tasks and then match the people to the skill requirements. When this is not possible, there are a number of alternatives you can consider to make things work.

Project Management Tip

✎ **The Combination of Players Is Always Important**—In addition to the skills of individual team members, the combination of personalities in a project is important. The people need to work well together. The people skills need to be complementary, especially in a long project where people will be working together closely. Consider this combination of personalities when you put together a project team. It's important that the sum of the team should always equal more than the total of the individuals.

Do the best you can with the people you have.

If your team doesn't have all the skills necessary, build training into the project. If your team is not qualified in all required skills and training takes too long, consider hiring a consultant or outside vendor to fill in the gaps (if you have budget to do this).

Also, before you decide that your team is incompetent, give them a chance. People can often do more than you think. Remember the self-fulfilling prophecy—if you believe people have talent, they will exhibit talent. If you believe they will fail, that's likely to happen. Be realistic about your team's ability, but don't charge the project with unnecessary negative energy before it even starts.

Compromise and negotiate for the team members you really need.

Don't just complain—be constructive. If some of the team members are not appropriate, suggest a different team to the people who made the original selections. If you have this option before the team is formally announced, consider alternative people for the team and discuss the alternatives with the appropriate decision makers. These people may be able to offer explanations for the staff selections that you never considered, making the choices more reasonable than you thought. If you have documented your own case with task requirements and skill inventories as suggested, a rational manager will usually listen. You may not get everyone you want, but if you identify the priorities, you might be able to negotiate for the people you really need.

Suggest an alternative team selection process for the next project.

Though this may not help this time, it may be that the other managers never considered having you involved in the selection process. Explain the advantages of having the project manager involved and offer a structured approach to the staff selection process. You may meet with political resistance if other people are afraid of giving up their authority for making project decisions, but you can explain to your superiors that they can make the final selections, you just want to be involved in the process.

There are many reasons why the project manager should be involved, including becoming familiar with the strengths and weaknesses of the team as early as possible and gaining insight into the skills and abilities of the staff. This insight leads to better schedules and monitoring and control systems that are geared toward the needs of the various staff.

As your managers become more confident in your abilities, the insightful ones will get you involved in early decisions about the project. If they don't, then you may want to consider career alternatives.

HOW SHOULD THE PROJECT BE ORGANIZED?

Even though there are infinite possible combinations of people involved, there are only a few basic ways you can structure the organization of a project. These include functional (or line) organizations, pure project structures, matrixed organizations, or mixed organizational structures.

The Functional Project Organization

In a project that uses people from the same organization, the existing line organization can be used to manage the project. This organizational structure is appropriate when the project is clearly the responsibility of one department. Many small projects use the functional organization as the project organization. (See Figure 4-4.) A functional project is assigned to the functional department or division in a company that has the most interest and technical ability to complete the project. Almost all tasks in a project organized as part of a functional organization will be completed within the one functional area. Existing managers in the department double as project managers.

The advantages of using a functional organization to complete a project are the following:

- **Familiarity of the team.** The team members are already familiar with each other and the skill levels of the staff are clearly understood.
- **Established administrative system.** The general administrative policies and procedures are already understood by the team.
- **Staff availability.** The staff is readily available to the project because the line managers control the staff assignments. Thus, there are few, if any, interdepartmental conflicts over the use of resources.
- **Scheduling efficiency.** The scheduling of staff can be highly efficient. As a staff member is required, the person can be immediately assigned to a task and then return to routine work without serious logistical interruptions.
- **Clear authority.** The lines of authority and communication are understood. Thus, the conflicts between project authority and line authority are minimized.

The disadvantages of a functional organization are the following:

- **Project isolation.** The project may be completed in isolation from other parts of the company and fail to realize larger strategic goals as a result.
- **Limited resources.** The project is limited to the technical resources within the department, which may not be adequate to complete the tasks required. Of course, outside vendors and consultants can be

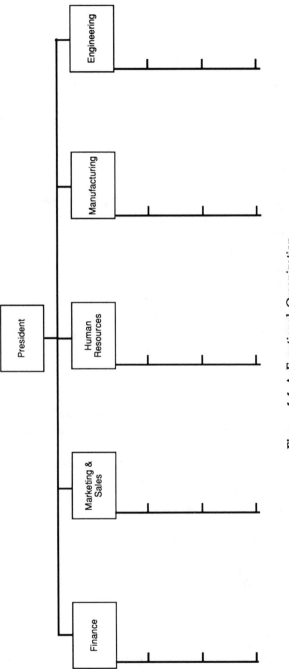

Figure 4-4 A Functional Organization

hired, but expertise within other departments of the company is not readily available. This may lead to inefficiencies or redundancies in the project organization.

- **Bureaucratic procedures.** There may be more levels of approval than really necessary for the project because of the established bureaucracy in the line organization. This impedes progress on the project or makes the decision-making process less efficient.

- **Lack of project focus.** The project may lack focus or priority in a functional organization because it is not the only work being done. Thus, routine departmental work may interfere with project work. In addition, motivation for project work may suffer because the project is considered "additional" or "optional" work, as opposed to a clear responsibility.

- **Department orientation.** The project may suffer from "department-think." This is where the priorities of the department become the project priorities, regardless of the actual goals for the project. Work outside the department's normal concerns are given little attention, and the "finished" project may not be complete or suffer quality problems as a result.

The Pure Project Organization

In pure project management a team or "task force" is put together to accomplish the project's goals. In a pure project organization, all the team members report to the project manager during the course of the project. (See Figure 4-5.) The team members do not have responsibility to other managers or jobs during the course of their work on the project. When a team member's responsibility for the project is complete, this person will return to another job or will be assigned to another project. Only one project and one job are assigned at a time.

In the direct version of the pure project structure, every project team member reports directly to the project manager. This is appropriate in small projects with fifteen or fewer people involved. In the indirect version of the pure project structure, the project manager may have assistant managers or supervisors to manage sub-projects or functional areas within the project. As in an ordinary line organization, the supervisors and assistants report directly to the project manager· and the various functional teams within the project report to the second level managers. Extremely large projects may have multiple management levels, just like a large corporation.

Pure project organizations are found in companies fulfilling large government projects or in some engineering-driven companies that produce predictable model updates for their products. Large construction projects often employ a pure project organization, as well. If work on a complex, priority project spans a year or more, then a pure project organization is often an advantage.

The advantages of the pure project organization include

- **Clear project authority.** The project manager has true line authority over the entire project. Thus, there is always a clear channel for resolving project conflicts and priorities. The unity of command in a pure project organization results in each subordinate having one and only one direct boss—a clear advantage in most situations.
- **Simplified project communications.** Communication and decision making within the project are simplified, because everyone reports to the same project manager and is focused on the attainment of the same project goals.
- **Access to specialized expertise.** If similar projects will be completed by the company on a cyclic basis, specific expertise in the component aspects of the project will be developed over time. It simply becomes a matter of transferring the experts to the right project at the right time.
- **Project focus and priority.** The pure project organization supports a total view of the project and a strong, separate identity on the part of the participants. This helps keep the project focused and integrated.

There are distinct disadvantages to the pure project approach, however:

- **Duplication of efforts.** If a company has multiple projects with important goals in progress at the same time, some efforts may be duplicated—making the overall cost of the projects higher than necessary.
- **Unclear loyalties and motivations.** Project members form strong attachments to the project and each other, which is good. However, when the project is terminated, the team must be disbanded, and this leads to uncertainty and conflict. Team members fear layoffs or anticipate assignments in undesirable projects in the future. Thus, keeping the technically qualified people happy in the company over the long haul becomes a major challenge.
- **Intracompany rivalry.** Political rivalry and competition may become strong between projects in a company that uses pure project organization for its major projects. This results in a company that competes with itself instead of with the competition—an ugly state of affairs.
- **Reintegration of resources.** Integrating a pure project group back into the functional organization can be fraught with problems of all kinds. People who were involved in the project may be considered

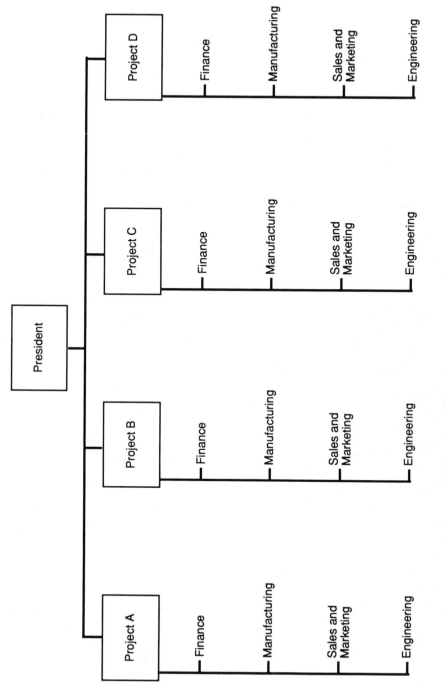

Figure 4-5 A Pure Project Organization

"outsiders" when their original jobs no longer exist, requiring the people to adapt to new job assignments.

The Matrix Organization

Defining projects in an organization and implementing project management techniques sets in motion a significant change in the culture of the user. One of the more complex results of using project management in business is the introduction of "matrix management"—the phrase used to describe the management of the web of relationships that come about when people join the project team and are subject to the resulting multiple authority-responsibility-accountability relationships in the organization. (See Figure 4-6.)

The matrix organization is an attempt to take advantage of the benefits of a pure project organization while maintaining the advantages of the functional organization. It is rare to find pure project or pure functional organizations in business—matrix organizations are the most common.

In a matrix organization, a clear project team is established that crosses organizational boundaries. Thus, team members may come from various departments. A project manager for this project is clearly defined and the project is managed as a separate and focused activity.

The project manager may report to a higher-level executive or to one of the functional managers with the most interest in the project. However, the specific team members still report to their functional departments and maintain responsibilities for routine departmental work in their functional areas. In addition, people may be assigned to multiple project teams with different responsibilities. The problem of coordination that plagues other project structures is minimized because the most important personnel for a project work together as a defined team within the matrix project structure.

The management responsibilities in these projects are temporary—and a supervisor on one project may be a worker on another project, depending on the skills required. If project managers in a matrix situation do not have good relationships with line managers in the organization, conflicts may arise over authority over employees work and priorities. Not everyone adapts well to the matrix structure for this and other related reasons.

The complexity a matrix organization causes is clear: people have multiple managers, multiple priorities, and multiple role identities. Because of these complexities, before an organization enters into matrix organizational structures, at least two of the following criteria for the project or the enterprise should be met:

- There is a need to share scarce or unique resources that are required in more than one project or functional area.

- High levels of information processing and communication are required across functional areas in order to complete the project.
- Pressure from the outside by customers or agencies is present to have one person or group centralize control of the project even though the project may be carried out by other groups in the organization.

In cases where projects meet at least two of these criteria, the matrix organization has distinct advantages:

- **Clear project focus.** The project has clear focus and priority because it has its own separate organization and management. Most of the planning and control advantages of a pure project structure are realized in a matrix organization.
- **Flexible staffing.** Staffing is relatively flexible in matrix organizations because resources from various line organizations are available. Scarce technical resources are available to a wide range of projects in a company that regularly employs matrix-organized projects.
- **Adaptable to management needs and skills.** The authority of the project manager can be specified as strong or weak, depending on the priority of the project. If a project manager has strong authority, this person has command authority over most of the project. If a project manager has weak authority for a project, then the line managers have a strong influence on project activities. Thus, the matrix organization can be adapted to a wide range of projects—some that need strong support from line managers and some that require independent management.
- **Staff development opportunities.** People can be given new challenges and responsibilities in a matrix organization that are not as likely in a purely functional organization. People can gain exposure to new technical areas, develop management skills, and have new experiences that maintain their interest and motivation at work. Ultimately these new experiences can lead to more effective employees with high degrees of independence and flexibility. This results in better overall corporate productivity because people tend to be more responsible for the quality of their own work in project-oriented groups.
- **Adaptable to business changes.** Matrix organizations can adapt more quickly to changing technological and market conditions than traditional, functional-only organizations. This is largely because of the high people-to-people contact in these organizations. In addition, matrix-organized projects encourage entrepreneurship and creative thinking that crosses functional responsibilities.

The flexibility and responsiveness of matrix organizations are important, especially as a way to encourage new ideas and individual responsibility within organizations. The complexity of matrix-organized projects within companies offers some specific challenges. These include the need for clear understanding of the matrix relationships, the requirement for open and consistent communication throughout the organization, and the demand for specific training for the line and project managers in the management skills that are required to make the matrix organization productive. Unfortunately matrix organizations sometimes deride into ambiguous, conflict-ridden entities if the authorities, responsibilities, and purposes of the people involved are not clearly understood and accepted.

The Three C's in Successful Matrix Organizations
• *Communication*
• *Cooperation*
• *Coordination*

The disadvantages and potential conflicts within a matrix organization must be understood and dealt with in order to take advantage of the benefits of matrix management. The more frequently reported problems in matrix-managed organizations are the following:

Built-in Conflicts

Conflict between line management priorities and project management priorities are inevitable. The question of who is in charge affects both the project and the routine departmental work. The division of authority and responsibility relationships in matrix organizations are inherently complex. Matrix organizations are no place for intractable, autocratic managers with narrow views of organizational responsibilities.

Resistance to Termination

Some of the same problems inherent in terminating pure project structures are shared in matrix organizations. Team members may prefer their project roles over their line responsibilities, creating interesting motivational challenges for managers. Because the team members have unique identities and relationships in their project roles, matrixed projects often resist termination.

Complex Command and Authority Relationships

There is no unity of command in a matrix organization—a clear violation of traditional management principles. The team member is often caught between conflicting demands of the line manager and the project manager. The discomfort and uncertainty of having more than one boss at the same time cannot be

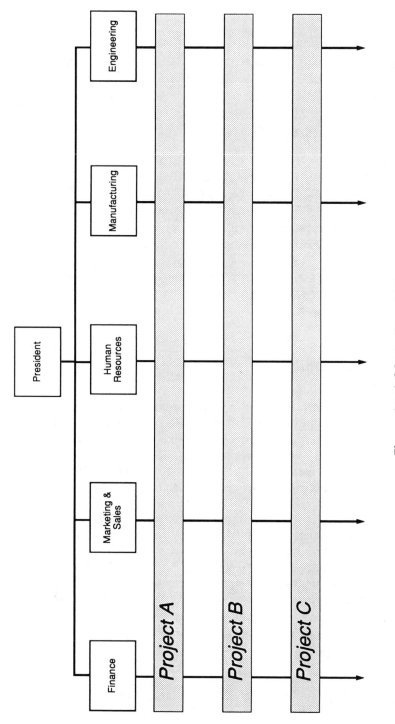

Figure 4-6 A Matrix Organization

adequately described to someone who has never experienced the situation. Of course, if the two bosses are adequately trained and open in their communications, then many of these difficulties can be resolved or eliminated.

Complex Employee Recognition System

In a matrix organization, which manager should assign the employee's performance review or make recommendations for raises? If the reward responsibilities and authorities of the project manager and the line manager are not clearly identified, the employee may feel unrecognized for outstanding project work. It is imperative that both line responsibilities and project responsibilities are accounted for in the employee's performance review process. And some form of reward system needs to be established for team members within the project—whether this is just public acknowledgment of quality performance or formal monetary rewards depends on the project and your budget. Again, communication, cooperation, and coordination are the keys to making the matrix system effective.

The Mixed Organization

There are some organizations that employ a mixture of functional, matrix, and pure project organizations to accomplish enterprise goals. In companies with a wide range of projects, a project office may be set up to help administer projects as well. This office offers expertise and assistance in planning and tracking projects. In other companies, the office may become a division in its own right, with full-time project managers and staff responsible for project-oriented activities.

Mixed organizations are not distinguishable from a matrix organization because of the complexity of relationships—and most of the strengths and weaknesses of a matrix organization apply to a mixed organizational structure. The unique problem in mixed organizations is one caused by the extreme flexibility in the way the organization adapts to project work—leading to potential incompatibilities, confusion, conflicts, and duplications of effort if the managers are not adequately trained to deal with these complexities.

Which Structure Should You Use?

The organization you choose for most ordinary business projects will probably be an adaptation of a matrix or functional organization. The people you choose for the project will determine the best organization structure. If multiple departments must be involved and the project is outside normal functional responsibilities, then a matrix organization is appropriate. If the project is relatively simple and uses people from one primary department, then a functional organization can work.

In the newsletter project, the organization of the project was developed primarily along functional lines that already exist, with the involvement of a few outside resources and vendors added to complete specific tasks. In the sales office project, a matrix organization is appropriate because of the wide range of involvement and on-going communication across functional areas required to complete the project.

IDENTIFYING OBJECTIVES FOR THE WORK TEAM

After the staff is selected and the project organization determined, these decisions should be documented as part of the project plan. Ultimately, the documentation will include a clear description of task assignments for each group and identification of specific objectives for the various team members.

The project already has clear goals—but these goals are not useful for directing individual work assignments. Goals specify only the end results required of an entire project. It is important that each member of the project team is aware of the goals and commits to them, but individuals need the end-results of their own work specified as well. Each member of the team will contribute only a part of the work required to meet the project goals; therefore, individual team members need subgoals, called objectives, that identify the end results required from their work efforts.

Goals establish directions, but objectives tell individuals what they need to do to contribute to the overall project. Objectives tell specific players or groups how you want to achieve a specific milestone. Objectives focus on the details of specific accomplishments by individual team members. They are guiding principles that direct the efforts of the project team in their work toward meeting the project's goal.

For expediency, it is usually best if the objectives are initially outlined by the project manager based on the project goals and the tasks. They should be discussed and refined in meetings with the specific team members. In this way, the project manager has direct input into the objectives, and the team members feel that they have participated in the development of their work assignments. Just handing team members a list of objectives without getting their input is autocratic, unfeeling, and inappropriate for project work.

Objective setting must be an interactive process that results in a clear understanding of objectives and responsibilities for each team member. Just like setting goals, the process may go back and forth a few times until specific objectives are established. The clarity of the project objectives is essential to effective project performance. Research indicates that when people understand their work objectives, their performance is more likely to be optimized.

Newsletter Team Assignments			
Team Manager	*Team Manager*	*Team Member*	Vacation or Work Constraints
Joe	Project Manager, Also Tasks 6, 8 and 13	Assure quality and completion of project on time and within budget.	
John	Articles, Tasks 1-5	Write interesting articles to fit format.	July 8-15
Gail	Mailing List, Task 15	Assemble a complete and current customer list in a timely manner.	
George	Articles and Design, Tasks 1-5 and 7-13	Assist John with articles and finish desktop publishing the newsletter within format specifications.	
Ingrid	Final Approvals, Tasks 8 and 10	Assure overall quality and corporate standards are adhered to.	July 28-31

Figure 4-7 Newsletter Team Assignments and Objectives

Objectives specify the quality and time frames for each task that are the responsibility of a person or group. When objectives for all the team members are added up, the complete list of project goals should be accounted for. The team members should understand how their individual objectives fulfill specific aspects of the overall project goals—and they should be clear on their responsibilities to fulfill these goals. Ownership of objectives is important because it leads to commitment and responsibility for the project.

Because some team members in a project may not be brought in until after work has been started, the objective setting process may be an ongoing process. If this is the case, the project manager should document the general objectives for each functional area of the team and then refine the objectives in the first meeting with the new team members as part of their integration into the project.

A list of team assignments and objectives for people involved in the newsletter project is provided as an example of one possible format for documenting the individual objectives component of the project plan. (See Figure 4-7.) It is also useful to note any work limitations for the team members on the chart, such as vacations, travel dates, or other commitments that may affect availability for the project.

The Project Team Goes Beyond the People Who Do the Work

There are always more people involved in a project than those who do the work. These people approve aspects of the project, review progress, and are often involved in high-level project decisions, such as establishing budgets or authorizing additional staff and equipment. They are also important to the project and should be considered part of the project team in the larger sense of the word.

Typical project team members who may be involved with a business project, but who will not be working on the project include

- Customers and clients
- Executive staff and managers
- Technical reviewers and analysts
- Government agencies

Because of the many other people potentially involved or interested in a project, it is important that responsibility and authority of all the team members are identified in advance, agreed upon, understood, and clearly communicated. To do this, the linear responsibility chart is a standard project documentation technique that can be very useful. (See Figure 4-8.)

The linear responsibility chart lists out all the various team members and their roles in a project. This responsibility chart then becomes part of the

TASKS

PEOPLE	Select Broker	Fund Office	Design Interior Changes	Arrange Utilities	Order Office Equipment	Business Permits	Bank Accounts	Stationary & Supplies	Phone System	Signs	
Ingrid, Vice President	5	6	5			5	6				
Roger, Regional Mgr.	6	3	6	5	6	6	3			6	
Dave, Sales Specialist	1	1	2	3	3	5			4	1	
Jennifer, Sales Admin.		4	3	1	1	5		1	3		
John, Support Specialist	2	2	1	3	3	1	1		1	4	

Linear Responsibility Chart for Part of the San Francisco Sales Office Project

Key
1. Primary Responsibility
2. General Supervision
3. Must Be Consulted
4. May Be Consulted
5. Must Be Notified
6. Must Approve

Figure 4-8 Linear Responsibility Chart for Part of the San Francisco Sales Office Project

project plan. As with all aspects of the project plan, it is a good idea to have this chart reviewed and approved before it is set in concrete.

DEFINING THE MATERIAL RESOURCE REQUIREMENTS FOR A PROJECT

In addition to a team, every project needs equipment and supplies. Some of this equipment is taken for granted, including the office space and business equipment you already have in place, for example, personal computers for writing reports, desks, filing cabinets, telephones, or fax machines. But most projects have additional unique resource requirements. For these needs, it is necessary to establish an inventory of equipment and materials requirements for your projects and a strategy for getting the resources you need. (See Figure 4-9.)

In some ways, establishing your material resource requirements is very similar to creating the skills requirements and skills inventories for your project team. But, instead of people skills required for each task, you will list your equipment, supplies, and other material requirements for each task. Then, for each requirement, note the tactic and steps for getting the required resources. Sometimes the steps required to get resources need to be added as tasks to your network because significant time will be spent locating and purchasing the required materials or equipment.

A description of the quality, quantity, and budget constraints for equipment and supplies is required in any project inventory, regardless of the size and complexity of the project. When the project schedule is completed (see the next chapter), date requirements for the supplies and equipment should be identified as well.

The format for listing inventory and supply requirements should be adapted to the needs of each project. In the office project, getting the equipment is a major component in meeting the project goals—in fact, selecting the phones, buying furniture, and other aspects of fulfilling the physical requirements for the project are actually projects in themselves. Each person responsible for these tasks should make a list of required equipment and supplies and have it approved. For the newsletter project, most of the operational equipment is already in place in the marketing communications department and only paper for the printing of the newsletter must be selected. The materials inventory for such a simple project can be completed by adding a column to the task list illustrated in the last chapter. In more complex projects, a worksheet like the one provided as an example may be used for documenting the resources required for each task or milestone in a project.

Getting the Things You Need

There are some fundamental, obvious ways in which resource requirements can be filled:

Equipment and Supply Worksheet

Project _____ Date _____

Completed By _____

REQUIRED	RESPONSIBLE PERSON OR VENDOR	HOW MUCH IS NEEDED?	WHEN IS IT NEEDED?	CHECK IF AVAILABLE
MATERIALS:				☐ ☐ ☐ ☐ ☐ ☐
EQUIPMENT:				☐ ☐ ☐ ☐ ☐
SUPPLIES:				☐ ☐ ☐ ☐ ☐
SPECIAL SERVICES:				☐ ☐ ☐
OTHER:				☐ ☐ ☐ ☐ ☐ ☐

Figure 4-9 Equipment and Supply Worksheet for a Project Task

- Buy the equipment or supplies from a known supplier
- Identify a new supplier and buy the equipment or supplies
- Send the requirements out to bid and have multiple suppliers compete for the business
- If equipment will be used infrequently, rent it or borrow it from another department

In addition to identifying the method for fulfilling your resource requirements, you will also need to assign responsibilities for getting these supplies and equipment. This can be done as part of the objectives assigned to other team members or can be listed on the staff inventory as a separate column.

If you will be managing similar projects, it is important to create a list of available suppliers and vendors for your resource requirements: rate them on price, quality, and service. This list will help you expedite the fulfillment of your material and equipment needs because you won't have to spend time locating specific vendors for commonly purchased supplies and equipment. Some companies develop approved vendor lists for this purpose that are maintained by a purchasing or accounting department.

For both your team and material requirements, you will want to go through the formal review and approval process that has been established for your project. At this point in your project planning, you should have complete, documented project goals, a work breakdown structure and network for the project, a description of your project team complete with skills inventory and a list of clear objectives for each team member, and documentation of required equipment and supplies. With these in hand, you are now ready to create the project schedule, and we'll show you how to do that in the next chapter.

Chapter Five

ESTIMATING DURATIONS AND SCHEDULING:
Six Steps to Realistic Dates

Using the list of objectives, the completed project chart, and the resource inventory developed in the last chapters, the next step in the project planning process is to develop the schedule. The budget is often completed in parallel with the scheduling process, but we'll cover that process separately in Chapter Six, so you needn't think about it until then. After years of trials, most project managers agree that it is more effective to complete the schedule before finalizing the budget.

Scheduling is the process of converting sequenced project tasks into an achievable timetable. An accurate, realistic schedule is the most important tool for controlling the implementation of a project. It is also the most important part of the project plan for coordinating resources and people. Still, too many project managers put together the schedule their superiors want to see—knowing full well that the schedule is too tight and the goals impossible to achieve. Other managers add too much room for error and look incompetent as a result. Managers using either of these scheduling approaches will fail to manage their projects optimally—either the projects will be late or they will cost too much or both.

In this chapter you will learn to estimate realistically the amount of time required to complete a project. A schedule based on realistic estimates will provide a superior framework for guiding your project to cost-effective, timely completion. Anyone can arbitrarily assign dates to a list of tasks—the trick to creating a realistic and achievable schedule is to use techniques that allow you to predict project outcomes in advance with an acceptable level of accuracy.

A realistic schedule is the key to managing people, time, and resources. In a large project consisting of many tasks and resources, the development of a complete schedule can be the single most time-consuming aspect of the project planning process. For this reason, the scheduling phase is often rushed or poorly executed. Even with computerized tools, scheduling a complex project can be a lot of work. Because an accurate schedule is essential to the professional management of any project, regardless of size or complexity, the schedule is not a place to cut corners. The more thought you put into a schedule, the more likely you'll meet your deadlines as planned.

THE SIX STEPS TO ACCURATE SCHEDULING

As stated before, scheduling begins after the list of tasks and a complete staff and resource inventory are complete. With these components of the project plan in hand, reliable scheduling involves six steps, which will be described in depth in this chapter. (See Figure 5-1.)

Step 1. Establish the scheduling assumptions.

Step 2. Estimate the time required to complete each task (activity) on the project plan based on available resources (regardless of charting technique chosen).

Step 3. Determine the critical path and task float. (The critical path and task float are important in larger projects. We will explain them and show you how to calculate them in this chapter, so don't be dismayed if you don't know what they are.)

Step 4. Determine the calendar dates for each task and create an ideal master schedule for the project.

Step 5. Adjust individual resource assignments and incorporate necessary changes into the schedule after review.

Step 6. Chart the final schedule for the project and distribute it to the team.

Scheduling Step 1. Establish the Scheduling Assumptions

Based on the material covered in the previous chapters, you already know how important it is to clarify objectives and expected results before a project plan is started. For many of the same reasons, it is important to specify scheduling assumptions before the schedule is completed. (See Figure 5-2.) The answers to the following questions can be used to clarify your scheduling assumptions:

- Are there a fixed number of resources to be used on the project or can they be added as required to meet schedule priorities?
- Is there an absolute fixed date when the project *must* be completed or is the completion date to be determined based on the planning process?

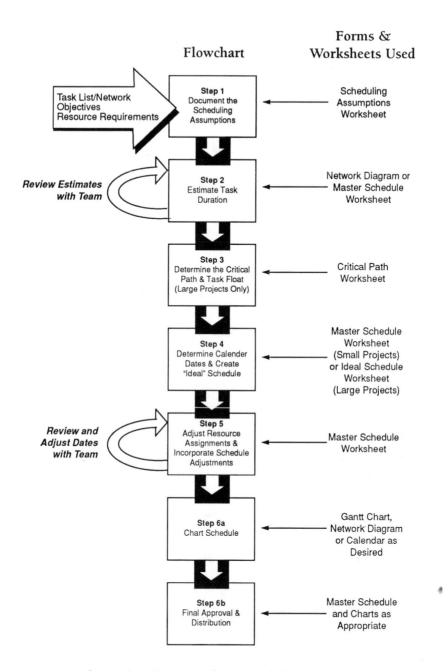

Forms &
Flowchart | Worksheets Used

Task List/Network Objectives Resource Requirements

Step 1
Document the Scheduling Assumptions
— Scheduling Assumptions Worksheet

Review Estimates with Team

Step 2
Estimate Task Duration
— Network Diagram or Master Schedule Worksheet

Step 3
Determine the Critical Path & Task Float (Large Projects Only)
— Critical Path Worksheet

Step 4
Determine Calender Dates & Create "Ideal" Schedule
— Master Schedule Worksheet (Small Projects) or Ideal Schedule Worksheet (Large Projects)

Review and Adjust Dates with Team

Step 5
Adjust Resource Assignments & Incorporate Schedule Adjustments
— Master Schedule Worksheet

Step 6a
Chart Schedule
— Gantt Chart, Network Diagram or Calendar as Desired

Step 6b
Final Approval & Distribution
— Master Schedule and Charts as Appropriate

Refer to this diagram of the scheduling process as
you proceed through the chapter.

Figure 5-1 The Scheduling Process

Scheduling Assumptions Worksheet

Project Name <u>San Francisco Office Project</u>   Date <u>May 22</u>

1. Are all the resources currently available for this project?

If no, list the resources required that are not available:

People   Leasing Agent Needs to Be Found

Equipment

☐ YES

☒ NO

2. Is there a due date when the project absolutely must be complete?

If yes, enter date:

Reason:

☐ YES

☒ NO

3. Will overtime be allowed?

If yes, how much?

☐ YES

☒ NO

4. Are there any holidays or other breaks during this project?

If yes, list dates: July 4

☒ YES

☐ NO

5. Have additional resources and people been approved for this project?

☒ YES

☐ NO

6. Have the work schedules and availabilities of all resources been documented?

☒ YES

☐ NO

Notes: Follow the Phildelphia Office Plan as Reference

Figure 5-2 Scheduling Assumptions Worksheet

- Will people work standard workdays or will overtime be allowed?
- What holidays will be observed by your company and your suppliers?
- Are all resources currently trained and available or will the project depend on hiring more people and purchasing new equipment?

In a large project, you should document the assumptions in writing before you complete a schedule and attempt to gain consensus with managers and key personnel working on the project. A completed Assumptions Worksheet is provided for the sales office project as an example of one format that can be used for this. In simple projects, with only a few people involved, the documentation is rarely necessary, but verbal agreement on the assumptions is still a good idea. The consensus gathering and approval process should be similar to the one discussed in the second chapter for establishing the objectives and the scope of your project as a whole.

The assumptions should be agreed upon by all key people involved in the project including outside suppliers. Obviously, you can't expect your advertising agency or your employees to work over Christmas holidays unless they have agreed to this in advance, and you can't hire new people or buy more equipment unless your boss approves the decision. However, many project schedules fall short because the manager producing the schedule forgets the obvious.

In addition to specifying the underlying scheduling assumptions, you will need to determine the level of detail for your schedule. In simple projects, like the newsletter example we've used, the project is specified at the general activity level. Therefore, the level of scheduling detail will also be very general. In more complex projects, the level of scheduling detail may vary by task and activity. Some activities will be scheduled down to the hour, other activities will be scheduled over a much broader period of weeks or months. In general it is the level of detail used in charting your project, as determined by the methods discussed in Chapter Three, that should dictate the optimum scheduling detail for your project.

Scheduling Step 2. Estimate the Time Required to Complete Each Task

After the assumptions are understood and agreed to, you can proceed to the key step in producing an accurate schedule: estimating the length of time each task (activity) will take to complete. In project management methodology, this is called estimating task duration. It is the duration of the tasks, when added together, that establish the length of time required to complete a project. You should enter the task duration estimates directly on the network diagram or on something similar to the Master Schedule Worksheet. (An example is provided later in the chapter.)

It must be emphasized that completing duration estimates for each task is the single most important aspect of the project scheduling process. Without accuracy at this stage, the entire plan is in jeopardy. If your task estimates are too long, the project may cost more in time and resources than it's worth. If your task estimates are too short, the project will not finish on time. This could affect the availability of resources, the success of the project, and your credibility as a project manager.

To complete the estimating process, it is necessary to work with the network diagram, task list, or activity chart developed for the project. Be aware that your task list and network diagram may need minor revisions as you go through the duration estimating process. You may think of a task you left out or decide that one task should really be broken into two.

Task duration estimates for business projects are most often based on the number of workdays required to complete each task. Some managers choose to estimate tasks in hours or weeks instead of days, depending on the nature of the project, its complexity, and its life span. As an operating rule, if any single task in a project takes 2 percent or more of the total project time, it should be listed on the task list and the schedule. If a particular task is very important but takes less than a few days, it should still be scheduled. In extremely cost-sensitive and/or complex projects, some tasks might be scheduled on a subhourly basis for each resource. Again, the level of charting detail used to represent your project will determine the level of detail for specifying task durations.

Estimating Skills and Techniques

In some ways scheduling and duration estimating are like trying to see into the future. After years of experience, many managers can accurately estimate time and resource requirements for common project tasks as if magically pulling numbers from the air. This "educated guess" technique, also known as the "guesstimate," is one of the most frequently used and abused forms of estimating. Fortunately, there are better techniques for estimating task durations that take the mystery and the mistakes out of the process. (See Figure 5-3.) Here are several dependable techniques you can use:

- **Estimating Based on a Similar Project.** One of the easiest estimating techniques is to find a successfully completed project plan for a similar project and base new task duration estimates on this previous project. If you use this technique you will need to account for any differences between the projects and adjust the scheduling times accordingly. For example, in the sales office project, the plan from an office opened last year in Philadelphia can be used as a reference. You note that it took a total of five weeks from start to finish to get the Philadelphia office opened. You also notice that the offices had been pre-screened before the project started so a property broker didn't need to be hired. Therefore, you will have to add time to the project to account for those differences. But the durations of the other tasks on the project should be similar, including time required to order the stationery, get signs installed, and build out the space to the specifications.

Project Management Tip

✎ **Two People Doesn't Mean Half the Time**—The number of people available to complete each task or activity must be one of your basic scheduling assumptions. Your duration estimates must therefore reflect the number of people working on each task. In the last chapter a sample form for listing your team members was provided—the information on that form is necessary for completing the task duration estimates and the final schedule.

The body count available for a task will obviously affect the duration estimate for that task. For example, if one person will be working on a task solo, it may take four weeks to complete the task. However, with two people working on the same task, it may only take two and a half weeks. It almost never takes exactly half as much time for two people to do what one person can do, because time is required to coordinate information and integrate the work.

Always allow for this extra management and coordination when you add additional resources to a project. If you divide only the single person time by additional people you could get yourself into a serious time crunch. As a guideline, divide a single-person time estimate by the number of people and then add 10 to 30 percent to account for coordination and management time. The percentage of time added depends on the complexity of the task, the egos involved, and the depth of organizational bureaucracy.

Your duration estimates should also take into account the quality and training of the people available for your project. If you need to hire and/or train people, this must be added as a subproject. Also, some of your resources will be better than others at getting work done. You may want to complete separate task duration estimates for the various people involved. The time required for the person who will take the longest becomes your "worst case" estimate and the time needed by the most experienced, efficient person becomes your "best case" estimate.

Project Management Tip

✎ **Working Backward from the Due Date to Understand Project Time Constraints**—You should never work backward from a fixed due date to estimate task durations or assign task schedule dates. If there is a "fixed" date, it will usually compel people to make estimates that fit the time allowed. This means either squeezing tasks into too little time or spreading the tasks out unrealistically.

If, however, you suspect at the onset that a project may take longer than the time dictated, you can work backward from the finish date, assigning durations to see if a "rough cut" of the project will take more time than is available. If this is the case, you must get the deadline extended, add resources to finish the tasks in less time, or reduce the number of tasks (accomplish less).

- **Assigning Standard Task Units.** If you manage projects in which many of the same kinds of tasks are duplicated over and over again, you may want to create a "standard task unit" for these common tasks. This technique is often used in construction and engineering, where the time to complete a standard operation has been established and proven over time. It is also useful in projects such as assembling products or editing manuals or in any project that uses predictable, recurring tasks. Creating a schedule using standard tasks is a simple matter of adding up all the standard task times and putting them on the calendar. For example, a construction company specializing in building suburban homes knows from experience how long it takes to complete each task in building a block of houses. When the project manager for this construction company completes a schedule to build five new houses, he simply lists the standard task durations in sequence.

  It is important to remember that standard task estimates may change over time. Standard task units should be measured and evaluated on a regular basis. Also be careful not to assign a standard task unit to a task that sounds similar but on further investigation is really quite different in scope. Some kinds of tasks are not easily standardized. These include tasks that are really subprojects involving multiple activities, tasks that involve a high degree of creativity such as programming or promotional writing, and tasks without a long enough history to be standardized.

- **Using Team Estimating Sessions.** It is often necessary and advisable when multiple people are involved on a project to consult with other team members when estimating task durations. Even if the political situation doesn't necessitate team estimating sessions to gain consensus, it doesn't hurt to have a meeting with your team to review the

Choosing the Best Estimating Techniques for Your Project

Technique	Best Application
Based on a Similar Project	When a previous successful plan is available with a high degree of similarity to the current project
Standardized Task Units	When repetitive tasks are duplicated in many similar projects; requires tasks with a history of consistent execution over substantial time period.
Team Estimating	Always advisable when multiple people are involved; mandatory if people have special or unique expertise.
Expert Assistance	When a manager is inexperienced or if the project is extremely cost and time critical and requires a high degree of reliability in order to succeed.

Figure 5-3 Choosing the Best Estimating Technique for Your Project

estimates. It's good for building a sense of shared objectives and open communication. An excellent method is to assemble the specialists and team members in a room to "rough out" a schedule. Start with the chart of known tasks and then ask for their advice on the time estimates. In a really large project, you may need to break the project into subproject blocks and have meetings for estimating each major segment of the project.

- **Getting Expert Advice and Assistance.** If you are inexperienced and managing a complex or important project for the first time, you may wish to engage the services of an expert or use the knowledge and expertise of more experienced managers to estimate durations, select resources, define tasks, and assemble the schedule. Experienced project managers work as consultants and you can locate one in the Yellow Pages or through the referral of business associates. Another source of expert advice is to ask experienced managers or specialists in your company who are not part of your project team to serve as project mentors. By watching a veteran in action, you can learn the ropes for managing your next project.

  Ideally you should use more than one estimating technique on a project. For example, base the estimates on your last project and then use a team estimating session to cross-check the schedule or to investigate the time required to complete a new, unfamiliar task. The final estimates, which take multiple sources into account, will usually be more accurate than will those based on only one estimating technique.

- **Compromising Between Best and Worst Case Scenarios.** In every task duration estimate, regardless of technique used, there should be some allowance for "error." Some project management methodologies, including PERT which was discussed previously, use three time estimates as part of a wide range of scheduling options and algorithms: the optimistic estimate, the most-likely estimate, and the pessimistic estimate.

  The optimistic estimate represents the project schedule if everything moves along perfectly. Because problems crop up even in the most carefully controlled projects, almost no project ever comes in on the best case estimate. The pessimistic estimate accounts for everything imaginable going wrong, though sometimes even these schedules

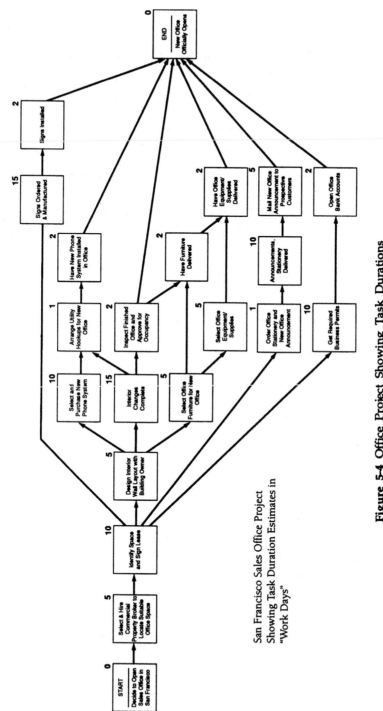

San Francisco Sales Office Project
Showing Task Duration Estimates in
"Work Days"

Figure 5-4 Office Project Showing Task Durations

Master Schedule Worksheet

Project Name _Customer Employee Newsletter_ Date _January 4_____

Scheduled Start _Jan 3_____ Scheduled Finish _February 4_____

Prepared by _Gail_____ Date _Dec 28_____

Approved by _M. Baxter_____ Date _Dec 31_____

TASK	Duration	RESPONSIBLE PEOPLE	START DATE	FINISH DATE	ACTUAL START	ACTUAL FINISH
1. Assemble story ideas	5	Gail	Jan 4	Jan 8		
2. Meeting to approve story ideas	1	Department Staff	Jan 11	Jan 11		
3. 1st draft of stories	5	Gail	Jan 11	Jan 15		
4. Stories reviewed	1	Dept. Staff & Mr. Baxter	Jan 18	Jan 18		
5. Final draft of stories	2	Gail	Jan 19	Jan 21		
6. Final draft approved	4	Mr. Baxter	Jan 22	Jan 25		
7. Layout stories with computer	3	Gail	Jan 25	Jan 27		
8. Layout approved	1	Mr. Baxter	Jan 27	Jan 27		
9. Final changes and proofreading	1	Gail & Dept. Staff	Jan 28	Jan 28		
10. Final sign-off	1	Ms. Smith	Jan 28	Jan 28		
11. Type output on Linotronic typesetter	1	Gail	Jan 28	Jan 28		
12. Camera-ready film to printer	1	Gail	Jan 29	Jan 29		
13. Review "blueline" proof at printer's shop and approve	1	Printer, Gail	Feb 1	Feb 1		
14. Finished newsletter delivered to office	1	Printer	Feb 3	Feb 3		
15. Distribution of newsletter	1	Gail	Feb 4	Feb 4		

Figure 5-5 Master Schedule Worksheet

turn out to be optimistic if a disaster strikes. A most likely estimate and the schedule that results should be a compromise between these best and worst case estimates.

Be more pessimistic estimating tasks that involve a lot of guesswork or new people, less so on common tasks using "tried and true" resources that you have experience with. As you gain confidence in estimating over time, a concisely scheduled and well-managed project should normally come in close to your "most likely" estimates. In all your estimating, remember that it's better to finish a project early and under budget than to deliver a project late and over budget! (See Figure 5-4.)

Determining the Degree of Confidence in the Estimates. Another way to accommodate potential errors in estimates is to assign a degree of confidence to each duration estimate. Some tasks will have a high degree of confidence because you are already familiar with them or because they are relatively simple. Other task duration estimates, either because the tasks are less familiar or more complex, will have a lower degree of confidence. Degrees of confidence can be expressed as percentages. A task with almost complete assurance of timely completion may have a degree of confidence of 99 percent. A totally unfamiliar activity might have a estimated confidence of only 20 percent or less. The degree of confidence can be used to express the overall scheduling risk and to determine the range between the optimistic and the pessimistic duration estimates.

For massive, complex projects, statistics-based estimating techniques can be used to calculate variances and determine the probability of achieving a particular time goal. These are not normally necessary for business projects, but if you find yourself responsible for a major engineering project, you will need to learn to use probability predictors in your scheduling calculations. (References that cover these statistical techniques are provided in the back of the book.)

Getting the Estimates Down on the Plan. You will likely need to make two or three duration estimate revisions as you work with your task list until you get exactly what you want. It is a good idea to make three or four copies of the task list to work on and keep a blank master for the final schedule (unless you are using a computer of course). Enter your task duration estimates on the scheduling worksheet and on the network diagram if you are using one. In a simple project, you only have to fill in the duration column on the Master Schedule Worksheet as shown in the example for the customer newsletter project. (See Figure 5-5.) A network diagram with durations has already been shown demonstrating the convention for displaying durations on the individual tasks. If you have developed a flowchart of the work breakdown structure to represent your project, then duration estimates for each task can be written right on the flowchart.

Scheduling Step 3. Determine the Critical Path and Task Float for the Project

Once the individual task duration estimates are complete, you are ready to get down to the business of putting together a schedule with real dates. On the larger, more complex projects, one step remains before that is possible, however, and that is calculating the "critical path." If you are going to manage small projects with only a few sequential activities, this step isn't necessary. But on most projects, multiple parallel paths and subprojects are involved. It is the critical path that determines the amount of time required for completion of a multipath project, and its identification is crucial to development of an accurate project schedule.

Project Management Buzzwords

☞ Critical Path—The path of longest duration as determined on a project network diagram. The critical path determines the total duration of the project. If a task on the critical path is delayed, the final completion of the project will likely be delayed.

☞ Critical Task—Any task that is on the critical path is called a critical task because if it fails to finish on time, it will delay the tasks following it. Critical tasks typically account for less than 10 percent of all the tasks in a large project.

By definition, the critical path is the sequence of tasks that forms the longest time duration of the project. Therefore, if a task on the critical path is delayed, it will add additional time to the project, that is, make the project late. Because you have to know the durations of the tasks to calculate the total project duration, you can't determine the critical path until the task duration estimates are complete.

To comprehend the concept of critical path better, go back to the simplified network diagram for the sales office project. As you've already seen in this familiar example, the tasks in complex projects do not necessarily occur in sequence. You've also seen that there are some tasks that absolutely must follow one another. The duration of tasks and the precedences shown for tasks on the network diagram define the "critical path." In a project with only sequential tasks, all activities or tasks in the project are on the critical path because one task follows another. If one task in a sequential project is late, all tasks following it will be late (if your duration estimates are accurate and can't be modified).

The critical path is "critical" because tasks that follow a critical task cannot be started until all the previous tasks on the critical path are completed. Thus, if a task on the critical path is delayed, all tasks following the delayed critical task will be pushed out in time. The critical tasks will have starting and finishing times that are fixed relative to the start of the project. Tasks not on the critical path will usually have some flexibility relative to when they can start and finish. This flexibility is called "float," or sometimes "slack." Float is the difference between the time available for performing a task and time required to complete a task.

In the sales office project, which has multiple paths, if suitable office space is not located and leased until ten days later than planned, most of the subsequent tasks can't be started on time. Letterhead can't be ordered without an address. A build-out on the space cannot start and office furniture and decoration can't be selected to fit in an unspecified office. Thus the leasing of the office is on the critical path.

Project Management Buzzword

☞   **Float (or Slack)**—The difference between the time available for performing a task and time required to complete a task. Total float is calculated as follows:

Total float   = Latest finish   − earliest start   − duration

If the total float for a task equals zero, then that task is on the critical path.

The phone set-up tasks, however, are not on the critical path. Based on the network, you can start ordering phones on workday 20 in the project, because all the precedent tasks should be complete by then according to the network diagram. However, if you wait another one to eight days before you start this task, you will still be able to get the phones installed by the opening day of the office according to the network. Thus, there are eight days of "float" or "slack" in this path that allow you to schedule the phone installation activities in a more flexible way, depending on the best use of your resources.

The bank account path also has some scheduling flexibility because these tasks are not on the critical path. This flexibility doesn't exist for tasks on the critical path because they have no float.

The identification of float is one of the advantages of network project planning. Networks allow float to be easily calculated and allow for more flexible scheduling of tasks that are not on the critical path.

This limited example shows that the critical path becomes the key to both scheduling and managing your project to a timely completion. Identifying the critical path will also help in prioritizing work as the project proceeds and problems are encountered. In most cases, tasks on the critical path will have priority over other tasks in the project. (See Figure 5-6.)

In a large project the critical path will include only a small percentage of the actual tasks in the project, typically less than 10 percent. In the example we are using, which shows only a subset of the sales office project tasks, the critical path uses a much larger percentage of the tasks because, for practical reasons, we are using a relatively small, simplified network to illustrate the techniques.

Calculating and Diagramming the Critical Path. To people new to project management methodology, the calculation of the critical path sounds technical and complex. However, as you'll soon see, it isn't difficult to calculate and it is vitally important to maintaining control of your schedule after your project begins.

To calculate the critical path on a small project, simply add up all the task duration estimates for each path in the network diagram. By definition, the path with the longest number of days for completion will be the critical path. Using this technique, the number of workdays estimated for completion of the sales office project totals forty-one, because this is the longest possible path in the project. In Figure 5-6, the critical path is shown with double lines drawn between the shaded critical tasks. If you add up the durations for these tasks, you'll find that they indeed total forty-one.

In large projects the critical path can be more easily calculated with the network diagram, your task duration estimates, and a form like the Critical Path Worksheet. (See Figure 5-7.) To calculate the critical path, you need to make a few fundamental calculations, based on the estimated durations for each task.

Using the Critical Path Worksheet to Calculate Critical Path and Float. The steps for using the Critical Path Worksheet to determine the critical path and the total float for tasks not on the critical path are

1. **List the tasks and estimated task durations on the worksheet.**
2. **Calculate the earliest start number for each task.** The earliest start is the earliest time an activity can be started if all the activities before it in the path have been completed. Begin from the first task in the network diagram and assume that the first task is day "zero." You

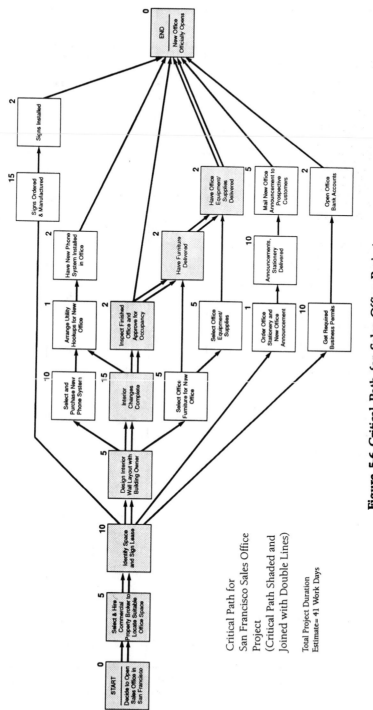

Critical Path for
San Francisco Sales Office
Project
(Critical Path Shaded and
Joined with Double Lines)

Total Project Duration
Estimate= 41 Work Days

Figure 5-6 Critical Path for Sales Office Project

Critical Path Worksheet

Project Name __San Francisco Sales Office Project__ Date __May 25__

TASK	DURATION	EARLIEST START	EARLIEST FINISH	LATEST START	LATEST FINISH		TOTAL FLOAT
Select and hire commercial property broker	5	0	5	0	5		0
Find office and sign lease	10	5	15	5	15		0
Design interior changes with the owner	5	15	20	15	20		0
Interior changes complete	15	20	35	20	35		0
Inspect finished office and approve for occupancy	2	35	37	35	37		0
Select and purchase phone system	10	20	30	28	38		8
Arrange utility hook-ups	1	30	31	38	39		8
Phone system installed	2	31	33	39	41		8
Select and order office furniture	5	20	25	29	34		9
Office furniture delivered	2	37	39	37	39		0
Select and order office equipment and supplies	5	25	30	34	39		9
Office equipment delivered and set-up	2	39	41	39	41		0
Order and manufacture signs for new office	15	15	30	24	39		9
Signs installed	2	30	32	39	41		9
Order stationery and announcements	1	15	16	25	26		10
Stationery and announcements delivered	10	16	26	26	36		10
Announcements mailed	5	26	31	36	41		10
Get business permits	10	15	25	29	39		14
Open bank accounts	2	25	27	39	41		14

All tasks with zero total float are on the critical path.

Figure 5-7 Critical Path Worksheet

should assume that each task begins immediately after the finish of the preceding activity.

Earliest start = Smallest number of days from the beginning of a project before a task can begin.

Day "zero" is the first day in a project for making calculations.

In the example, the earliest start for the task "Select and Purchase New Phone System" becomes $0 + 5 + 10 + 5 = 20$, because 20 is the total of all durations that immediately precede the beginning of that task on the network diagram.

3. **Calculate the earliest finish number for each task.** To do this, add the task duration (as a number of days) to the earliest start number.

Earliest finish = Earliest start + task duration

Thus, the "Select and Purchase New Phone System Task" is calculated as $20 + 10 = 30$. The earliest day this task should be started on is workday 30 in the project.

4. **Calculate the latest finish for each task.** The latest finish is the last day a task can be completed without changing the end date of the project. The latest finish is calculated by first noting the largest number in the Earliest Finish column. This number is the total number of days in the project. Assign this number to the last task in the project and subtract the duration from the number of duration days in the path. Thus, to calculate latest finish, you work backward from the last day of the project. (In essence, it is the same as calculating earliest start, only in reverse.) So, the latest finish for the "Select and Purchase New Phone System" task becomes $41 - 2 - 1 = 38$ because these are the total of the durations between the task subtracted from the number of the last day of the project.

5. **Calculate the latest start for each task.** The latest start is the last day in a project a task can begin and still be completed without affecting the end date of the project. In other words, if a task hasn't been begun by this date, the project will be late. Determining the latest start is simply a matter of making the following calculation:

Latest finish – Duration = Latest start

For the "Select and Purchase New Phone System" task, this becomes $38 - 10 = 28$. Thus, if this task begins after workday 28 in the project, the project will be late if all the other task durations are correct.

6. **Determine total float for each task.** Total float is determined by the following simple calculation:

$$Total\ float\ =\ latest\ finish\ -\ earliest\ start\ -\ duration$$

The tasks with zero float are on the critical path. Check this with the network diagram illustrating the critical path shown earlier. Tasks with float have scheduling flexibility. In the "Select and Purchase New Phone System" task, the total float calculation is $38 - 20 - 10 = 8$. Thus there are eight days of scheduling flexibility associated with this task.

If you still aren't clear on the calculations for determining the critical path, go over the previous section one more time and refer to the network diagram with each calculation on the sample Critical Path Worksheet. The concepts of float and critical path will become clearer if you refer to them in relationship to the network diagram.

On large projects with many hundreds of tasks, you can see that these calculations, even though simple, may become tedious. This is why computerized programs were developed for drawing networks and calculating schedule dates. Some of the computerized project management options available to you will be covered in Chapter Ten.

Even if you do use a computer to help you with your network diagrams and calculations, it is important that you master the basic scheduling principles as they have been presented here. If you don't understand the underlying principles of float, start dates, finish dates, and critical path, you won't understand how the computer derives the schedules it produces, and you won't be able to modify the schedules to suit your needs and priorities.

Scheduling Step 4. Determine the Calendar Dates for Each Task and Create the Ideal Schedule

When the tasks, durations, critical path, and relative start and finish calculations are complete, an actual schedule with calendar dates can be produced. To list the schedule dates, use the Master Schedule Worksheet or something like it for simple projects. On more complex projects, like the sales office project, it is advisable to work on a form similar to the Ideal Schedule Worksheet before producing a final master schedule.

The starting date of the project is determined by you and your project team. Using a calendar, preferably one with spaces for making notations, number each workday in the project, beginning with zero for the first day. Don't number weekends unless you work on these days. Also, skip holidays or other days you will not be working on the project (as noted on the Assumptions Worksheet).

Using the completed Critical Path Worksheet as your guide, fill in the dates that correspond to each workday number on the scheduling worksheet. In the example, the sales office project is started on Monday, June 3—this is day 0 on the Critical Path Worksheet. Workday 5 is Monday, June 10; workday 14 is Friday, June 21; and so on. Remember, for tasks on the critical path the

Ideal Schedule Worksheet

Project Name _San Francisco Sales Office Project_____

Scheduled Start _June 3_____   Calculated Finish _July 31_____

TASK	RESPONSIBLE PEOPLE	DURATION	EARLIEST START	EARLIEST FINISH	LATEST START	LATEST FINISH
Select and hire commercial property broker	John, Dave	5	June 3	June 10	June 3	June 10
Find office and sign lease	Agent, Dave	10	June 10	June 24	June 10	June 24
Design interior changes with the owner	John, Dave, Agent	5	June 24	July 1	June 24	July 1
Interior changes complete	Owner	15	July 1	July 23	July 1	July 23
Inspect finished office and approve for occupancy	John, Dave	2	July 23	July 25	July 23	July 25
Select and purchase phone system	John	10	July 1	July 16	July 12	July 26
Arrange utility hook-ups	Jennifer	1	July 16	July 17	July 26	July 27
Phone system installed	Phone Co.	2	July 17	July 19	July 29	July 31
Select and order office furniture	Jennifer	5	July 1	July 9	July 15	July 22
Office furniture installed	Jennifer	2	July 25	July 29	July 25	July 29
Select and order office equipment and supplies	Jennifer	5	July 9	July 16	July 22	July 29
Office equipment delivered and set-up	Jennifer	2	July 29	July 32	July 29	July 31
Order and manufacture signs for new office	Dave	15	June 24	July 16	July 8	July 29
Signs installed	Dave	2	July 16	July 18	July 29	July 31
Order stationery and announcements	Jennifer	1	June 24	June 25	July 9	July 10
Stationery and announcements delivered	Jennifer, Printer	10	June 25	July 10	July 10	July 24
Announcements mailed	Jennifer	5	July 10	July 17	July 24	July 31
Get business permits	John, Jennifer	10	June 24	July 9	July 29	July 31
Open bank accounts	John	2	July 9	July 11	July 29	July 31

Figure 5-8 Ideal Schedule Worksheet

"earliest start date" and the "latest start date" should be the same, as should the "earliest finish" and "latest finish" dates.

Tasks that aren't on the critical path will have an earliest start date, latest start date, earliest finish date, and latest finish date. This variance in dates is a result of the amount of float (or slack) you calculated earlier. Of course, in simple sequential projects, you will have no float, so you will only have start dates and finish dates for the tasks.

Project Management Tip

✎ **The Mythical Man-Month**—If adding additional resources is an option, in labor-intensive operations, including assembly work, ditch digging, or typesetting, it is possible to add people and gain productivity and reduce task time. Labor-intensive tasks can be speeded up with additional workers sharing the labor, though an extra layer of management may also be required to coordinate the additional resources. This usually affects the budget more than the schedule.

As we've said before, adding more people may not always result in increased productivity. Tasks requiring brain power and creativity may be negatively impacted by adding resources. Egos may get involved and integration of the tasks may suffer because extra time is needed to ensure quality, coordinate finished work between participants, and manage the overall work flow.

A classic example of this problem is trying to speed up the development of a complex computer program. The writing of large computer programs requires that the work must be broken down among members of a (large) programming team. Finished pieces must be assembled into a complete program where all the parts function together in perfect harmony. To achieve this harmony, the programmers and their managers must work closely together to avoid duplicate efforts and to make sure each section of the program dovetails into other work. This integration process eats up a lot of time in meetings, coordination, and testing.

So, if it takes one person one month to do the programming (a man-month), it might take two people eight weeks to get the same job done because of coordination, creative conflicts, and problems in integrating this kind of work (four man-months to do the same job). In fact, as you add more people to a project, it can finish later and later. This principle of losing productivity by adding additional people was well documented by Frederick P. Brooks in a classic study of IBM in the 1960s titled *The Mythical Man-Month: Essays on Software Engineering*. It's a book worth reading, as its principles and insights are timeless.

Once all the dates are entered on the schedule worksheet, you will have a complete ideal schedule. (See Figure 5-8.) The ideal schedule is just that: the best case schedule if all resources are available and ready as planned. It is the optimum schedule possible using your available resources. The ideal schedule will need to be reviewed and modified to incorporate any resource constraints or adjustments necessary because of scheduling conflicts with other projects or other constraints you may not have considered in the first go around.

Some people ask why they should create an ideal schedule at all if they know it will need to be modified. The ideal schedule is important because it represents the baseline schedule for making all future scheduling adjustments. The ideal schedule is the bottom line you should adhere to when quoting a date for project completion—because you can't do better than this unless you change the project assumptions.

Scheduling Step 5. Adjust Individual Resource Assignments and Incorporate Changes into the Schedule after Review

The next step to accurate scheduling is to use the ideal schedule to make specific resource assignments from your resources list. After individual assignments are finalized and reviewed by the project team, the schedule must be adjusted to accommodate any other necessary changes. In most projects you will probably also need to get the schedule approved by a boss or project committee. This may be done as a separate step or as part of a total project plan approval coordinated with the budget approval process.

The shortcoming of the ideal schedule as we've created it here is that it does not consider resource availability or conflicts with other projects and priorities. In complex projects you may have to rearrange task assignments as you go through the scheduling and task assignment process, because the schedule shows conflicts in their availability. For example, Jennifer may be your preferred person to select office space in San Francisco, but it turns out that she will be on vacation when the schedule calls for the office selection. Because Dave is also acceptable for this task, you can assign him to the task instead of Jennifer, even though she was your first choice.

Resource Loading and Resource Leveling for Optimizing Resource Utilization. After creating a preliminary resource schedule using your first-choice selections, you may often find that some people and resources are over scheduled and others are not scheduled enough. The level of time commitment individual resources have to project is called resource loading. If the resource loading is high it means that a major portion of a resource's time (people or equipment) is being used by the project. This means that the person in question can't be working on other projects with high resource loading at the same time—because he or she will become overcommitted.

Options for Adjusting the Schedule

Problem	Options
Not Enough Time	Change the scope of the project or add resources.
People or Resources Not Available as Needed for a Task	**Stretch** the task by adding more time; **split** the task into two to accommodate scheduling constraints; **reprofile** the task to use more or different resources.
Resources Over Utilized	Assign or hire additional resources with similar ability; stretch, split or reprofile the tasks to level the resource loading.
Resources Under Utilized	Reassign individual schedules to smooth utilization; assign resources to other projects if available; hire as part-time employees or consultants.

Figure 5-9 Options for Adjusting the Schedule

Adjusting resource assignments for better overall scheduling and cost effectiveness is called **resource leveling**. Resource leveling in complex engineering projects with hundreds of people and many kinds of equipment can be difficult and is usually handled with the help of computers and heuristic algorithms. In most business projects, however, resource leveling can be accomplished by critiquing people's schedules and reassigning people for better utilization of their time. (See Figure 5-9.) If you need more information on resource allocation and resource leveling techniques for complex projects, there are references listed at the end of the book that explain resource leveling theories and calculations in more detail than is possible in a book of this scope.

Theory and calculations aside, the goal of the final resource allocation process is always to (1) assign the best suited, available people to each task and (2) to assure that resources are used efficiently, with few (if any) gaps in people's working schedules. Remember to consider holidays and vacations on the individual working schedules. Note also that projects tend to slow down during the Christmas holiday season and during other predictable times of the year for a variety of reasons. You may need to adjust the schedules to accommodate these factors as well.

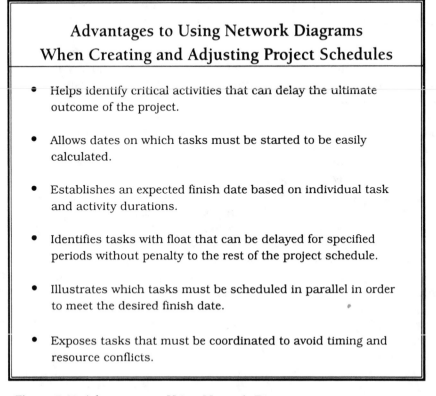

> ## Advantages to Using Network Diagrams
> ## When Creating and Adjusting Project Schedules
>
> - Helps identify critical activities that can delay the ultimate outcome of the project.
>
> - Allows dates on which tasks must be started to be easily calculated.
>
> - Establishes an expected finish date based on individual task and activity durations.
>
> - Identifies tasks with float that can be delayed for specified periods without penalty to the rest of the project schedule.
>
> - Illustrates which tasks must be scheduled in parallel in order to meet the desired finish date.
>
> - Exposes tasks that must be coordinated to avoid timing and resource conflicts.

Figure 5-10 Advantages to Using Network Diagrams

In cases when you only have one person available to do a specific task, this person's availability will dictate the schedule of the tasks to which he or she is assigned. If this presents a problem, then attempt to locate a qualified substitute to fill in for this person. When no one is available on staff, you may choose to hire temporary help or freelancers to keep the schedule on track.

Don't forget that material resource constraints can also affect project scheduling. For example, even if you have a qualified operator available for typesetting your newsletter, if the typesetting computer isn't available because it is committed to another department's project you still have a scheduling problem. You will need to adjust the schedule to accommodate the availability of the typesetting equipment, rent equipment of your own, or negotiate with the other department for time on the machine when you need it. (See Figure 5-10.)

Adjusting the Schedule to Meet Forced Deadlines. Other schedule adjustments might be necessary because of imposed project deadlines. Absolute deadlines are a reality in every business. In the customer newsletter project, for example, it may be necessary to finish the newsletter for a trade show before a specific date. In this case, if the newsletter isn't finished on time, it may have little value after the trade show and will represent money wasted and a failed project.

If your master schedule says you need four weeks to produce a two-color newsletter with photos and you only have two weeks to do it, you must make adjustments to your tasks, durations, and schedule. However, you can't change the minimum amount of time required to get a job done right. You might be able to take a day or two out of the writing and review process, and you might shorten the newsletter from eight pages to six, but you can't cut the printing and binding time—as those are fixed processes that can't be shortened. (You could pay "rush charges" in some cases but this means blowing your budget to save the schedule.)

It is important to go through the ideal master scheduling process first, before you accept a "forced" schedule because you will get a more accurate picture of the actual time required to complete a project of the scope defined. If necessary, the ideal schedule can serve as a negotiating tool to communicate and explain the need for more time to complete a project.

If you have done a credible job of estimating your task durations, and if your network diagram is a true representation of the order the tasks must be completed in, then the earliest finish date determined for your project by the procedures presented in this chapter is probably a good one. If, however, you go through your tasks and check everything and review every task and network precedence and squeeze every possible day out of the estimates, and there still isn't enough time available to complete the project by the mandatory date, then you have only two basic tools available to you:

1. Change the scope of the project, or

2. Add additional resources, in the form of more people or better/faster equipment

This example elucidates one of the single most important concepts in project management and an obvious one—you can't complete something in less time than it takes to get it done. Yet every day managers in every kind of business accept unworkable schedules because they are forced into it by management, customers, government requirements, or budgets. Some managers consistently fail to bring projects in on time and within budget because it was never possible to do it in the first place. No one looks good for failing. There are alternatives to buying into an unworkable schedule and the humiliation that results.

These alternatives include

1. Going over the task estimates and schedules with your boss, using his or her guidance and expertise to seek alternative ways to complete the project.

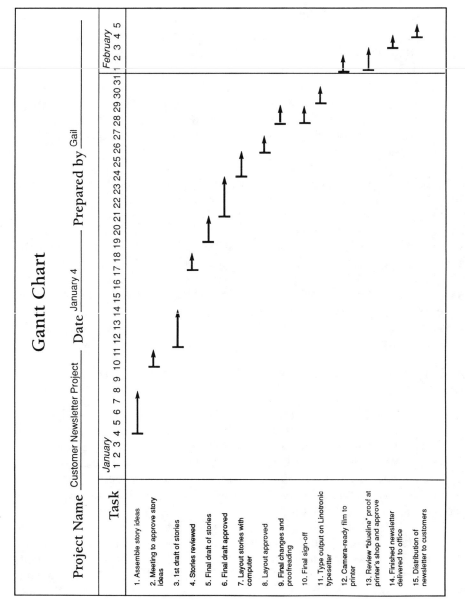

Figure 5-11 A Simple Gantt Chart

2. Holding a team strategy session to develop ways to modify the scope and objectives of the project in ways that will make the dictated schedule more feasible.

3. Gaining approvals for additional people and resources, usually done after the budget is completed, which will be discussed in more detail in the next chapter.

4. Requesting that someone with more experience and authority be responsible for the schedule and the project. This is a last resort, but it often gets the point across that you think the completion date is unworkable, given the current scope and objectives of the project.

In most organizations you will be thanked for bringing the facts to management and refusing to accept a project doomed to failure. In less progressive companies, you may get shown the door. If you've done all your project planning work up to this point, you may make some points by explaining why the requested completion date is unlikely. If they won't listen and the next manager fails to bring the project in on time, you will only be able to say, "I told you so." While it's an empty feeling if you end up losing your job because of politics, if you're that good at project planning, you have better career opportunities ahead of you elsewhere. And, if the company management is truly unreasonable when faced with the facts, the business may not be around long anyway.

Scheduling Step 6. Chart the Final Schedule and Distribute It to the Team

The form used to chart and document the final schedule will greatly influence how useful the schedule is to project participants as a tool for tracking and prioritizing their time. In many projects you will find it beneficial to translate your schedule listing into a weekly or daily **Gantt chart.** The development of the basic Gantt chart is attributed to Henry Gantt, an official in the Army Bureau of Ordnance during World War I, who used the charts to help control the scheduling of munitions production.

Gantt charts, sometimes referred to as project time lines, ordinarily have a list of dates at the top and a list of tasks down the left side. A line on the Gantt chart shows the date when each task begins and ends based on its precedence and duration. The level of scheduling detail you display in your Gantt charts will be determined by the time periods you use on the top: daily, weekly, hourly, monthly, or whatever is appropriate for your project. If a project takes a year or more to complete, you may want to use a monthly or weekly Gantt chart. If your project takes only thirty days or fewer, a daily chart will provide more useful information.

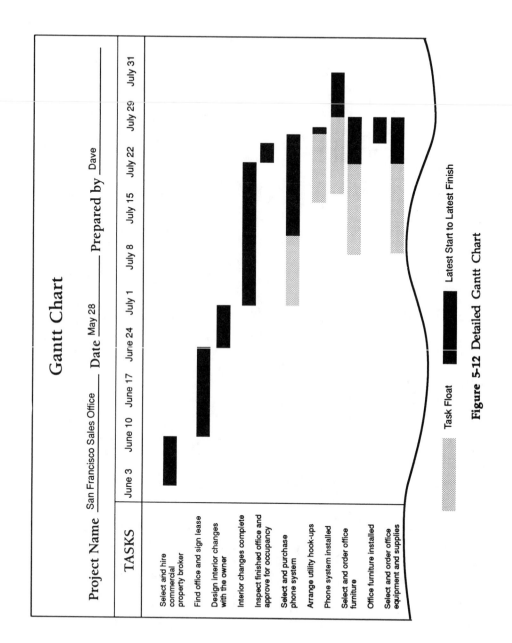

Figure 5-12 Detailed Gantt Chart

Gantt Chart

Project Name San Francisco Sales Office   Date May 28   Prepared by Dave

TASKS

- Select and hire commercial property broker
- Find office and sign lease
- Design interior changes with the owner
- Interior changes complete
- Inspect finished office and approve for occupancy
- Select and purchase phone system
- Arrange utility hook-ups
- Phone system installed
- Select and order office furniture
- Office furniture installed
- Select and order office equipment and supplies

June 3 June 10 June 17 June 24 July 1 July 8 July 15 July 22 July 29 July 31

Task Float   Latest Start to Latest Finish

151

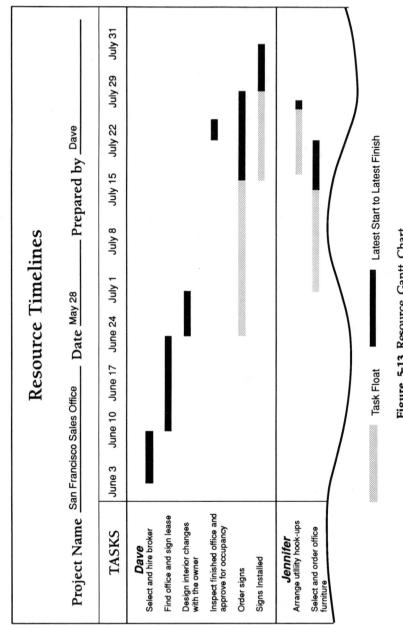

Figure 5-13 Resource Gantt Chart

A simple Gantt chart, like the one shown for the customer newsletter project (Figure 5-11), shows only start dates and completion dates. A more complex Gantt chart, as for the sales office, shows float times as well as the absolute latest finish dates by using different kinds of lines: dotted, solid, or shaded. There are even more detailed, complex Gantt charting possibilities using additional symbols for milestones, current project status, and changes which are used to monitor and control the project after it is initiated. (See Figures 5-12 and 5-13.)

Project Management Tip

✎ Schedule Charting Pros and Cons

Listings—Schedules that follow the existing formats in the sample forms are useful for most projects and necessary for keeping track of progress compared to the schedule as the project proceeds. For manageability and control, it is useful to break these schedule listings into subprojects if the project is extremely large and combine them with a milestone schedule.

Calendar Charting—Notated calendars can be extremely useful for keeping track of schedules for many small projects. Multiple projects or different team member tasks can be entered in various colors on the calendar. Calendars are a good communication tool when displayed in a central location where many team members can see the dates. Large display calendars with reusable, washable surfaces are available in many business supply stores for this purpose.

Gantt Charts—Gantt charts are best used as a visual overview of project time lines. However, they don't show task relationships and should not substitute for a network diagram or master schedule listing. Gantt charts can be very useful in initial schedule planning, for simple projects, or for individual timelines on a complex project involving many people. These are also good for comparing project progress to the original schedule.

Milestone Schedule—In the last chapter it was demonstrated that milestones can be assigned to summarize major paths on a network. Milestones can also be used to chart an overall project schedule. A milestone schedule doesn't have enough information for managing a project, but can be useful in communicating an overall schedule on a large project to upper management or other people who need an overview of the project without task details.

In addition to creating a Gantt chart, some people like to notate the schedule dates directly on the network diagram. Although this is a good reference tool for reviewing the entire project, it is awkward to use as a working schedule when assigning responsibilities to individual team members. Therefore, you should also use a schedule listing like the Master Schedule Worksheet in addition to the network diagram to display and communicate the schedule details.

Of course, many variations of schedule formats may be used to accommodate individual preferences. It is important that the key information, including task descriptions, start dates, expected finish dates, and assigned people, is easy to read and interpret. Each individual who will be working on the project needs to be able to create a personal timetable from the master schedule.

In complex projects, most project managers use more than one schedule format because it allows them to view the project in different ways, depending on the focus of the analysis that is required. Gantt charts are good for an overview, the network diagram is useful for the details, and individual schedules are needed for unambiguous communication to team members about their respective responsibilities.

Gantt charts showing the time lines separately for each person on a project team are also very useful for visually representing overall resource usage in a project. These charts allow you to visualize resource loading without using complex algorithms. The individual resource Gantt charts immediately show if any people are being used too much or too little on a project, or if significant gaps in a resource's scheduling exist. An example of an individual resource Gantt chart for the sales office project is provided as an example of this schedule charting option. (See Figure 5-13.)

SCHEDULING MULTIPLE PROJECTS

Scheduling decisions for one project often affect the schedules of another project. Resources used on one project are often needed for other projects. If the commitments for time and resources required for other projects are not considered, the schedule and resource allocations for a project can be unrealistic. It is rare that people are responsible for managing only one project at a time. Because it is common to manage multiple projects simultaneously, special steps need to be taken during scheduling to assure that conflicts between projects are minimized.

To solve the problems associated with coordinating multiple projects, the following steps are required:

1. Determine the relative priorities for the projects. Scheduling and resource allocation decisions should be based on these priorities.

2. Create the ideal schedule for each project as documented in this book.

3. Create Gantt charts or bar charts (histograms) to display the time lines and resource utilization of multiple projects on the same chart. (See Figure 5-15.) Color the time line for each project differently.

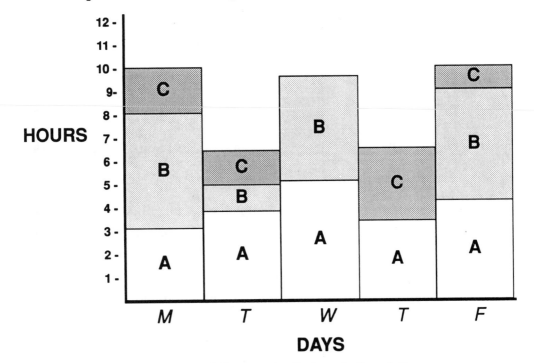

Figure 5-14 Resource Load Diagram for Projects A, B, and C

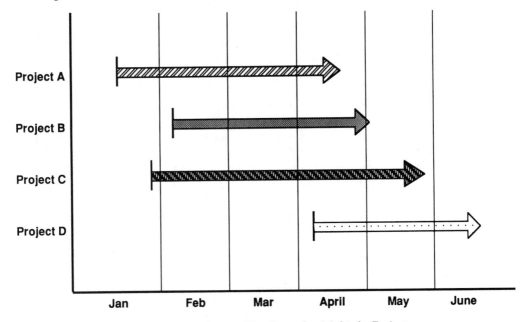

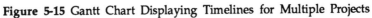

Figure 5-15 Gantt Chart Displaying Timelines for Multiple Projects

Final Schedule Checklist	
Assumptions	No assumptions are violated.
Critical Path	Clearly marked on the network diagram.
Consensus	All major participants have reviewed dates for completeness and accuracy.
Dates	All holidays and special events have been noted appropriately; No resource conflicts exist.
Chart	Clearly specifies tasks, durations, individual responsibilities, and target start and finish dates.

Figure 5-16 Final Schedule Checklist

4. Adjust the schedules for the projects based on the overlapping time lines and reassign people who are over committed or underutilized. In the example charts, you will see that a bar chart can display the relative commitment of each resource. Some project managers include commitments for day-to-day activities in these bar charts as well, so overall work load is indicated for each resource. The resource and schedule overlap may dictate changes in the team assignments for projects in order to optimize timing and work flow.

If you are responsible for more than one complex project, the manual process and calculation complexity of identifying schedule conflicts and resource allocations can be time consuming, awkward, and fraught with error. As a solution, it is advisable to choose a computerized project management program that can assist you in integrating and adjusting the resource allocations and schedules across multiple projects. (See Figure 5-16.)

THE SCHEDULE APPROVAL PROCESS

With the final approval and distribution of the scheduling charts, your schedule is complete. The approval process will depend largely on your organization and the scope of the project. For small projects no approvals may be necessary and large projects may have many layers of bureaucracy. We offer additional detail on recommended preparations for the approval process in the next chapter on budgeting, since the approval for the complete project plan, including the schedule and the budget, is frequently completed as an integrated process after the budget is calculated. However, it is a good idea to get the schedule reviewed by the project team before the final project approval process begins.

No matter how the approval process is handled in your organization, be prepared to discuss your scheduling assumptions and the process you used in creating the schedule. If people feel confident you have done your homework in producing a schedule, the approval process will go more smoothly. If you are working on a large project, you should have the key members of the project team review the schedule, whether they are part of the approval process or not, to identify any conflicts, problems, or errors that may have been accidentally incorporated. If you have time before the schedule must be approved and distributed, put it away for several days and then study it again. After a few days away from the charts, you may notice errors that eluded you previously.

A complete, realistic schedule for a complex project should go through at least a couple of rounds of reviews before it is finalized—so don't get frustrated if you have to make changes and revisions before it's approved. Not even the most experienced project manager produces the perfect schedule the first time around!

Chapter Six

BUDGETING:
Reliable Procedures
for Establishing
Costs and Expenditures

If there isn't enough money to complete a project, it doesn't matter how well the rest of the project is planned or managed. If you can't pay people or buy materials, work on the project stops. Because of this, the budgeting process seems to instill more fear and anxiety in managers than any other aspect of project management.

The budget and the other components of the project plan are deeply intertwined. The budget is always affected when there are changes in a project's tasks, resources, or schedule. If you forget to list a key piece of equipment required, your budget will be grossly inaccurate. If a project takes longer than anticipated, it will cost more than you thought. If more people are required to complete a task than originally planned, the project again will use more money than was allocated in the budget.

Cost estimating is mystifying to many project managers. The process seems fraught with error—and even when project managers "pad" the estimates with a little extra just to make sure there is enough approved budget to get things done, the money always seems to run out before the project is finished. Whether appropriate or not, project managers are almost always evaluated on their bottom line performance. Even when the final end results are positive, if the project costs more than originally estimated, the project manager is sure to hear about it.

The reason the budget gets top billing in most projects is because of simple economic realities. The allocation of money between projects and general operations in a business is one of the fundamental decisions affecting the company's profitability and future. The allocation of funds to every project and organization has strategic implications for the entire enterprise. Thus, the success of a project is usually associated with the ability of the project manager to bring the project in within the original budget estimates, regardless of what happens to change the project during its implementation phase.

The budget is not just a planning tool, either. It is one of the central components driving project implementation and control—and as such, it is critical that the budget reflects the reality of monetary resources available to and required for the project. The budget will be used as a baseline for comparing actual versus planned expenditures as the project progresses. It, together with the schedule and work objectives, guide the project through to completion.

Projects depend on accurate budgeting, cost control, and accounting of costs throughout the life of the project. This chapter presents reliable, unambiguous methods to estimate costs, gain budget approvals, and make the necessary project modifications to deal with limited funds. The knowledge presented here, it is hoped, will help relieve some of the anxiety and uncertainty endemic to the budgeting process.

THE STEP-BY-STEP BUDGETING PROCESS IN REVIEW

As part of the project plan, the budget is a forecast of the future. Forecasts don't need to be correct to be useful—they just need to predict future events closely enough to guide actions and decisions as the project progresses. Plans should have flexibility built in to be adjusted to changes in the business environment as the project is implemented. But, this flexibility is least evident in the budget. It is the cost estimates more than any aspect of a project plan that get set in concrete in the minds of managers and customers.

Schedules change and specifications may be adjusted, but the budget remains the budget. Even when more money is allocated to a project, the progress of the project is tracked to the original estimates—and your project becomes burdened with the label of "over budget." Though this isn't an ideal situation, it is a reality and project managers must learn to live within the constraints of the budget they establish—and it is why a structured budgeting process is required for even the simplest of projects.

Every aspect of the project plan that has been created to this point has a cost associated with it—the tasks, people, equipment, and the schedule. The equation for budgeting a project is a conceptually simple matter of combining these costs to come up with a total estimate for the project's price tag.

Based on this simple budgeting algorithm, it is readily apparent why the rest of the project plan must be completed before a final budget can be produced. Though the budget may cause the other parts of the project plan to be modified if the final cost estimates come in too high, budgeting should be viewed as the critical final step in completing the project plan, and often the most difficult portion to get approved.

The Conceptual Budgeting Process

People + Resources + Time = Budget

The budgeting process can actually start very early in the project conceptualization phase. During the project selection and goal setting of the conceptualization phase, very rough budget guidelines and financial expectations for the project are often established.

As project planning begins, it may be appropriate to make conscious adaptations to the initial plans based on these rough guidelines. Certain components of the project plan, including task sequences, project team selections, and resource specifications, may be adjusted based on monetary considerations to meet basic project goals. For example, because one of the project goals for the newsletter is to keep the cost of the newsletter down to conserve advertising funds, you may recall that the initial choice of a designer for the newsletter project was made partially for financial reasons. In this case, however, the overall quality of the project will remain the same, because the person chosen was still well qualified to meet the overall goals of the project.

Only in cases where monetary decisions will not affect the stated goals of the project is it appropriate during initial planning to consider the budgetary constraints. Otherwise, it is inappropriate to specify a budget during the initial work planning and resource selection process because this may force the project to be adapted to the budget before the real demands have been identified.

WHY BUDGETS GO AWRY

Before we go into the right way to complete a budget, let's consider the problems that can occur during the budgeting process. Though the things that can go wrong with budgets are countless, there are standard problems that can be avoided.

The learning curve is not considered when scheduling resources

This results in an inadequate budget for labor as well as an inaccurate schedule. Simply add project tasks for training employees to account for this requirement and budget them accordingly.

Managers play games with the budget

Because managers in the past have "padded" their budgets, an arbitrary amount is subtracted from the amount allocated to your project to compensate for this practice, even though your budget was not padded. The solution to this is to train managers that it is best to provide accurate budgets and through honest interactions, to convince your team members that your estimates are not inflated.

Other games that need to be identified and minimized include political uses of the budget—such as managers who knowingly underestimate the budget to look good or a group that manipulates costs in their favor to win a contract. If costs are purposely being over- or under-estimated for any reason, it is usually not difficult to gather data that will expose the problem. If people know this is happening, the bias in the estimates will usually be reduced.

Waste and spoilage are not considered when ordering materials

No project uses exactly the amount of materials estimated. For example, in the newsletter project, some paper will be wasted, and in the build-out of the office space in San Francisco, some lumber and drywall materials will surely be required that are not directly measurable on first estimate. Be sure enough budget for these "extra" materials is included; otherwise you might end up with a hole where a wall is supposed to be.

Easily-measured costs get exact budgets, and difficult-to-measure costs get little attention

This is exactly the opposite of what should happen, but because it takes more time, people just guess about the amounts they don't know. The difficult-to-measure costs should get additional research so the amounts allocated to them will be more precise.

There are also problems in budgets that are not predictable, due to changes in the environment of business. Some of these errors in budgeting must simply be tolerated, because there is no way to predict them with certainty. These include:

Outside supplier or material costs increase during the course of the project

The effect of this increase can often be minimized if detailed contracts with committed prices are negotiated in advance. If it is obvious that material prices are rising, allow for this by increasing the budget by a fixed percentage over the length of the contract to allow for predicted price increases. This is a potentially serious problem in projects that run longer than six months.

A key person leaves the project and must be replaced
with expensive consultants or a higher-priced employee

The trick is to identify the key employees in advance and make sure they are happily retained by the company. Another alternative is to have cross-trained employees available to fill gaps when this is possible. When this is not possible, or employees leave for unpredictable reasons, you must just bite the bullet and find another person for the job—or consider canceling the project altogether.

The economic or corporate climate changes along with the priority for
the project

This can work both for you and against you. In some cases the changes may be so monumental that the project may be canceled for lack of demand. Consider the impact a major corporate layoff would have on the sales office project. In other cases, more money may be required to expedite the project. For example, if a competitor unexpectedly enters the market with a new product, you may need to get your product out faster to maintain market share. In either case, the budget for the project must be changed along with the rest of the project plan.

Of course there are other unpredictable economic occurrences that can wreak havoc with a budget including radical changes in foreign exchange rates, stock market crashes, and severe changes in inflation rates. For these, you can only cross your fingers and hope that the world remains relatively stable for a while.

Now that you know what can go wrong with your budget, let's consider the structured approach used by successful project managers that allows them to put together a budget with a relatively high level of confidence, in spite of these potential problems.

FOLLOW THE PREFERRED PROJECT PLANNING SEQUENCE TO ESTABLISH YOUR BUDGET

For expedience, many unwary project managers constrain their project plans with the budget at the very beginning. Some think it is faster to do this, since the project will eventually be limited by the budget anyway. Other times project managers are forced to accept a budget dictated by their superiors before the work plans are understood. Thus, the project planning process is inappropriately implemented as follows:

- Establish budget.
- Establish goals.

- Disregard the goals and force tasks, team, and resources to fit the budget.

Though this process is prevalent in modern business, the results are usually ineffective. If the budget is established first and the project is forced into it, people evaluating the project will assume that the original goals and prescribed end results are still operative—even if you try to state otherwise. The trade-offs made during the planning of schedules, resources, and final quality of the output will not be clearly communicated. The goals cannot be renegotiated to account for budget constraints because the process is not cyclic and no review of the budgetary constraints on the goals ever occurs. Businesses have failed to reach their goals for years because of this kind of planning and never realize how relatively easy it is to solve the problem.

The preferred planning sequence, which may take a bit longer, but will have more satisfying results in the long run, is the one espoused in this book:

- Establish project goals.
- Define tasks, team, and resource requirements to meet the goals.
- Establish the costs of meeting the goals based on the documented requirements.
- If the costs exceed budget expectations you have two choices:
  —Increase the budget because the project is worth it.
  —Modify the project goals and adapt the project plan accordingly.
- If, after further evaluation, the project is still unworkable or infeasible because of the budget, scrap it before more time and effort are expended. It's better to stop now than to try to do something that will fail in the end anyway because of lack of resources.

This is goal-driven project planning, as opposed to the budget-driven project planning described earlier. Ultimately, the budget constrains the project plans in both cases, but in the first case the compromises being made because of the budget are rarely negotiated or understood. The compromises being made in a goal-driven project plan are easily documented and communicated as the project plan goes through multiple iterations. It is also possible to negotiate an increase over the original budget goals because the plan clearly documents the necessity for more resources.

You're right—this is more work at first. But after the process is well understood and becomes part of the company's culture, the benefits in increased profitability, quality, and performance will be worth the effort of goal-driven planning.

Given that the majority of the budget will be developed after the other components of the project plan are complete, including the WBS and network, the resource requirements, and the schedule—the ideal budgeting process requires

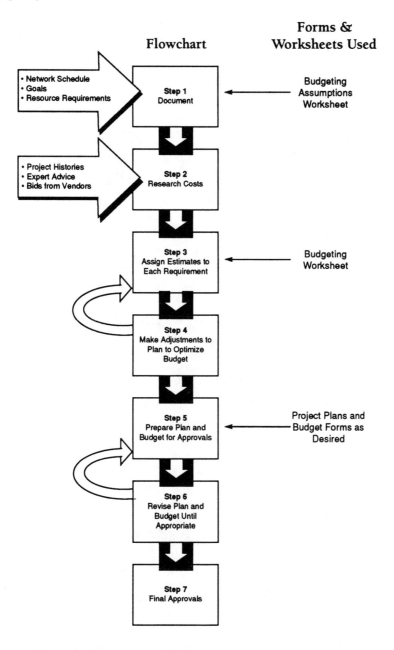

Refer to this diagram of the budgeting process as you
proceed through the chapter.

Figure 6-1 The Budgeting Process

the following steps, which will be described in detail in the chapter (see Figure 6-1):

Step 1. Establish the initial budgeting assumptions.

Step 2. Research the specific costs associated with each aspect of the project plan.

Step 3. Assign costs to each task and resource.

Step 4. If necessary, make adjustments to the WBS, team assignments, resource lists, and schedules to optimize budget utilization.

Step 5. Prepare the budget and project plan for approval.

Step 6. Revise the project goals and plan, if required, to accommodate budget constraints established during the approval process.

Step 7. Resubmit the project plan (including the budget) for final approvals.

Budgeting Step 1. Establish the Initial Budgeting Assumptions

Costs are tied to the project assumptions—and these assumptions must be documented as part of the budgeting process. Project assumptions that will influence the project budget are the following:

- Quality of the final output or end results of the project
- Quality of the materials used to meet project goals
- Quantity of materials required to meet project goals
- Time frames specified to meet project goals

These are all specified in other aspects of the project plan, but where these affect specific budget amounts, they should be noted again on the budgeting worksheets.

Just as scheduling assumptions are tied to the availability of resources, there are also assumptions specific to the budget process. These assumptions are tied directly to the ongoing availability of funding for the project. Budgeting assumptions include the sources of funds for the project, the approval levels for the budgets, and corporate performance criteria, such as sales or growth, that will affect the availability of funds. In the final form, budgeting assumptions list specific constraints on the budget that will affect the funds available to the project—including timing of revenue receipts, projected sales, and projections for inflation.

As a project proceeds, a change in business conditions that affects the validity of the budgeting assumptions may seriously impact the source of funds available to support the project. When this is the case, it is necessary to reevaluate and perhaps renegotiate the project priorities, the budget, and the source of funds for the project. For example, in the sales office project, a continuous, growing demand for the company's products is an underlying

Budgeting Assumptions Worksheet

Project _San Francisco Sales Office_   Date _May 27_

Completed By _Roger_

---

1. What has priority—schedule or cost control?
   - ☒ Schedule
   - ☐ Cost Control

2. Is there a fixed overhead rate for this project?
   - ☒ Yes
   - Amount _27%_
   - ☐ No

3. Is there another similar project that can be used for budgeting comparisons?
   - ☐ Yes
   - Name _Philadelphia_
   - ☐ No

4. Has a general budget amount been allocated to the project?

   When ? _To Be Completed with Plan_   By Whom? _____

   How Much? _____ When is the money available? _____

   Is it adequate to meet current project goals?
   - ☐ Yes
   - ☐ No

5. What financial and economic assumptions are being made that affect the budget?

   Sales continue to increase in the region.

   Inflation at 4%.

   No earthquakes.

Figure 6-2 Budgeting Assumptions Worksheet

assumption in the budgeting for the project. If company sales plummet before the office is open, the project goals may need to be reevaluated, because the underlying source of financial support for the office is no longer available.

The initial assumptions about the budget are relatively easy to identify, such as sources of funds for the project. Other assumptions cannot be documented until the budget is approved. During the budget approval process, additional or modified assumptions should be noted as specific compromises or decisions are made, as this will document the changes you must make to the project outcomes in order to work within an approved budget or identify potential problems if funds become short during the course of the project. A worksheet like the one shown for the sales office project can be used to document budgeting assumptions that are known at the beginning of the budgeting process and those that develop as the budgeting process proceeds. (See Figure 6-2.)

Budgeting Step 2. Research the Specific Costs Associated with Each Aspect of the Project Plan

As each of the planning components for your project is completed, the budget and monetary goals should be in the back of your mind, guiding choices about the people to use, the vendors to work with, the supplies required, and the facilities to select. You should not assign specific costs to these choices, however, because you don't want to influence your selections or constrain your thinking based on the budget. Still, you should make informed decisions when you know a less expensive alternative will still meet project goals.

When the initial plans are complete, including tasks, team, resource requirements, and schedule, the decisions you have made can be translated into actual estimates of the overall cost for the project. When approved, this becomes the baseline budget for the project.

The first step in this translation process is to research the costs for each aspect of your project, including people, supplies, and time. Similar to the techniques covered in the last chapter for researching schedule estimates, information on costs can come from the following sources:

- Expense histories from other projects
- Team estimating sessions
- Expert advice and assistance
- Quotes from outside vendors on specific aspects of the project
- Standard pricing guidelines or allocation methods established for specific resources

If cost estimates are based on projects the organization has a lot of experience with, then the research for establishing cost estimates is relatively routine. For example, the newsletter project is a relatively routine project for the marketing communications department of TechMore, so the costs will probably be based on similar projects that have been completed by the department in the past. A few phone calls may be made to printers or designers to verify the estimates, but most of the other costs are well established because of the department's experience with similar projects.

If a project involves work that is not standard or in which the company or department has little experience, more research should go into the estimating before final budgets are assigned. In the sales office project, even though a similar project was completed recently in Philadelphia, more time should be spent researching office prices and establishing the operational costs in San Francisco because the company has little direct experience in this city and labor is especially expensive there. Though it was appropriate to base the schedule on the Philadelphia experience, it is inappropriate to base the budget on the Philadelphia office because of the different costs of doing business in the two locations.

Budgeting Step 3. Assign Estimates to Each Project Requirement.

After initial cost research is done, specific estimates need to be assigned to the project elements. The estimate for specific costs in a project can and should be directly related to the WBS (or network) and the schedule. Each milestone in the WBS should have a specific cost estimate associated with it. If the planning process has been followed up to this point in the book, the specific people, material resources, and time for each task have already been identified. Using this information, specific costs can be filled in for each task and resource required, using a worksheet like the one shown. (See Figure 6-3.)

This step sounds simple, but there are many choices to make and many estimates to consider. The challenge in budgeting is to assign the correct cost estimates to each of the elements of people, time, and resources, but this is fraught with risk and uncertainty because of the nature of the task. Because you can't see into the future, you must estimate costs associated with work and schedules that are themselves based on estimates and guesses.

To eliminate some of the uncertainty in budgeting, there are a number of established and appropriate ways in which project budgets can be completed. These include top-down budgets, bottom-up budgets, and zero-based budgets (discussed earlier in Chapter Two). The method you choose for final cost assignments will depend on your organization, the complexity of the project, and the amount of money involved in the project. The budgeting methods also get team members involved in different ways, so the choice of budgeting approach has political ramifications as well as financial ones.

Top-Down Budgeting. In this approach the managers at high levels establish the budget amounts based on their own research and collective experience, priorities for this project, and corporate strategies. Then, the project budget is allocated to the other managers in the project who will divide the costs between

Budgeting Worksheet

Project __Sales Office Project__   Date __March 12__

Completed By __Roger__

TASK	DURATION	STAFF OR VENDOR REQUIRED	SPECIAL EQUIPMENT & SUPPLIES	ESTIMATES
Broker and Lease	15	Use Dave or John		$87,000
Build-Out	22	Building contractor	Provided by contractor per specifications	$12,000
Phones	13	Dave, John, and Jennifer	Wall jacks, 8 4-line units, Reception unit	$6,000 plus $1000. installation
Furniture	10	Jennifer	See List	$8,000
Recruitment	45	Walter Agency		$31,000
Public Relations	15	Jennifer, PR Agency	Mailers, Folders, Postage	$17,000
Office Supplies	10	Jennifer	See List	$14,000
Equipment	10	Dave, Jennifer	See List	$63,000

Figure 6-3 Budgeting Worksheet

the various project components. If the cost research has been done effectively by the people dictating the budget amounts, this approach has validity and is often the most expedient way to get a budget completed. However, if an arbitrary or insufficient amount is assigned from above, the project runs the risks, already discussed, of forcing the project into the budget before the compromises are fully understood.

In top-down budgeting situations, people are often afraid to tell their managers that something will cost more than their managers expect. Thus, they tell their managers what they want to hear. The thinking is that the company will not let an important project die, so when budget runs out, which it will certainly do in this situation, the company will make up the difference. And who do you think loses his job in this case when the project expenditures exceed the budget?

Bottom-Up Budgeting. In bottom-up budgeting, the team members directly involved with the work are asked to assign costs to each of their own tasks. This requires a process similar to the group scheduling process discussed in the last chapter, or the budgets can be completed independently for each area and then integrated.

This approach is the most reliable in incorporating detail and direct experience into the budget. It also has advantages of encouraging a wide range of participation in the project, resulting in higher levels of project commitment by the team members. However, in bottom-up budgeting, it is typical for people to overstate their individual budget needs because they suspect higher management will cut the budgets arbitrarily, which they often do, as shown in independent research.

The Combined Top-Down/Bottom-Up Approach. A hybrid approach to budgeting, that of combining top-down and bottom-up estimates, works well in many projects, especially large, high-risk ones. In this approach an overall budget is researched independently by upper management, but not disclosed to lower-level management. Then, the bottom-up budgeting takes place as described, except the players know that a "target" has already been established by management. The two budgets are then compared and reviewed. Discrepancies in the two budgets are discussed in team meetings, and differences are negotiated. Final estimates are established for the project based on the results of the discussions.

The advantage of this approach is that the two budgets can be compared—and if they are both very similar, there is a good chance that the budget is *on target*. If the two budgets are very different, it is apparent that the goals and objectives of the project are not clear to everyone or someone is providing contrived figures.

Top-down budgeting is good at including corporate limitations, strategies, and overall resource availability in the estimates, which are not always considered in the bottom-up approach. And, because bottom-up budgeting is good at including detailed operational considerations and direct information on specific resource requirements, a budget that melds the two approaches is more likely to be realistic and appropriate than is a budget that uses only one source of estimates.

The trick to making this kind of approach work is a trusting environment with open communication. If the higher-level management is intimidating in the negotiating process, nothing will be gained. If the team members are skeptical, the process will degrade into a political struggle for resources and position.

High- and Low-Point Budgeting. The high- and low-point budgeting method allows the estimator to assign a lowest and highest estimate to each budget item. These kinds of estimates are useful if new manufacturing or production processes are involved in developing an end product. The high-level estimates assume maximum productivity and the low-point assumes lowest imaginable productivity. Thus, the organization allocates a range of resources to the project based on the actual productivity realized.

The Bidding Process. In budgeting large projects, you may need to send specific components of the project out for final bid. This affects both the team selection process and the budgeting process. If you send a specific aspect of the project out to bid, clearly specify the time requirements, quality, and desired end results of the work to be completed or the equipment/materials to be purchased in a "request for bid" proposal. At least three vendors should be considered if you send out for bids.

A ZBB to Determine Budget Priorities and Cut-offs

In many business projects there are optional choices that affect the budget in different ways. Each of the choices has different costs associated with it. In these projects it is often useful to establish the priorities for various decisions, add up the total costs for all the components, and then mark a budget cut-off where the features are at an acceptable level to meet the project goals.

This process is similar to the ZBB process described in Chapter Two for selecting projects—the difference is that individual features of cost are prioritized and ranked, instead of ranking whole projects. The basic steps in completing a ZBB for budget items are

- Prioritize the features or activities in relationship to the goals of the project.
- Establish the costs of the relevant features or activities under question.
- Establish the budget cut-off point, making sure that enough features are included to meet the project goals and verify that any optional features are still financially viable.

Project Management Buzzwords

☛ ACCOUNTING TERMS FOR PROJECT COSTS—Accounting and finance departments use many different terms to describe the costs associated with your projects. The ones you encounter will depend on the type of projects you manage and the accounting procedures used in your company. Here are some of the common cost terms that you may run into when planning your projects:

Labor Costs—The salaries and benefits paid to people who work on your project.

Materials and Supplies Costs—The costs of purchasing additional supplies and minor equipment for your project. These are usually separate from capital expenditures, which are large or expensive equipment purchases required for a project.

Vendor Costs—The costs of using consultants, outside companies, or service providers to complete work on a project.

Fixed Costs—These costs are unaffected by the volume of work being performed. Fixed costs are incurred on a predictable basis with the passage of time. Examples include rent or lease payments, most salaries of permanent employees, insurance premiums, and other expenditures that do not vary radically.

Allocated Costs—Charges that are assigned to a project by the company, usually as a percentage of operational overhead.

Overhead Costs—The cost of doing business which is not directly attributable to your project. Most allocated costs are also overhead costs. Overhead includes charges for facilities, support staff, general supplies, insurance, and benefits.

Direct Costs—Costs that are a direct result of work, services, or materials used on a project.

Indirect Costs—Indirect costs is another term used to describe overhead.

Variable Costs—Costs that change with time or volume. For example, hourly workers and materials can be variable costs. Salaries are not variable.

Semivariable Costs—They are costs that vary with the work performed but not in a directly proportional way. Examples include short-term labor costs which are semivariable because day-to-day changes in production rarely affect the overall cost of labor, but long-term hiring and layoffs will.

Capital Expenditures—The purchase of large, permanent machines, facilities, or equipment. For tax purposes, these purchases are noted separately, because their value must be depreciated instead of applied as a direct cost.

The ZBB can also be modified slightly to choose among rated features and costs as well. As an example of an application of the modified approach to ZBB analysis, consider the problem of choosing a paper to print the newsletter on. The quality of paper used in the newsletter covers a wide range of costs and attributes. Some of the choices are obviously inappropriate—but for others it is unclear whether the impact of this paper or that one will make any difference in the overall results. However, there are arguments for and against each choice of paper. Some paper is more durable. Some paper takes ink better and the colors will be brighter. After a list of the papers and the trade-offs is made, the team can decide on the appropriate set of features and associated costs that will result in an acceptable choice of paper for the newsletter.

This modified ZBB process of ranking features and budgets can be applied to a whole range of budget decisions. When the ZBB is complete, the compromises are clearly documented, making it easy to see how the budget decision affects the project goals.

CHOOSING THE BEST BUDGETING APPROACH FOR YOUR PROJECT

All of the following factors must be considered when deciding on the budgeting approach for your project:

The accounting procedures and processes already used by your organization. Obviously the methods of budgeting and accounting already established in a company or organization will affect how and when a project will be budgeted. Some projects may be budgeted in advance, during fiscal budgeting, for example, before the actual projects are planned for implementation. Other companies establish budgets for projects on a case-by-case basis as they are approved for implementation. Budgets and cost reports produced for other projects in your organization should be used as guidelines for creating your own project budgets.

Before you establish the perfect budgeting format for your project, realize that it is usually more appropriate and more expedient to use the formats that have already been approved for other projects in your company. If these budget formats are unacceptable for some reason, this should be discussed with your managers and the accounting department in advance—because it is likely that the cost accounting in your company relates directly to the established budgeting formats. Since you will depend on this cost accounting to verify project expenditures and payments as the project proceeds, it is important that you match your budget to the tracking system already established in the company, even if you choose different forms.

Cost allocation methods may also be established for parts of the project budget. For example, if a fixed percentage is used to assign overhead to labor costs to cover general supplies, benefits, and facilities to the department plans in a company, then the same algorithm can often be used to calculate these costs in the project budget.

If you're not sure about preferred budgeting formats or established cost allocation methods, take a trip down to the accounting or finance department and talk to the people there to determine their preferences and procedures.

The size of the project. The larger the project, in terms of costs, the more budgeting control is required. Also, the priority and visibility of the project affects the level of detail and approach used in budgeting a project. If a project has high corporate priority, more people will be involved in developing and approving the budget.

The organization of the project. If the project is relatively simple and confined to one functional organization, the budgeting process will probably require fewer approvals and interactions than a project organized within a matrix or pure project structure.

The reporting and approval levels in the project. The kind of budget reports you produce should relate to the responsibility of the managers involved in approving your project, reviewing its progress, and completing the work. The approval levels can be documented and tracked in a linear responsibility chart, presented in Chapter Four.

The types of costs associated with your project. Projects have different kinds of costs and these need specific budgeting and tracking. The more kinds of charges and activities, the more detailed the budgets need to be.

The risk and priority associated with the project. If a project is high priority and high risk, more time and detail will go into the budgeting process. If the project is relatively routine or based on recurring activities, then less time will be spent in researching and finalizing budget estimates.

The overall project goals. As with all other aspects of the project plan, the goals of the project are central in shaping, defining, and approving the budget.

Budgets have levels of detail associated with them, just like project networks. Some project activities can be effectively budgeted at the milestone level. Other aspects of the project need specific task-level cost analysis. And various parts of the plan may be budgeted at different levels, depending on the cost sensitivity and monetary risk associated with that aspect of the project.

For example, in the newsletter project, the in-house labor costs for writing and coordinating the project are considered fixed overhead, so these are not budgeted explicitly. The design, printing, and materials costs are all estimated in detail because they are costs that can be attributed directly to the project.

Project Management Tip

Budgeting Tips—Here are five time-proven guidelines to help you perfect your budgeting efforts and avoid rounds of changes:

- Always include labor costs, even if the resources come from within the company. In this way the true cost of the project to the enterprise is reflected in the budget. Even if labor cost is allocated as "fixed overhead" in your company, it is still important to specify this cost in the budget.
- Never "pad" the budget or add a "fudge factor." Make your estimates as reliable and accurate as possible. It is just as bad to overestimate a project as it is to underestimate one. If everyone pads the budget, then the company will have less money to allocate to other projects. This could materially affect the ability of the company to take advantage of new opportunities. Of course, if everyone underestimates his or her projects, the company will surely be in trouble.
- If the budget amount involves choices, establish a range for the budget. Make sure the criteria affecting the range can be specified.
- Never underestimate the budget just to get the job. Some managers mistakenly think they can make up for the budget shortage by working harder, skimping on quality, or changing materials. If this is agreed to in the goals and project specifications, fine. If you don't change the specifications, disaster will be the final result. Work of a certain quality costs a certain amount to produce. Do your best to look for alternate plans and sources, but never compromise the budget without letting people know about your change in assumptions.
- If the cost estimate for the project is too high on the first go-around, try adjusting the labor requirements or making changes in the schedule that won't affect the end results of the project. Sometimes a simple change in vendors or a modification in task sequencing can have incredible impact on the price of a project.

In the sales office project, the budget includes diverse elements, for example, capital equipment, fixed overhead of in-house personnel used to complete the project, fixed costs, variable costs, vendor costs, and a variety of other items. A form like the one shown might be useful for documenting the budget for this project. (See Figure 6-4.) Complex budgets are typical of larger projects.

Sample Budget Form

Project _____   Date _____ Completed By _____

TASK NUMBER	RESPONSIBLE PERSON OR VENDOR	DATES		ESTIMATED COSTS				ACTUAL
		START	END	EQUIPMENT	MATERIALS	LABOR	TOTAL	

Figure 6-4 Another Sample Form for Budgeting

Budgeting Step 4. If Necessary, Make Adjustments to the Plan to Optimize the Budget

As the cost estimates are made, it may become apparent that work can be reordered or reassigned in ways that will still meet the overall project goals and save money in the process.

For example, as the budget for the San Francisco sales office project was being developed, using a combination of top-down and bottom-up budgets, the project manager realized that the steps for the grand opening were left out of the project plan and needed to be added to the schedule and the team assignments.

The budgeting process may also expose problems with scheduling or resource utilization that should be adjusted to optimize the budget. For example, a change in the order of task sequences may have little effect on the end results of a project, but may be significantly cheaper because the resources are used more efficiently.

After all the planning for the project, the final project budget may still be too high, even after adjustments and compromises. Sometimes the project will lack the profitability stated as part of the objectives—or will impact other enterprise objectives, causing its priority to be reevaluated. This reevaluation process can be frustrating to a project manager who has just spent a month or more planning a complex project.

Based on the project selection criteria discussed earlier in the book, you may recall that a project that is not profitable may still be appropriate for implementation for a number of reasons, including

- To gain knowledge in a new area of the business or gain expertise in a new technology important to the company's future growth
- To gain follow-on business that will be profitable
- To develop an improved competitive position in terms of product line, knowledge, technology, and/or industry relationships

Decisions to fund expensive or nonprofitable projects should be made by executive management in the company, based on a review of the complete project plan, the company's strategic goals, and long-term commitments. It is the project manager's or planner's responsibility to accurately and honestly report the estimated costs associated with a project, even if the estimates make the project less desirable or less viable.

Charting the Budget to Understand Cost Relationships. How you present the detailed budget along with the other plan elements will be important in the budget and project approval process. There are many formats for organizing a budget, and usually companies already have a preferred format for presenting financial data, as we've discussed previously. It is usually best to use this preferred format because it is already understood by the managers reviewing it.

If your company doesn't have a preferred budget format or one that is appropriate for your project, the example formats already illustrated in this chapter can be used for a variety of projects. Most computer-based project management programs offer a wide range of other budget reporting formats to choose from as well. As with the project schedule, a visual representation of budget data can be quite useful in understanding the relationships between various aspects of the budget. These graphs are often included in a project plan in addition to budget details.

Bar charts, pie charts, and line charts are very useful budget representation tools. There are three standard ways to chart the budget that are especially useful in representing project costs:

1. Charting total project costs over the life span of the project with a line chart
2. Graphing milestone costs as a bar chart or pie chart
3. Graphing component costs of the project, including labor costs, materials, and capital expenditures in a bar chart

Several examples of budget graphs for the sales office project are provided as examples. (See Figure 6-5.) These charts make it easy to visualize where the most money is being spent. This is important, because these areas will require the most cost monitoring as the project proceeds.

Budgeting Step 5. *Prepare the Budget and Project Plan for Approval*

After the budget estimates are made and the project plan is "tweaked" for final adjustments to the schedule and resource specifications, it is time to integrate all the elements of the budget and the project plan for final approvals.

The complete project plan should now include the following:

- A narrative description of the project, along with the project goals, as documented in Chapter Two.

- A summary of project assumptions.

- A work breakdown structure for the project was documented in Chapter Three. A network or milestone summary of the network for projects requiring may also be included, if warranted.

- A list of team members and resource requirements as documented in Chapter Four.

- A project schedule, documented as described in Chapter Five.

- A detailed budget and budget graphs.

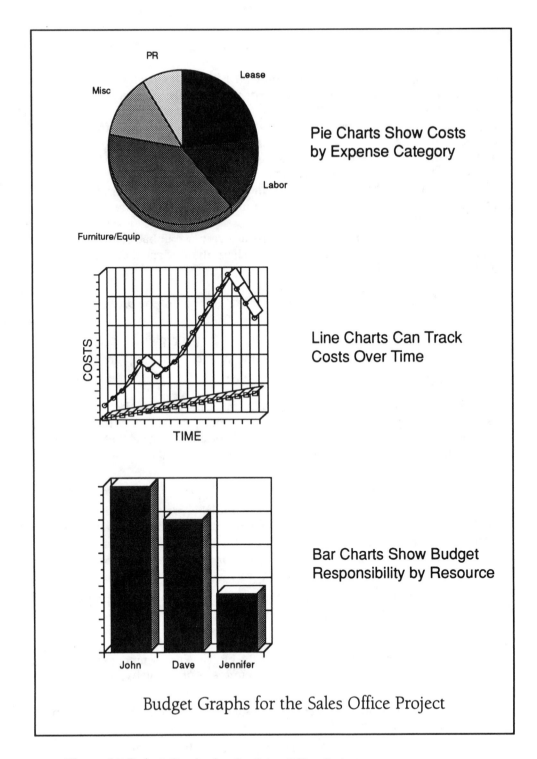

Figure 6-5 Budget Graphs for the Sales Office Project

Project plan elements are usually summarized in a cover memo or executive summary. This summary should specify the project goals, overall costs, time frames, and resource requirements for the project. Unless you approve your own projects, this memo should specifically ask for permission to proceed on implementing the project. For large or complex projects, it is typical to submit the plan for review a few days before a formal review meeting is held to discuss the project. If you're lucky, the project will be approved at this meeting. If not, you may be asked to make changes or revisions to the project.

If you have done a thorough job of planning up to this point, the revisions should be minor—because the project team will have been informed and involved during the preparation of the plan components, so the final plan shouldn't come as a big surprise to anyone.

If major changes are desired, however, it is negotiation time. If the changes are unnecessary or political in nature, negotiate and defend your position with data and clear explanations. Remember, you have put significant amounts of thinking and preparation into this plan—don't compromise now just to get the plan approved.

Beware when a senior manager insists on maintaining his or her budgetary and project schedule positions based on his or her "extensive experience with similar projects." An inexperienced manager may be threatened by this position, or arguments may ensue instead of logical, reason-based debates. Worse, the interactions may be met with silence. Try to keep the discussion focused on the issues, the thinking, and the logic of the presentation. You may find that there are valid reasons to adjust the budget, schedule, or other parameters of the plan. Remember that compromises are almost always necessary with large projects. There is usually more than one way to handle a project and still meet objectives. Keep your mind and the discussions as open as possible to alternatives.

If the personalities clash, have another meeting when people have had time to cool down. And, if you know something is absolutely wrong, don't buy into the plan if you know the changes will cause the project to fail. (If you need more tips on handling negotiations of this kind, read Chapter Eight.)

If, after reasoned debate and open discussions, it is decided that there are valid reasons for changes to the budget or other aspects of the plan, proceed to the next step.

Budgeting Step 6. Revise the Project Goals and Plan to Accommodate Budget Constraints Established During the Approval Process

The plan should be revised as agreed in the meetings with senior management and the project team. In a large, complex project, many of the steps covered throughout the last four chapters of this book will need to be reiterated—including reassessing the project goals, the work, the schedule, and of course, the budget. This may require individual and group meetings to make the changes and come to consensus on the new plan. Don't rush the replanning effort. Make sure the ramification of each change in the plan is *fully* understood.

If the project requires major revisions because of a change in company strategies or in economic environment, this is not something you could have predicted—so it is important to put it in proper perspective and accept the changes, as long as they are reasonable. If your assumptions are well documented, changes based on these assumptions should be relatively straightforward.

If you are forced to accept certain changes that you believe are inappropriate and you are to remain the project manager, make sure you document the changes that affect the goals and end results of the project, as well as those to budget items and schedules, before the plan is approved. If you don't clearly communicate the changes and the effect they have on the project, people may expect the original end results to be achieved, even though the schedule and the budget were changed. At this point, you should know why this presumption will get you into trouble.

Budgeting Step 7. Resubmit the Project Plan for Final Approvals

Finally, when the signatures are put on paper, the project is ready to proceed to the next stage—implemenation. The planning components will guide your project throughout implementation and will form the baseline project plan that all progress, expenditures, and evaluations are compared to.

THE CRASH PLAN AND THE OPTIMAL PLAN

Sometimes it is useful to prepare two budgets, especially if projects are high priority or have absolute deadlines. In these cases, it is appropriate to prepare an optimal budget and a "crash" plan. The crash plan is used as an alternative if something goes wrong during implementation. "Crash" plans can also be used to show how bigger budgets can be used to buy labor or other resources to shorten schedules. The optimal budget is the budget that estimates what things will cost if everything goes as originally planned. The "crash" budget is a pull-out-the-stops approach that gets things done as quickly as possible without worrying about money or resources.

Using the sales office project as an example, it is possible to get a full seven weeks out of the schedule if an expensive executive search firm is contracted to find the staff for the office. However, the firm's fees increase the cost of the project by more than $150,000. Because the expected revenue from the office is very important, it is decided that using a search firm would be more expedient and appropriate than taking the extra time to staff the office using in-house resources. If time is more important than direct cost (and it often is), then the "crash" approach to budgeting is appropriate.

Of course, there are only certain places in the project plan where "crashing" can be done. These include adding resources to mechanical processes or using more expensive vendors who get things done faster. As we discussed earlier in the chapter on schedules, adding more money, more people, or more equipment does not always decrease the time required to complete a project. Throwing money at a project is only a solution if it actually accomplishes something that wouldn't happen otherwise.

Use the network diagram to assist in calculating the true impact of adding more resources to the project. If you use a computerized project management program, many of the more sophisticated programs can accomplish "what if" analyses by displaying the costs of different schedules and resource allocations. If the payback is worth it, make the schedule adjustments and spend more money—or keep the "crash" budget and schedule in the top drawer if things start running late or if your boss asks for the project to be completed earlier than originally planned.

Finally, with your project plan in hand, you are ready to begin work. So, on to the next chapter, where we will cover the process of initiating the project and the steps in monitoring and controlling the project to completion.

Chapter Seven

GETTING STARTED AND ASSESSING PROGRESS: Processes for Keeping Projects on Track

---

After completing the steps in the last six chapters, you have a complete project plan approved and ready to implement. This chapter shows you how to use the plan developed for initiating a project, along with simple charts, graphs, meetings, and checklists to maintain control of the ongoing progress of a project. Regardless of technique, charting method, or project complexity, no project management system will succeed if the project plan isn't used as a tool for controlling the project during implementation.

In the same vein, a project plan is useless without a project manager. Since people will complete the work, project managers must employ appropriate methods to motivate, coordinate, facilitate, and administer the project team. Otherwise, the work will never get done. As a project manager, you must also identify and implement the appropriate management style for keeping the team motivated. This chapter provides guidelines for achieving your objectives as a project manager.

Using the management, reporting, and charting techniques presented in the chapter, you will be able to stay abreast of the status of every activity and cost. In addition, tips for organizing meetings and managing communications both up and down the project ladder are provided. Together, these techniques allow you to make necessary changes in a timely fashion, thereby maintaining control of the schedule, resources, and the costs—and ultimately guiding your project to completion on time and within budget.

ESTABLISHING YOUR ROLE AS LEADER AND MANAGER

Before you do anything else on your project, consider both your leadership style and your management tactics—the two are intertwined and central to the implementation of projects. Your leadership skills and the appropriateness of the management tactics you adopt for each of the various people on your project team are of paramount importance in achieving project goals.

Management of the project and leadership go hand in hand. As a manager, people identify you as the responsible person for the project. As a leader, you command both the authority and the responsibility you need to guide the project. You will also be a trusted and reliable source of information on the project. As a leader, your team will expect you to be honest, competent, and inspirational. As a manager, you will direct and guide the project through to completion—using specific techniques and procedures that establish the framework and structure of the project. It is possible to complete the management part of the project—the meetings, assignments, audits, reports, and other communications—and not attain the status and influence of a leader. (See Figure 7-1.)

What Kind of Leader Are You?	Never	Sometimes	Always
I am fair in my dealings with others.	☐	☐	☐
I consider the motivations of my staff before assigning tasks.	☐	☐	☐
I use a different management style with different people.	☐	☐	☐
I am available when my team needs me.	☐	☐	☐
I support my team with other managers.	☐	☐	☐
I acknowledge the team for work well done.	☐	☐	☐
If you answered five or more as "Always," you are among the most adaptive leaders in the world.			

Figure 7-1 What Kind of Leader Are You?

As a successful project manager, you must be both a manager and a leader. You must gain the trust and respect of the project team, so people feel comfortable taking your direction. You must also develop procedures and administrative tracking for assuring that work is getting done on time and within budget. This is as important for small projects as it is for the large, complex ones.

The management tactics you employ include the communications, reports, and administrative procedures you use in guiding the project to completion. We will discuss these tactics in more detail later in the chapter. For now, let's consider your role as the leader of the project. It is this leadership role that allows you to motivate, adapt, and influence the people working on your project. Without these abilities, the rest of the project management "bag of tricks" is useless.

Leadership can be defined in many different ways. John Kotter in his book *The Leadership Factor* (Macmillan, 1988) defined leadership as the process of moving a group of people in some direction through mostly non-coercive means. He added in a later book that leadership is the process that helps direct and mobilize people and/or ideas. Other management theorists have recently defined leadership as the process of creating an environment in which people become empowered. Empowerment is a popular management concept for getting people committed and excited about the work they do so they achieve their own objectives with little direct supervision.

For many years, the attributes of effective project managers as leaders have been debated. Theories abound that tout the traits and behaviors of effective leaders. These theories search for biological, personality-based, emotional, physical, psychological, and other personal characteristics that affect leadership ability. The relationship between intelligence traits and effective leadership has been considered. Even diet and exercise levels have been explored as ways to identify and classify effective leaders.

Regardless of semantics and theoretical points of view, leadership comes down to one thing—the ability to meet the project goals through other people. Project managers must be leaders by definition. In almost all projects, they must get work completed through others. The question then remains: How can you accomplish this?

Recently, theorists have moved away from innate traits that make effective project managers to an emphasis on styles that people can learn and adopt to become successful leaders. It became apparent as business researchers and theorists looked at the issue of leadership that there are a wide range of effective leadership styles that can be adapted effectively to meet the needs of different people, organizations, and projects. These include

- **Task-oriented leadership.** This style emphasizes getting the job done and concentrating on methods for assigning and organizing work, making decisions, and evaluating performance.

- **Employee-oriented or people-oriented leadership.** This leadership style concentrates on open communication, the development of rapport with team members, and an ongoing direct concern for the needs of subordinates.

- **Reward-based leadership.** Reward-based styles tie positive feedback and other rewards directly to the work accomplished. The reward-based style assumes that a high level of performance will be maintained if work results in meaningful rewards that correlate directly with the quality of the person's efforts. Rewards include pay and promotion, of course, but also encompass support, encouragement, security, and respect from the project manager.

As a project manager, don't assume that because you like something done a certain way that your team members will have the same preferences—this is a common management fallacy. Individuals differ from one another by experience and personality. Each person has a different conception of how the job should be done, who should get credit for the effort, and how each individual should be rewarded for his or her work. Because projects also differ by goals, size, and complexity, different methods must be used to monitor and coordinate projects.

It is the project manager's responsibility to adjust management and leadership style to produce the desired effect or work from the project team. This approach of matching management style to the specific needs of a situation is often called situational management or contingency theory. Project managers must effectively apply task-oriented, employee-oriented, and reward-oriented systems as appropriate for the project, the objectives, and the individual team members. Choosing the styles to use on your project will depend on a number of factors:

- **The type of work being completed.** Structured tasks require simple specification of the work. But an overly directive style may be redundant because the work is already well defined. In fact, if work is routine and potentially monotonous, it may be important for the project manager to display open support of the team efforts to keep people motivated. Creative tasks, on the other hand, may require less specification, and if the work is already highly satisfying to the worker, the project manager may be best to let the person alone to be creative. The trick with creative tasks is to monitor activity and progress on the task without seeming autocratic, or making team members feel constrained.

- **The level of experience and independence of the team member.** Obviously, less experienced team members need more guidance than experts. But always be cognizant that people on your team are intelligent and knowledgeable, even the less experienced people. Acknowledge the fact that your team members know things that you don't. Just because you are the project manager doesn't mean you need to know how to do everything on the project. That is why you have a team.

- **The person's own preferences for level of feedback and communication.** Some team members require more feedback than others. Some will resent you looking over their shoulders; others will want you to check each activity. Learning to adapt your communications to individual requirements is something that comes with experience. The ability starts with basic awareness and observation of people working on your team.
- **The cohesiveness of the group.** For a number of reasons, some teams are simply more or less cohesive than others. Some team members only have limited contact together. Other team members may have established relationships. Less cohesive groups need more ongoing communication and support from the project manager. More cohesive groups will generally be more self-directed and require less direct intervention from you.

Project Management Tip

✎ **Learn to Listen to Your Team**—The ability to listen is one of the most important skills a project manager can possess. Focused listening helps keep you abreast of project progress better than any status report. Observant listening can also help you foresee political issues, before they start bogging the project down. Here are some hints to make you a better listener:

- Stop talking and let others tell you what they want to say.
- Let people finish what they are saying. Try not to interrupt, because you'll never hear the complete intent of the person if you do. If there is a brief pause in the discussion, don't jump in prematurely. Make sure the other person has finished before you take your turn.
- Eliminate distractions, such as telephone calls or people coming in and out of the office. Give the person your full attention.
- Listen with purpose and intent. Try to hear between the words for the underlying meaning of the message. Notice body language and facial expressions as people talk. These are often the clues to dissatisfaction or issues that are not being addressed. If you see something wrong in the faces, ask some probing questions to get at the real concerns.
- Restate what you heard the people say to make sure you got the message right. You must receive and understand the message for communication to occur.

Worksheet Identifying Management Approaches for Team Members

WHO	RELATIONSHIP WITH YOU	REASONS TO COOPERATE	REASONS TO RESIST	MANAGEMENT STRATEGY
Dave	Subordinate	Wants to Advance, Very Creative	Has Hidden Agenda	Encouragement & Acknowledgement —Don't Over-Manage
John	Subordinate	Competitive with Dave	Set in Ways	Acknowledge His Expertise—Ask for Advice Frequently
Jennifer	On Loan to the Project	It's Her Job, Very Enthusiastic	Bureaucracy and Paperwork	Play on Long-Term Opportunity
Lease Agent	Outside Vendor	Wants Us as Client	Schedule Too Demanding	Promise Business in the Future if Deadline Met
Furniture Representative	Outside Organization	Wants to Make a Sale	None Apparent	Negotiate Prices
Facilities Manager	Different Department	Pressure from Group President	Traditionally Resists New Programs	Negotiation and Communication. Use Boss if necessary.

Figure 7-2 Worksheet Identifying Management Approaches for Project Team Members

A worksheet can be used to identify the management styles and tactics appropriate for motivating the people and facilitating the efforts of team members on your project. (See Figure 7-2.) Starting with the skills inventories you created earlier for your team, and based on your own experience with each team member, you can identify styles that seem appropriate for each person who will work on your project. A simple example of such a worksheet is provided for the some of the sales office project team. Notice the wide range of communication preferences and support requirements for the members of this team.

ESTABLISHING OPERATING GUIDELINES FOR THE PROJECT

One of the first things you need to communicate to your project team is how the project will be administered and coordinated. Before you gather your project team to start work on their respective objectives, you need to do some thinking about the way you will administer, coordinate, track, and update your project.

As the project manager, you need to complete the following ongoing administrative, coordination, and control activities during the project:

- **Coordinate activities between groups and vendors involved in your project.** Coordination is one of the major uses of a project manager's time in large projects. This involves managing the interfaces between people, vendors, managers, and clients who are involved with a project, as well as controlling schedules.
- **Monitor progress on the project against the plan.** Managers must compare the time, cost, and performance of the project to the budget, the schedule, and the tasks defined in the approved project plan. This must be done in an integrated manner at regular intervals, not in a haphazard, arbitrary way. Any significant departures from the budget and the schedule must be reported immediately—as these anomalies affect viability and success of the entire project.
- **Adapt the project schedule, budget, and work plan as necessary to keep the project on track.** As the project progresses, changes in the original plan may be required for a number of reasons. It is the project manager's responsibility to make sure that these changes are appropriate, valid, and approved.
- **Document project progress and changes and communicate them to team members.** The quality and level of detail for your reports and communications needs to be consistent, reliable, and appropriate for each level of the project team.

SUCCESS CRITERIA FOR PROJECT CONTROL

The success you have in completing the administrative activities will directly affect the end results your project will achieve. Success in meeting your project goals depends on these basic criteria:

- **The quality of the plan you have put together with your project team.** A major portion of this book is devoted to the preparation of the plan because of its centrality in the project management discipline. If you diligently followed the steps laid out in previous chapters, your plan is likely a good one.
- **The consistency with which the plan is monitored and updated.** A plan that stays in the top drawer of your desk will not help you guide your project to a successful conclusion. Instead, it must be updated regularly to be useful. It must also reflect the current status of the project and any changes that become necessary because of new information, budget constraints, or schedule modifications.
- **The level and clarity of communication maintained throughout the implementation of the project.** The amount as well as the quality of communication is important. Every person on your linear responsibility chart for the project requires ongoing communication at various levels of detail. Higher level management requires summary reports on the project. Operational members of the team require more detailed information. Some communication will be formal and some will be informal. The objective of communications is to keep people informed, on track, and involved in the project.
- **The rapport you establish with the project team.** This depends largely on your success in applying the leadership styles we discussed earlier.

ESTABLISHING PROJECT ADMINISTRATION PROCEDURES

If your project is one of many similar undertakings in your organization there are probably established operating and administrative procedures in place already to help you complete your ongoing responsibilities to the project. These include report formats, time frames for project review, and other tracking procedures. If these procedures and administrative reports are not already well established in your organization, you need to develop basic operating procedures before you begin work on your project. To establish the operating procedures, answer the following questions:

- How will you assign the work? If team members are already clear on "who is going to do what" because of their involvement in the planning process, how will you coordinate these efforts?
- How will you measure progress on the project?
- What kind of information do you need to assess progress?
- What standards will be used for evaluating the quality of project deliverables?
- How many project meetings will you have? Which people need to attend?
- How often will you update the project plan?
- How often will reports on the project be made?

The number, frequency, and detail of the reports and procedures you use will depend on the management requirements for your project, your manager's preferences, and your own need for ongoing information on the project. The chart included here identifies some typical operational guidelines and administrative procedures for small and large projects. (See Figure 7-3.)

ACTION	DAILY	WEEKLY	MONTHLY	QUARTERLY OR LESS FREQUENTLY
Informal Discussions with Team	S	L		
Staff Meetings with Managers		B		
Project Review Meeting with Team		S	L	
Status Report		S	L	
Project Audit (optional)				L
Team Building Activity			B	
Report to Management			B	
S = Small Project				
L = Large Project				
B = Both Small and Large Projects				

Figure 7-3 Operational Guidelines for Small and Large Projects

INITIATING THE PROJECT—GETTING STARTED ON THE RIGHT TRACK

After identifying appropriate leadership styles and operational procedures for your project, it is time to get the project going. With the complete, approved project plan in hand, you are ready to initiate work. For small projects, the initiation might involve sending a memo and making a few calls or personal visits to the team participants to get them started on their objectives. For larger projects, a project initiation or "kick-off" meeting is usually desirable.

Whether handled formally or informally, the project initiation needs to accomplish the following objectives:

- Clearly communicate the goals of the project to all team members to assure that everyone is clear on his or her own objectives and responsibilities to the project.
- Explain the level of commitment you need to the project, and get people enthusiastic to make things happen.
- Identify critical deadlines and critical phases of the project.
- Review the overall schedule and work plan with the team.
- Explain basic operating procedures including reports, meetings, and other ongoing communications required between you and other team members.
- Explicitly give the people responsible for the initial tasks the go-ahead to begin work on the project.

TRACKING PROGRESS THROUGH THE IMPLEMENTATION PHASE

Once the project is initiated, you are in the project implementation phase. During this phase, as a project manager you will coordinate the work effort, monitor progress, and initiate control activities to keep the project on track.

Monitoring progress is completed to establish your current position compared to the planned position. Some of this monitoring will be formal, in the form of reports and meetings. Other monitoring will be informal, in the form of just talking to people and maintaining relationships with people on the project.

What Should You Monitor?

The following must be monitored for every project:

- The status of work being performed compared to the plan
- The volume of work being completed
- The quality of work being performed

- Costs and expenditures compared to the plan
- Attitudes of people working on the project and others who are involved with the project, including customers and management
- Cohesiveness and cooperation of team members

In this list there is more to be monitored than just the schedule and the budget. The level of communication and cooperation between team members and the quality of the work being performed are also obviously important aspects of the project. In addition, you must monitor the use and availability of capital equipment and machinery. For example, you may be responsible for the usage of computer equipment or heavy machinery in a large project. You also want to make sure the equipment doesn't "walk out the door," so to speak.

Every project should have both formal and informal monitoring. The larger and more complex the project, the more monitoring is required. The goal is to keep your team working toward the final deadline, within the budget, and in line with the goals specified for the project. In a large, complex project, the effort required to monitor and control it may take more time than you actually spend "working" on the project. This is all right. It is your job as a project manager to guide the project to a successful conclusion. Of course, on smaller projects, the degree of monitoring and control should be much less time consuming.

One thing that helps minimize time spent in monitoring activities on both small and large projects is the use of simple reporting formats. Keeping reports clear and succinct is more important than is getting hundreds of pages of narrative on each aspect of the project. In addition, the use of appropriate project management software that is adapted to your project needs help reducing the time required to understand the impact of current activities and changes on the project plan. (See Chapter Ten for more on choosing an appropriate software program.)

The tasks, milestones, and budget you documented in the plan for your project are the starting point for project coordination. These tasks and milestones form the checkpoints to be used to monitor progress. Whether formal or informal, monitoring serves one or more of the following basic functions:

- To communicate project status and changes to other project team members
- To inform management (and clients or customers) about the status of the project
- To provide the justification for making project adjustments
- To document current project plans compared to the original project plan

Consistency is very important in the monitoring and control process. The project must be monitored from start to finish, because problems can occur anywhere along the way. Some project managers start out full of energy and monitor everything during the first few weeks. Then, when things seem to be going all right, the monitoring falls off. These managers often end up with a big mess at the end of the project, because they've failed to keep track of progress and problems. Don't let it happen to you! Be consistent. Monitor things, even when you trust your team and things seem to be going well. Problems have a way of happening when you least expect them.

FORMAL MONITORING APPROACHES

The size and complexity of the project, along with the culture of the organization, determines the extent of formal monitoring to use. Formal monitoring includes reports, audits, and project review meetings.

Status Reports

Most formal monitoring is in the form of project reports and status reports produced by various members of the project team. The most typical formal project tracking is the monthly or weekly progress report—monthly reports for long projects, weekly reports for short projects. Status reports should be completed by each team member (or supervisor) and then compiled and summarized by the project manager. The project manager then adds his or her own comments to the summary report, draws conclusions on the status of the project, makes recommendations for actions and changes, and sends the report on to other managers, executives, or customers who need to be kept apprised of project status. In addition, status reports are provided to team members to keep them informed of activities by other members of the project team. (See Figure 7-4.)

There are three potential audiences for status reports: the team members on the project, company management, and customers (if there are any involved). The report to management and customers is typically more formal, but less detailed, than the report made to the team members.

Project status reports should generally include the following information:

- Work performed since the last status report
- Any changes required to the schedule or objectives
- Problems encountered and actions taken to resolve them
- Problems or issues that require further action
- Work planned for the next period
- Questions or items that require other people's approval or input

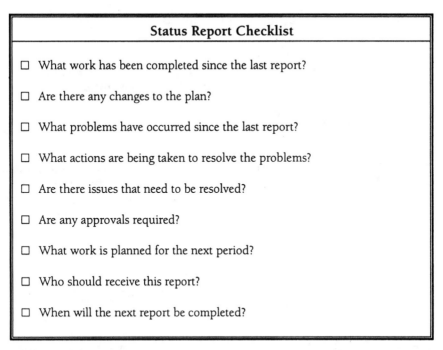

Status Report Checklist
☐ What work has been completed since the last report?
☐ Are there any changes to the plan?
☐ What problems have occurred since the last report?
☐ What actions are being taken to resolve the problems?
☐ Are there issues that need to be resolved?
☐ Are any approvals required?
☐ What work is planned for the next period?
☐ Who should receive this report?
☐ When will the next report be completed?

Figure 7-4 Status Report Checklist

The status report should always relate to the original project plan. One way to do this is to include the current schedule or budget next to the original project plan as part of your status reports. The key to effective status reports is to keep them simple while maintaining enough information to identify problems, actions, and changes. (See Figure 7-5.)

Other Project Reports

In large projects, there may be other reports produced to keep track of project status. These include cost variance reports, load leveling reports, supply inventories, and other formal documentation that is specific to track individual projects. The need for these other reports should be identified during the project initiation process, if possible. For each report, the following should be documented:

- How often is the report produced? Some reports are produced weekly. Others are submitted monthly or quarterly. In very large projects, there may even be daily updates in the form of production reports or supply reports.
- What is contained in the report?
- Who is responsible for producing the report?
- What is the objective of the report?

- Who will follow up on action items identified in the report?
- Who is the intended audience for the report?

In addition, before any report becomes part of the bureaucratic process associated with your project, ask yourself the following question:

- Is a report the best way to communicate this information, or is there some other form of communication that would be more expedient and just as useful?

In other words, is the report really necessary? Some reports are produced because they have always been required, not because it is really necessary for a specific project. This kind of mindless bureaucracy wastes time and energy.

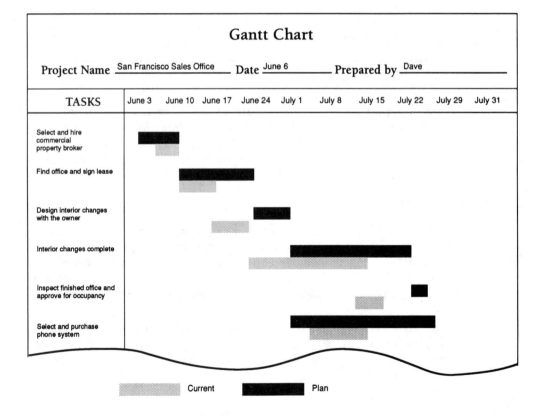

Figure 7-5 Current Project Schedule Compared to Plan

If a report is redundant, too frequent, or too long, don't be afraid to ask for it to be changed or eliminated altogether. There are better things for people to do with their time than produce reports that no one reads.

The Project Review Meeting

For some projects, a regular project review meeting is a good alternative to a lengthy project report. It is difficult to resolve issues with reports, so meetings are necessary. The project review meeting is an opportunity for key team members, not just managers and supervisors, to get together to resolve issues. It is also a time to discuss current project status and review performance toward meeting objectives. Project review meetings are often held at the completion of a major milestone, or before or after a key phase of the project. Some project review meetings are held on a periodic basis, in place of formal reports. For example, the newsletter project is best handled with brief reports and regular meetings, because the project is of a short duration. The sales office project has less frequent meetings until the end of the project, then more coordination is required.

If a project meeting is necessary to resolve issues, have one. It's best to take action as soon as you know of a problem, instead of waiting for the regularly scheduled meeting.

Guidelines for Making Meetings Effective

Meetings are both inevitable and important in project management, but they can be a drain on limited time and resources if improperly handled. Here are guidelines for keeping project meetings productive:

- **Keep them as short as possible.** No one wants to spend a half day or more in a meeting. After the first hour, meetings typically lose impact and focus.

- **Specify a time limit and stick to it.** If you schedule an hour for the meeting, the meeting should last no longer than an hour. In this way people can schedule their own time with confidence.

- **Invite only the people who need to be there.** Other project personnel can be informed of meeting results through the meeting minutes.

- **Always prepare and distribute an agenda in advance.** Get input from appropriate team members when preparing the agenda, to make sure the important issues will be covered.

- **Hold meetings only when they are necessary.** If there is nothing important on the agenda, cancel the meeting.

- **Identify the specific objectives to be achieved.** This is more than putting an agenda together. You need to also identify the specific deliverables you want from the meeting. For example, an agenda item might be a report on locations in San Francisco for the sales office. The specific objective of the agenda item might be to narrow the locations down to three possibilities from the list provided.

- **Keep things moving.** As the project manager, this will normally be your responsibility. Don't let the meeting get bogged down in politics, irrelevant issues, or personal agendas.

- **Use visual aids to get your point across.** The use of simple and clear visual aids, charts, and graphs can help clarify important issues and keep a meeting focused.

- **Assign action items in the meeting when further research or planning is required.** Don't resolve complex issues in a meeting without adequate information and preparation. Clearly identify the person who will be responsible for following up on the action item. Sometimes the assignment of a small task force is appropriate. Make sure a report of the work completed on action items is on the agenda for the next meeting.

- **Distribute short minutes or summaries of the meetings.** These should be completed within two working days after each meeting. These minutes should identify the results of the meeting, action items assigned (with names), and the time and location of the next meeting.

- **Remind people in advance about the next meeting.** Even though you have sent out minutes, remind people about the meeting. Usually this is accomplished when the agenda is distributed in advance.

The Project Audit

The most formal type of project monitoring is the audit. An audit is performed on large projects by objective outsiders who review progress, costs, and current plans. After discussions with team members, reviews of reports, and direct observations, the objective auditors then report their conclusions on the current status of the project based on their audit to the project manager or to executive management. Audits may be initiated both during and at the end of a project. Internal audits may also be performed by project managers and team members at key milestones in a large project. The goal of a project audit is to get a true and accurate picture of the quality of work, the current expenditures, and the schedule of the project.

Audits are typically performed in large government projects, projects involving multiple companies and big budgets, and projects involving customers who need outside assurance that work on their work is proceeding as planned. Managing the relationships and interfaces among people, the project, and the outside world during an audit is an important project management function.

MONITORING THE BUDGET

Reports and meetings are great for tracking schedules and performance, but budgets and cash outlays require special monitoring techniques. The way the budget tracking is set up depends on the accounting systems already in place in your company. As you make expenditures, or sign contracts with vendors, you need to establish some formal tracking method to measure your actual commitments. These should always be compared to the budget in your plan.

In most companies, if you rely on expenditure reports from the accounting department to provide financial status on your project, you will likely go over budget or think you have more money than you actually have. Money is often "spent" in the form of contracts or agreements long before it is accounted for in the billing and invoice cycles of the corporation. Accounting reports typically report on invoices that have been "paid to date." Unfortunately, they don't usually report on monies that have not yet been billed.

For this reason, you must track actual expenditures to date, in addition to reviewing the accounting reports. Ultimately, your expenditures and the accounting department documentation should match, but it might take as long as ninety days for the two systems to be reconciled.

You, and each person on your project team who will be making financial commitments to vendors or suppliers, must account for all monetary commitments as they occur. These expenditures should appear on the formal status reports. A simple way to do this is to have each person provide a photocopy of each contract, agreement, or order for your project as it is approved. These copies should be sent to you or a person designated by you. The total of these expenditures then becomes a part of the actual expenses committed to your project. As vendors specify new prices or change their bids, these must be put into the file as well, and budget figures adjusted accordingly in the next status report.

When you get reports from accounting that do not match those in your budget file, you will have clear documentation of the expenditures to reconcile the differences. (See Figure 7-6.)

(Amounts in $Thousands)	Lease (Broker & Deposit)	Build-Out	Phones	Furniture	Recruitment	Public Relations	Supplies	Equipment	Total
Planned	$87	$12	$6	$8	$31	$17	$14	$63	$238
Actual	$94	$21	$6	$6	$27	$16	$18	$58	$246
Variance	$7	$9	$0	($2)	($4)	($1)	$4	($5)	$8

Figure 7-6 Final Expenditures Report for Sales Office Project

INFORMAL MONITORING APPROACHES

Never rely on written reports alone to assess progress on your project. People often leave the problems out of reports because they don't want to put them in writing. Or they fail to report schedule slips in meetings because they think time can be made up later. People often don't want to expose a problem in front of others for fear of reprisal or embarrassment.

For example, John, the customer support manager, was late on writing the articles for the newsletter project. Still, in the weekly report he stated that the articles were "on schedule," even though they hadn't been started. John reported this way in good faith, fully believing he would be able to make up the time next week. Unfortunately, this kind of reporting causes many problems, especially if the person never does find the time to get back on schedule. If Joe, the project manager, fails to realize the problem until it is documented or reported, the entire newsletter project could be in jeopardy.

The quality of performance on a project is also subjective—so performance reported as outstanding by one group may really be substandard to another. In the sales office project, the contractors assembling the new office walls reported that everything was completed "to specifications." It wasn't until Roger, who was responsible for the project, actually visited the site, that he realized two of the offices had doors in the wrong place and the baseboards in the conference room were missing altogether.

For reasons like this, you need to review progress informally on the project on your own through direct observation and direct communication with the team members. Informal monitoring is completed by simply listening, observing, and communicating on an ongoing basis. The goal is to spot problems before they become unmanageable.

Management by Walking Around

One of the most useful informal project monitoring processes is "management by walking around." Often called MBWA for short, this technique simply involves informal talks and meetings with people working on the project. Progress can be assessed objectively through your own observations instead of through the filters of others. If your observations and the progress reports don't jibe, perhaps a formal meeting with a few of the key players is a good idea. Then, you direct the team to alternatives to keep work on track.

> *So much of what we call management consists in making it difficult for people to work.*
>
> —Peter Drucker

If any of your vendors or project participants is at a different location, a phone call now and then just to see how things are going is vital. This is also a good time to provide positive feedback about accomplishments to date.

Don't be a pest in your MBWA program, however. You want to be encouraging and motivating. If you are perceived as a spy, then the results of your monitoring efforts will backfire. People don't want you standing over their shoulders, especially if they have creative or thought-intensive work to complete. Think how you would feel if your boss came over two or three times an hour and asked you how you were doing. Make the visits unpredictable, spontaneous, and sincere for best results.

Informal Meetings and One-on-Ones

Not all meetings need to be formal and planned to be effective. Just inviting a team member or a few people who are working on the project to your office to sit and chat over coffee may be appropriate.

Another useful technique is to schedule regular one-on-one meetings with staff members so they can go over their own concerns, not just yours. Giving team members an opportunity to tell you about the project from their point of view can be very enlightening. People will often let you know about problems and concerns in a one-on-one situation that they would never reveal in a meeting or report.

Communications—Up and Down the Organization

The project managers who consistently succeed in bringing their projects in on time and within budget are those who effectively manage the interfaces and communications between people and organizations. The people working on your project, and other members of the project team, need to be comfortable with bringing issues to your attention. This goes for people who report directly to you, their managers, and your managers as well.

As a project manager, you need to make a conscious effort to maintain open communications with the people and organizations involved with your project. There are three types of communications that must occur for a project to be managed effectively:

1. **Vertical communications.** These are the up-and-down organizational communications based on the hierarchical relationships established on an organization chart.

2. **Horizontal communications.** Horizontal or lateral communication involves communicating and coordinating activities with peers.

Though formal authority is absent, the relative power or position of one party may dominate that of another. As a project manager, it is your goal to see that this doesn't happen.

3. **Diagonal communications.** The diagonal relationships are rarely shown on organization charts. They include upward diagonal communications with managers and officers from other areas and with subordinate groups in other departments. They also include downward diagonal communications with third parties such as contractors, suppliers, or project consultants.

If you have established the requisite communications in all three dimensions before conflicts occur, when the inevitable conflicts do arise between organizations, styles, procedures, or priorities, there will be an established channel available for resolving issues. Since conflicts must be resolved through communication, if you have established the basis for discussion before the conflicts arise, the resolution process will usually be easier.

GUIDING THE PROJECT THROUGH THE IMPLEMENTATION PHASE

To implement a project, you must establish control over the tasks being performed. You do this partly through your authority and responsibility for the project. You use leadership and control techniques to assign, direct, and prioritize work that needs to be completed on the project.

Of course, as you monitor your project you will find that things don't always go as planned. The project monitoring process may expose that a project is veering off course for a number of reasons. These include

- The budget in the original plan was not adequate.
- Things are taking longer than planned.
- The team members are not able to deliver the quality desired.
- Unexpected events in the outside world that cannot be controlled by you affect the project.

Again, control comes into play. Control is the process of assigning and modifying work, expenditures, and objectives in order to complete a project successfully. Control often involves making adjustments and changes to the original plan. We will cover more about making changes and adjustments in the next chapter. For now, just remember that adjustments are a normal and expected part of project management.

The implementation of the project thus becomes a cyclic process of directing work, monitoring work, and controlling work. The project is monitored, controlled, and adjusted as necessary until completed. (See Figure 7-7.)

Flowchart   Inputs

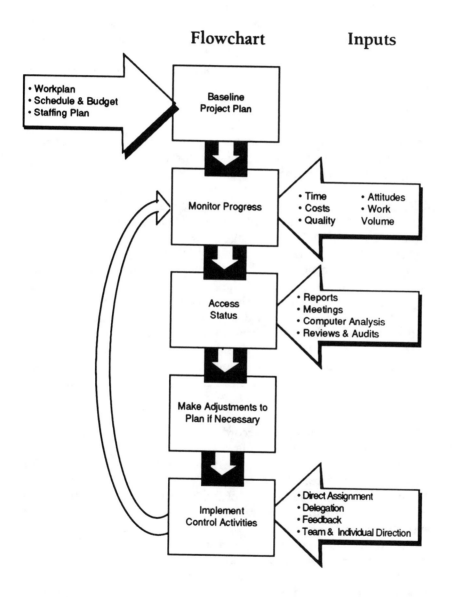

Figure 7-7 Project Monitoring and Control Process

Direct Control of Work Priorities

The most direct way for project managers to control a project is by assigning individual tasks to team members. Direct control can be used to adjust people's work priorities and make changes to schedules. In this way the project manager "steers" the project to completion. "Steering" must be done with tact and discretion, however. Otherwise, the team may become resentful of being overmanaged. The amount of direct control a project manager exercises depends on the independence of the project members and the creativity of the tasks. The more creative the tasks, the less direct control is feasible.

Delegation

Delegation is defined as the act of assigning formal authority and responsibility for completion of specific activities to a subordinate or group. In practice, delegation is an art. Delegation involves giving other people responsibility for completing specific aspects of the project. Rather than directly controlling a person's objectives and tasks, delegation involves assigning specific objectives to a person or group of people and letting them determine the best way to meet those objectives.

Delegation is often difficult for managers, especially inexperienced ones, because some of the "control" is given to others. In most projects, however, delegation is the best way to get work done—because it balances your power as project manager with the autonomy of the people responsible for the work.

For work on a project to be effectively controlled, delegation of objectives should occur with no overlaps between delegated objectives, no gaps between objectives, and no splits of objectives. Thus, all the work on the project should be assigned and the authority and responsibility for the objectives must be unambiguous—otherwise confusion will result.

Project Management Tip

✎ **Don't Be a Power Monger**—According to researchers, a common denominator in ineffective or underachieving groups is the manager who hoards power and information. Still, project managers often complain of too little authority or control of the projects they manage. But power is not something just given to you because of the job title or your experience. The power you need to manage any project is something that is available to any person. This is the personal power that inspires others to follow your lead. You won't need fancy titles or a bigger office. Personal power inspires commitment and loyalty. This kind of personal power is something you can share with your project team to empower them to do their best on the project. So don't threaten your team members or punish them when things don't go your way. Instead, gain their respect and trust. Be a leader, not a dictator. You'll get more work done in the long run.

Regular Feedback

Direct person-to-person feedback is one of the most powerful control mechanisms in the project management toolbox. People need to know that you notice what they are doing and that they are doing it right. Feedback is a key component of keeping people motivated and on track. Feedback allows the manager to acknowledge work completed and identify work that still needs to be done. Ideally, with appropriate feedback, motivated team members direct themselves to complete the work in the right way.

Feedback can be both positive and negative. In managing people, it is important to emphasize the positive feedback and control the negative feedback. Positive feedback can be in the form of thanking a person for a job well done, acknowledging a team in a meeting in front of other people, or doing something tangible, like taking someone to lunch for special effort or giving out a monetary award for outstanding performance.

Negative feedback is best handled discreetly and privately. Berating someone in a meeting or embarrassing an individual in front of others will not accomplish anything—and may alienate other people who are doing a good job. Negative feedback should be direct, but should not be personally derogatory. You should ask the person questions about the problem and get their side of the situation. Discuss alternatives and come up with a plan for fixing the problem, if possible.

For example, when John's failure to start the newsletter stories was discovered, Joe could have roared into John's office and called him a liar and an incompetent manager, demanding action on the stories be taken immediately. Instead, Joe took him out to lunch to discuss the problem. Joe was direct in stating that he was concerned about the stories and understood he hadn't started them yet. He asked if there was something he could do to help John. John pointed out that a new customer installation had taken more of his time than anticipated. In the discussion, it was suggested that Sarah, in sales development, could help by contributing a story she had suggested for another issue. Thus, John would only have to write two stories, instead of three. Later, Joe asked Sarah about writing the article, and she committed to get it done. All the stories arrived on time.

In very large projects, a formal performance review or performance appraisal system may be appropriate to provide ongoing feedback to project personnel, but a formal system is usually more important to promotions and raises that are outside the domain of the project per se. Even in projects where a formal performance review system is in place, it is important that performance feedback is frequent and continuous, because projects must adapt to immediate needs and circumstances. You can't wait for an annual review to tell someone to change working priorities or improve communications with another team member in a project—the project will suffer if you do.

Individual and Team-Oriented Direction

Both an individual component and a team-oriented component are required for optimum project coordination, whether using direct assignments, delegation, or feedback to keep people on track. Project work is not completed in isolation, and no person works on a project alone. People need to be aware of the impact their individual efforts have on other team members and on the project as a whole. Getting individuals to share objectives, concerns, and status is critical to the success of the project. The individuals must feel like a team with shared objectives to work optimally to reach those objectives—and it is the responsibility of the project manager to facilitate this team approach to the project.

Team Building as a Control Mechanism

Establishing functional interrelationships and interfaces between project team members is a major function of project management. Though a project manager should attempt to inspire team spirit through positive feedback and open communication, it isn't always possible for a project manager to get team members to work together effectively without intervention. A team-building session is a technique that can be used with a group of people working on a project to improve their own interteam interfaces and behaviors. The goal behind a team building session is to improve team achievement and productivity.

Team building is a formal process for diagnosing barriers to effective team performance in order to improve the overall effectiveness of a team in meeting the project objectives. When a project manager determines that teamwork is a problem in a project, diagnostic meetings are used between an entire team or a subteam to identify strengths and weaknesses in the communications, processes, and behaviors between team members. Ideally, team building sessions should be held away from the workplace and mediated by an outside consultant or neutral third party.

The mediator for the team building session directs the group to examine the issues that are affecting team effectiveness. These may involve interpersonal dynamics, conflicts in priorities, territorial issues, differing styles, or unclear objectives. These issues are then ranked in order of importance, and the team members prescribe a course of action for bringing about the necessary changes. After a set period of time, usually a month or more, the team is brought together again to evaluate the success of the action plan in improving teamwork, and a new set of action plans is developed.

Team building sessions are useful in larger projects where severe communication problems or group conflicts are evident. In smaller projects, miniteam-building sessions, held during a project review meeting, for example, might be in order to get people on track and resolve general intergroup issues that are affecting the project outcomes.

One final note about team building: as a project manager, you must support your team if you expect the team to support you. You need to review the team's work, of course. But you also need to be available to the team when they need questions answered or conflicts resolved with an outside resource. The team members need to feel you will back them up. The team attitude and the effectiveness of people on your project will depend largely on your ability to lead and communicate. If you fail to do that, no amount of monitoring or meetings will help you get the project done.

In this chapter you have learned about initiating, managing, and directing your project through the implementation stage. The most common formal and informal monitoring and control techniques have been presented, including reports, meetings, delegation, and direct observation. In Chapter Eight we discuss more ways to manage the inevitable changes and conflicts in a project as the implementation stage proceeds.

Chapter Eight

DEALING WITH CHANGES
AND CONFLICTS:
Procedures for Avoiding
the Traps and Staying in Charge

All projects, especially large ones, involve changes, conflicts, and problems that weren't anticipated in the original plan. This chapter covers ways to deal with those inevitable changes and problems. Specific recommendations are provided for handling the most common project management crises. In addition, techniques are illustrated for making timely and appropriate updates to the project plan so it always accurately represents the project in its current state.

CHANGES—PLANNING FOR AND DEALING WITH THEM

There is nothing permanent except change.
—Heraclitus

Even after careful planning and obtaining consensus from the project team, you may find yourself in the middle of a project that requires significant changes to the original plan. These changes are necessitated for a variety of reasons:

- A change in corporate priorities changes the priority of the project.
- A reorganization in the company requires staffing on your project to be adjusted.
- The board of directors dictates a cutback in expenditures, requiring the budget for your project to be significantly reduced.
- A major new competitor makes completion of your project even more imperative.

The list of legitimate reasons for changing projects is endless. Change is almost inevitable in project management. However, if you've done your planning correctly, you have a way of dealing with change systematically and rationally. Your project plan is your first line of defense when dealing with the uncertainty of project change. If the original project plan is complete and well documented, the impact of changes to it can be assessed and clearly documented.

In spite of the countless reasons for making changes, there are really only four factors that can affect a project plan: changes in goals (or objectives), staffing levels, budget allocations, and schedules. Each of these affects other aspects of the plan, as was documented in the first six chapters of the book. In essence, making a change to a project is a matter of replanning it to accommodate the change.

A change in staff will likely affect the schedule and perhaps the budget. A change in schedule may affect the budget and the staffing requirements. A change in budget may affect the objectives that can be accomplished, and this will affect everything else in the plan in some way. A project is an interrelated system. As you know well by now, you can't change one part of the system without affecting the others.

To make a change in a plan, the project manager must work through the original interrelationships in the plan and adjust everything that will be affected by the change. As these adjustments are made, each change is documented clearly, so they can be communicated to managers and team members alike.

Now, this all sounds relatively straightforward—if you make a change to the project, you make a change to the plan. In theory, it is straightforward; but project management most often fails when managers don't take time to understand the impact that one change has on the rest of the project plan. And, when these changes aren't communicated through the organization, other people still expect the original results from the project, even though changes have been made.

A Simple Case Study Makes the Point

Let's review a situation with the sales office project for a moment to illustrate how changes can affect a plan. Ingrid, the Vice President of Sales runs into Roger's office and frantically explains that the sales office must get done two weeks earlier because an important investor wants the office opened immediately to support the West Coast before he will invest in the company. Ingrid explains that the CEO has promised to have the office opened by July 15. Ingrid is frantic. She unfortunately told her boss, the CEO, that it would be okay, but she has no idea if it is possible or not. Now, Roger must figure out what to do, since he is the project manager for the sales office project.

Roger has two choices. He can agree to get the project done according to the new schedule and let everyone believe that the project will be done as originally specified, only two weeks earlier. If he does this and the sales office can't be opened on time, he will have committed himself, and his project team, to failure. Fortunately, Roger says he'll get back to Ingrid by the end of the day. He then changes his schedule and takes a few hours and reviews the project plan to understand the impact of the schedule change on the rest of the project.

Since the project is already in progress, he sits down with each of the key team leaders in the project and discusses the situation. After manipulating the tasks, assignments, priorities, and assumptions, the team realizes that there is a way to get things done earlier, but it will cost a bit more money.

Since the office has already been selected, Dave says it may be possible to expedite the signing of the contract and hire additional contractors on a rush basis to speed up the build-out of the office space. This will cost more than originally planned, but could shave two weeks from the critical path of the schedule. Dave has to make this his first priority. The phones, signs, and stationery will then become the problem. Since the office has to have phones, their priority will be moved up. This requires a change in Jennifer's schedule, and she has to re-prioritize other projects she is working on. The office can wait for a sign, however, which will be installed later. Everything else on the project will remain as originally scheduled, including the announcement opening party. Dave comes back a few hours later and verifies that for an additional $8,800 he can get the office built out in time.

Roger documents all the changes in a memo to Ingrid and the CEO. A new schedule and budget are included that compare the original schedule and budget to the new plan. (We provided examples of the new schedule and budget in the last chapter to demonstrate project progress reports. Now you know where the changes came from.)

Roger asks for approval to proceed with the new plan. The CEO grumbles about the increase in costs, but goes ahead and approves it anyway. What choice is there? He has already committed the date to the investor.

Imagine what could have happened if Roger hadn't reconsidered the plan before going ahead with the new schedule. When the increased costs were tallied and the signs weren't ready, he would have been blamed. Without communicating the impact of the schedule change on other aspects of the project, both Ingrid and the CEO would expect the rest of the plan to be implemented as originally planned—and that simply wasn't possible with the change in priorities. Roger's staff would have been angry at not being informed or involved in the decisions, as well, and might have undermined the project or refused to support the new schedule.

Instead, Roger took control of the situation, in spite of the CEO and Ingrid who already committed to the changes without checking. Roger could have been angry at them for doing this, and deep down he was, but instead of refusing to implement the changes, he came up with a rational approach that accomplished the major objective of adjusting the opening date for the office without compromising other aspects of the project.

Project Management Tip

✎ **Project Management Proverbs to Remember When Dealing with Problems and Changes**—Dr. Harold Kerzner included these proverbs, of unknown origin, in his comprehensive volume *Project Management: A Systems Approach to Planning, Scheduling, and Controlling* (Van Nostrand Reinhold, 1989). They are a distillation of project management wisdom.

- You can't produce a baby in one month by impregnating nine women.
- The same work under the same conditions will be estimated differently by ten different estimators or by one estimator at ten different times.
- The most valuable and least used word in a project manager's vocabulary is "No."
- You can con a sucker into committing to an unreasonable deadline, but you can't bully him into meeting it.
- The more ridiculous the deadline, the more it costs to meet it.
- The more desperate the situation, the more optimistic the player.
- Too few people on a project can't solve the problems—too many create more problems than they solve.
- You can freeze the user's specs but he won't stop expecting.
- Frozen specs and the abominable snowman are alike: they are both myths, and they both melt when sufficient heat is applied.
- The conditions attached to a promise are forgotten, and the promise is remembered.
- What you don't know hurts you.

THE RULES IN MAKING PROJECT CHANGES

This simple example based on the newsletter project illustrates some of the basic rules dealing with changes in a project including:

- Never get angry when your boss comes in and asks you to make changes. It won't do any good. Ask questions and try to understand the rationale for the changes. Concentrate on understanding the need for the change, not on less productive, negative behaviors. If you can see alternatives to the change that would have less negative impact on the project, suggest them.

- Never commit to the changes until you understand the impact they will have on the project. Always ask for time to review the plan and look at alternatives.
- Always know that there is more than one way to complete a task or sequence of tasks to accomplish an objective.
- Always get team members involved when alternatives and adjustments are required. If you don't do this, the team won't understand or support the changes. Besides, the people closest to the work are best suited to offer their opinions on other ways to get things done.
- Always work from the original plan and document the changes in relationship to the plan. The current project plan is always the baseline for making comparisons and analyzing alternatives.
- Always consider the impact on the entire plan, not just the component that is being changed.
- If changes in objectives, schedules, or budgets are involved, always ask for approval of the new plan before proceeding, unless you have authority to make the changes on your own.
- Always evaluate the risks associated with the new plan and make sure they are documented and communicated to the decision makers.
- Always make sure the changes are clearly communicated to the entire project team after they are approved.

TRADE-OFF ANALYSIS—HOW TO DECIDE WHAT CHANGES TO MAKE

The world hates change, yet it is the only thing that has brought progress.
—C. F. Kettering

A step-by-step methodology is helpful to understand the trade-offs in making project changes. In any analysis of project changes, three fundamental parameters are involved: time, cost, and performance. Understanding the trade-offs in a project change are always a matter of understanding the impact a change to one parameter has on the others. The following steps summarize an easy-to-follow method for analyzing project changes. During each of the steps in the trade-off analysis it is important to get the project team, functional managers, and customers (when appropriate) involved to determine their views and priorities regarding the impact of the problems and changes.

Trade-off Step 1. Gather information on the problems or the change.

Determine the reason for the problem or situation that is motivating the requirement for a change. The underlying rationale behind making changes

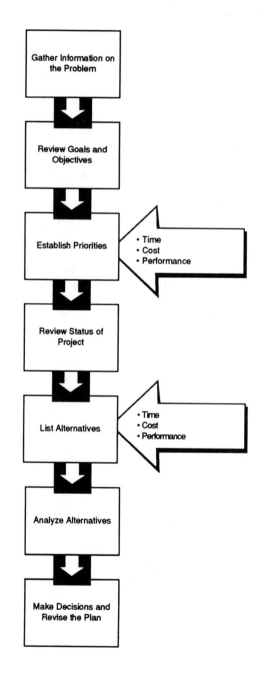

Figure 8-1 The Tradeoff Analysis Process in Project Management

in the project must be fully understood before the best decision can be made. Are the problems related to human errors or failures, unexpected problems, or outside environmental changes? Are the changes required because the project isn't going as planned or because the plan has fundamental flaws? Why are the changes required now but weren't when the project was originally planned?

Trade-off Step 2. The project goals and objectives should be reviewed.

It is important to verify that the project goals and objectives are still valid and appropriate, in light of the new problems or environment conditions. If changes and modifications to the goals are required, this is the time to do it, so the rest of the project plan can be adjusted to fit the new requirements.

Trade-off Step 3. Establish the relative priorities for time, cost, and performance criteria in the project.

If the project has high priority in the company, determine the impact of project changes on the firm's profitability and strategic plan. Is a cost overrun acceptable? Would it be better to change the specifications for the completed project? What would be better, incurring more costs or being late? Would "crashing" costs be appropriate in order to shorten the time required to complete the project? Without answers to these questions, the course of action cannot be determined.

Trade-off Step 4. Review the status of each aspect of the project.

Review schedules, quality of work, work priorities of team members, task sequences, and costs. Make sure the information is current and complete. If you've been doing your job in monitoring the project up to this point, this step shouldn't be any extra work.

Trade-off Step 5. List alternatives that will accomplish the objective of the changes or solve the problems.

This is a good time for a brainstorming session with the project team. List out every alternative you and the team can think of. Be creative. Don't hold back.

Depending on the problems facing the project, all project modifications involve one or more of the following general options. These options can be mixed and matched in various degrees to accomplish the desired result:

- **Hold the performance specifications for the project constant.** In this option, the goals and objectives are kept constant. This may require additional resources to make the original date, and thus increase the budget for the project as well. In some cases, the schedule may be lengthened or otherwise modified to maintain performance without adding additional resources.

- **Freeze the budget for the project.** If the budget is fixed, typically the first thing that is impacted is the performance specifications or goals for the project. In addition, adjustments to the schedule may be required.

- **Freeze the schedule for the project.** This may require adjustments to the specifications of the project, the budget, or both.

- **Adjust a combination of goals, budget, and/or schedule.** This is a matter of adjusting everything or some combination of the three factors to arrive at a compromise project plan that optimizes budget, schedule, and performance criteria. This is the most complex type of change to make, so it is best to look at the impact of each individual change first, before combining them into a new project plan.

- **Change the project team.** This may include training existing team members, adding people, changing assignments, or shifting staff priorities. The impact on the schedule and budget and specifications of the project will depend on the changes required.

- **Add equipment.** Additions or changes in equipment may solve performance and schedule problems in production-oriented projects, but sometimes have a significant impact on the budget.

- **Change operating and administrative procedures.** Sometimes excessive reporting or unnecessary administrative procedures can bog a project down. Simple changes in reports, meetings, or other procedures can often free up time that would be better spent on completing project tasks, thus minimizing the requirement for schedule changes.

- **Scrap part or all of the project.** This reduces budget and schedule requirements and affects performance criteria. If the project goals and objectives are changed radically, a completely new project plan is in order. If the project is scrapped because of new corporate priorities or environmental changes, then the current project must be terminated, as described in the next chapter.

Trade-off Step 6. Analyze the alternatives.

Use charts and graphs like those used to create the original project plan. Analyze the impact of each viable alternative. Make sure management and team members are involved in this analysis. A ranking system like the one used to prioritize projects in Chapter One is a useful approach in analyzing alternatives. Complete a risk analysis of each change as well, before determining the best alternative.

Trade-off Step 7. Make the decision and revise the project plan.

The changes should be documented and approved, just like the original project plan.

DEALING WITH RESISTANCE TO PROJECT CHANGES

Unfortunately, implementing the changes in a project is not always as simple as changing the plan. Change is a common source of tension and resistance in projects. Resistance to change is a common and natural reaction of human beings when they're asked to do something in a new or different way. Some of this resistance comes from the planning that goes into a project in the first place. People become attached to the plan and may reject alternatives that alter the outcomes or sequences that are originally approved for a project. Resistance to change in a project also comes from political self-interest, misunderstandings about the reason for the changes, and fear of the unknown.

You know you are dealing with resistance to change when you hear things like, "But we've always done it this way," or "We already planned it that way and that's the way we're going to do it," or "Let's talk about something else, things are going just fine the way they are," or "I liked the plan better before." The manifestations of resistance to changes include attitudes of skepticism, lethargy, procrastination, and declining performance in general.

Changes to a project plan must be communicated effectively, understood by the people affected, and accepted as necessary and appropriate. (See Figure 8-2.) If all three of these actions are not fully accomplished, it is unlikely that the change will be effectively implemented.

Here are some tactics for dealing with resistance to project changes:

- Openly discuss any tensions or frustrations associated with making a change to the project. This may be done in a group setting or in one-on-one meetings, depending on the personalities of the players involved.

- Use your leadership abilities to motivate enthusiasm and shared vision for the changes. If you have developed the positive, communicative relationships with your project team as emphasized in the last chapter, your project team will naturally follow your lead.

- Focus people on the positive aspects of the changes and minimize the negative impacts when possible, but at all costs be honest about the situation.

- Clearly define any new expectations, measurement criteria, or rewards that are associated with the changes. Be tough when you need to be.

- Don't let personal agendas get in the way. Accept the change and let your team know that you are supportive of the new direction. Remember that your team will follow your lead in the wrong direction if that's where you point them.

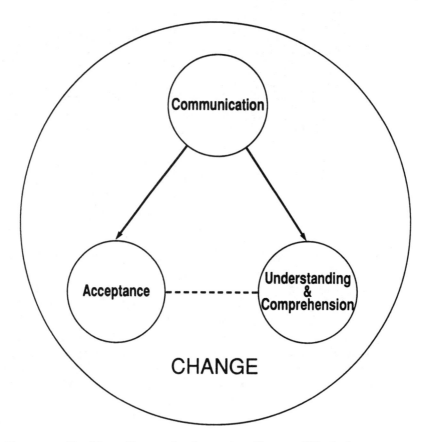

Figure 8-2 The Three Keys to Implementing Changes Effectively

---

Project Management Tip

✎   **Creative People Get Bored with Rounds of Changes**—The most difficult people to control are often the most creative. Depending on the project, they may be programmers, engineers, writers, illustrators, or architects. Many of these people are poor time managers (the more creative the individual, the worse they are at responding to time and budget commitments), and making them do the same work over and over bores them. Forcing creative people to make rounds and rounds of miniscule changes to a job will frustrate them quickly. As a result, the work they come back with each time will contain less creativity and may lack accuracy. Avoid this problem by keeping other team participants and managers away from their work whenever possible. Limit the number of change cycles and corrections to no more than two or three—and only to those that are absolutely necessary.

CONFLICT IN PROJECTS—WHERE IT COMES FROM AND HOW TO MANAGE IT

Conflicts are as inevitable in projects as changes are. Projects always involve many interactions between people and groups—even small projects. When the people involved in a project interact during the course of completing their tasks, there is always a potential for conflict. In fact, it is virtually impossible for people to work together, make decisions, and attempt to meet objectives without conflict.

In the past, managers thought of conflict as something to be avoided, caused by the failure of leadership or by personality defects. But, in contemporary project thinking, and management theory in general, it is understood that conflicts and disagreements in a project are not only unavoidable, they are also desirable in most cases. A project without conflicts is a project without priorities. If something is not at stake, there can be no conflict. Conflict between people is evidence of commitment and caring. People argue about things they care about. If the project is important enough to do in the first place, then there should be differing opinions and attitudes about the work and how it should be done.

Even though conflict itself is desirable and expected, the results of conflict can be either good or bad for a project. Conflict can result in positive choices and changes in the project. Conflict can inspire new thinking and creativity. Conflict can help identify problems that would otherwise remain unknown to a project manager. Conflict can also degrade into negative behaviors that reduce the performance and motivation of people working on a project. Conflicts left unchecked can cause undue stress and an unproductive atmosphere.

When confronted with conflict, it is obviously the positive outcomes that are desired. Conflict must be managed to positive conclusions. In all conflicts it is the project manager's responsibility to guide contrary thinking into positive agreements. In fact, some project managers instigate conflicts by pushing dates and demanding results that encourage team members to be creative in their approach to solving problems and achieving project results. (Make sure you have the skills to manage this before you try it.)

Conflict can occur at four levels in a project—at the intrapersonal, interpersonal, intergroup, or intragroup level. Intrapersonal conflicts stem from personal or professional expectations that are not met. As long as intrapersonal conflicts don't become projected onto other people, they may not affect the project at all—except to impact the motivation and productivity of a particular individual. Interpersonal conflict can be between specific team members or between one person and an entire group. Interpersonal conflicts are most often based on differences in personality, style, communication skills, or competing personal aspirations.

Group conflict can be either **intergroup** or **intragroup** in nature. In other words, between groups of people in the project team or between the project team and groups outside of the project. When one team or group is pitted against another, there are usually some interpersonal conflicts involved as well. In fact, individuals are at the root of all conflicts in projects—despite the underlying reason for the conflict.

The reasons for conflicts in a project, whether group oriented or interpersonal, are many. The most common project conflicts fall into the following categories:

- **Goal incompatibility.** Goal conflicts involve differences in project priorities and the criteria for evaluating task accomplishment. Differing opinions about the sequence of tasks and events are also goal conflicts. Functional managers and project managers may have very different goals, expectations, and performance criteria as well, causing conflicts between project tasks and functional responsibilities.

- **Task uncertainty and information requirements.** The higher the degree of task uncertainty, the higher the possibility of conflicts over the task and the information required to complete the task. If tasks are relatively routine, the source of conflict will usually be centered on who completes the task rather than how it should be handled.

- **Administrative procedures.** The frequency, number, and content of reports and forms are common sources of conflict in projects. Disagreements about the levels of administrative support required for a project are also typical. In addition, people may disagree about the report recipients and how the reports should be used in managing the project.

- **Role uncertainty.** The relative responsibilities and authorities of the project manager, team members, and line managers in an organization are a constant and regular source of conflict, especially in matrix organizations.

- **Technical alternatives.** People often disagree on the best way to do things. If new technologies are involved, the conflicts are more intense and the players more opinionated.

- **Staffing.** How many people are required? Where do the people come from? How many people can we hire? Who has to do the "grunt" work and who gets the "fun" tasks? The answers to these staffing questions are usually controversial and open to heated debate.

- **Resource allocations.** The people allocated to a project may be a source of conflict, because other groups may need the same people for their work. The equipment or facilities allocated to a project may be a source of similar conflicts, especially if space and equipment are in short supply.

- **Budgets and costs.** Is there ever enough money for anything? And don't projects always cost more than they should? Budgets and costs are a frequent and insidious source of conflict for all kinds of projects.

- **Schedules.** People invariably have different ideas about the length of time required to complete a task. The schedule is thus a constant

source of conflict and anxiety. Tension also centers on the sequencing
and priorities of schedule items, especially when people must prioritize
one project's activities ahead of those of another project.

- **Personalities.** Styles, attitudes, and egos are guaranteed to clash at
  some time, even among friends. And when you add power, self-esteem,
  motivations, and status to the equation, you're likely to see firework
  displays where the project team used to be.

All these potential conflicts can be summarized as one of three types:
goal-oriented conflicts that have to do with end results, priorities, and objectives;
authority-based conflicts that are based on questions about who has the authority
and responsibility for tasks, functions, and decisions; and interpersonal conflicts
that stem from the different work styles, egos, and personalities of the participants.
It is common for a particular conflict situation to be based on two or more
types of conflict.

The sources for conflicts include the project team, the clients or customers
for the project (if there are any), and functional managers, senior managers,
and other departments in the organization that are not directly part of the
project team. Any and all of these sources can be involved in a conflict.

CONFLICTS OVER THE LIFE CYCLE OF THE PROJECT

In research it has been shown that the sources and intensity of conflicts
have a specific and predictable pattern over the course of the project life cycle.
During the project initiation phase of the project, when goals are being set
for the project, most conflicts concern goals and authority for the project. (See
Figure 8-3.) Costs of the project are controversial at the onset of project planning.
As the project enters the planning stage, most of the conflicts center on priorities
and schedules, and as the plan takes more form, conflicts about technical
implementation and task sequencing issues become common. Personality conflicts
become more intense as each person tries to shape the direction and specifics
of the plan. Procedural conflicts are very common during the initiation and
final planning of the project, but become less important as the project proceeds.
During the main implementation stage, schedules become a greater source of
conflict, especially later in the project implementation as more pressure is put
on team members to meet date commitments. As the project is terminated or
phased out, personality issues often become a central aspect of conflict, as the
results of the project are evaluated and as the stresses and anxieties of leaving
the project become an issue.

Individual conflicts, of course, vary by project and the players involved.
But, if a project manager is aware of the primary sources of conflicts during
each phase of the project, many of the negative aspects of conflicts can be
eliminated by planning for them in advance.

TYPE OF CONFLICT	CONCEPT	PLANNING	IMPLEMENTATION	TERMINATION
Schedules	High	High	Very High	Low (unless late)
Priorities	Very High	Very High	High	Low
Staffing	Medium	High	Very High	Low
Technical	Medium	Medium	Very High	Low
Costs	Medium to High	Very High	High	Low
Procedures	Low	Low to Medium	High	Low
Personality	Medium	Medium	Medium	High

Figure 8-3 Conflicts Through the Project Life Cycle

THE STEPS FOR MANAGING PROJECT CONFLICTS

Though not a definitive methodology for resolving conflicts, the following steps are almost always useful in resolving project issues:

Conflict Resolution Step 1. Identify the type of conflict.

Is the conflict one of goals, authority, or personalities—or some combination of these issues? The conflict should be described in objective terms, with a minimum of opinion.

Conflict Resolution Step 2. Identify the players and the personalities in the conflict.

Who are the people and/or groups that are contributing and fueling the conflict? All of these individuals must ultimately accept the resolution to the conflict, or it will continue and have a negative impact on the project.

Conflict Resolution Step 3. Establish the underlying cooperativeness and assertiveness of each of the players involved.

Conflict handling starts with identification of the two dimensions of cooperativeness and assertiveness. The degree of cooperation is the degree the person wants to satisfy the other party's concerns or make the other party satisfied. Assertiveness is the degree with which the other party wants to satisfy its own point of view or concerns.

Conflict Resolution Step 4. Determine the background information on the conflict.

Talk to the other players and listen to their side of the issue. If there are many people involved, get the various points of view before you get everyone together to resolve the conflict.

Conflict Resolution Step 5. Establish an appropriate conflict resolution mode.

The choice of an appropriate mode for conflict resolution depends on a broad range of factors, including the relative importance of the conflict, the time pressure for a resolution to the conflict, and the positions of the players involved. Conflict handling possibilities are based on the combination of assertiveness and cooperation of the other party in the conflict, and on the type of conflict being handled. These include:

- **Forcing the situation.** This conflict resolution mode involves overpowering someone with force or using one's position of power to promote one's own concerns at the expense of the other's point of view. Rationality does not always prevail in a conflict situation, especially when the two parties are both highly assertive and uncooperative. Logic and reason do not always lead to a clear solution that is agreeable between two uncooperative parties. If two points of view are so divergent that a common ground on which to bargain and negotiate is not possible, then sometimes the only answer is to use your position as a project manager to resolve the conflict. If an issue is vital to the well being of a project, and you know you are right, you must simply dictate the action that must be taken so things can move forward. This approach may also be appropriate during emergencies when quick decisions are required or when unpopular issues, such as cost cuts or staff cutbacks, are necessary. For most project conflicts, however, this is a mode of last resort.

- **Accommodating or smoothing.** This conflict resolution mode involves avoiding areas of difference and emphasizing areas of agreement. Smoothing is a form of appeasement because one of the parties is unassertive and very cooperative. It is also appropriate when the issues are more important than your personal position or aspirations. You can also use smoothing when harmony is important in the short term. Unfortunately, most of the time the conflict will reappear again in another form. Accommodations rarely offer permanent solutions to conflict.

- **Avoiding or withdrawing from the Conflict.** Withdrawal involves ignoring the conflict as much as possible. It simply means giving up in some cases. Both your own concerns and the other's concerns are ignored. If the problem is trivial or tangential to more important issues, then avoidance is a definite possibility. This is appropriate when the other party involved in the conflict is both unassertive and uncooperative. If someone else is better suited to resolve the conflict, avoidance can also be appropriate. Also, if people need time to cool down after a heated debate before other negotiation is possible, a short withdrawal can be in order. However, if the issue is of immediate concern or very important to the successful conclusion of a project, avoidance is the last mode you should accept for resolving a conflict.

- **Compromising.** When a compromise is arrived at, people have each received something in exchange for something else. The goal of a compromise is to reach an acceptable agreement and end the conflict. If your concern is important, but not worth the risk of more assertive modes, then compromise can be a good option. If a compromise is accepted by all parties, a resolution to the conflict will have been accomplished. The problem with compromises in a project situation is that important aspects of the project might be compromised in order to achieve personal objectives. Compromising, like smoothing, often results in only temporary settlements.

- **Collaborating.** When something is too important to be compromised, an integrative solution, called a collaboration, might be an appropriate resolution to the conflict. A collaboration incorporates insights from people with different perspectives and incorporates multiple viewpoints. Collaboration is a good opportunity to learn from others. Consensus and commitment are possible after a collaboration because everyone has contributed to the resolution. Collaboration doesn't work when the conflict involves mutually exclusive points of view or more than a few players.

- **Negotiating and problem solving.** Negotiation and problem solving, also called the direct confrontation approach, requires a give and take attitude between the parties, meaning that both parties are somewhat assertive and somewhat cooperative. Problem solving involves searching for solutions that bring some degree of satisfaction to all the parties involved in the conflict. In most cases, negotiation or problem solving is the favored technique in project management to resolve conflicts. Training in the procedures, nuances, and skills of professional negotiation are beyond the scope of this book. However, some additional guidelines for negotiating effectively are presented next in the section.

The Problem-Solving Negotiation

The goal of negotiation is to arrive at an acceptable agreement that resolves two points of view so work on a project can continue. Negotiation and problem solving may involve the other resolution modes of collaboration and compromise. Both parties must accept the end result of the negotiation, and ideally, neither party should feel that he or she is better or worse off after coming to agreement. In fact, winning a victory should never be a goal of true negotiation over a project—in fact, winning is an inappropriate concept when trying to resolve a conflict. The desired outcome of a negotiation is the optimization of overall project goals.

As in any conflict resolution mode, the conflict must first be acknowledged. Then, negotiation and problem solving can begin. The process starts with communication. Negotiations often start by establishing common ground or shared goals. The idea is to create some common point of reference for discussing the conflict. The problem must then be separated from the people involved. The problem should be clearly defined and agreed to by the parties in the dispute. The problem should be explained in objective, functional terms—not in terms of egos and personality traits.

When the problem is clearly identified, the alternatives can be listed for solving the problem. People should list as many as possible.

Then, using objective criteria, not opinions and attitudes, it is possible to rank the solutions—the pros, cons, and so on, to each. This process is very much like the trade-off analysis described earlier for dealing with project changes. The goal of negotiation is a win-win compromise that enables the project to move forward. Unfortunately, other people may play another game—where they want to win so you, and the project, can lose. This win-lose approach, along with psychological pressuring, threats, and other negative tactics must be identified early in the negotiation, so alternative strategies for working with these people can be identified. Body language is important in determining the underlying intent of a person in a negotiation, and a project manager needs to be aware of not only the words, but also the postures and nonverbal messages that are being used in a negotiation situation.

It is interesting to note that research has shown that managers see themselves as compromising or negotiating a conflict, while they perceive the other parties in conflicts as competing or forcing their point of view in a situation. Opponents are almost always seen as uncompromising. This point of view explains why conflicts continue in so many projects.

Conflict Resolution Step 6. Be decisive and take action.

Don't wait too long or draw the conflict resolution out needlessly. It is better to take action quickly than to overanalyze the conflict and make little or no progress. If the conflict resolution requires changes to the project plan, follow the steps for trade-off analysis, detailed earlier, before making the project changes. Ultimately, all conflict resolution tries to come to agreement on what should be done, who should do something, or how things should be changed.

THE MOST COMMON PROJECT PROBLEMS AND HOW TO DEAL WITH THEM

Many project problems and conflicts can be anticipated. Forward thinking is one of the best ways to minimize the impact of these problems. A problem anticipated is a problem avoided. Here are some of the most common project problems and some tactics for minimizing their impact on your project.

The Floating Start Date

Some projects just never seem to get off the ground because other priorities keep getting in the way. Unfortunately, even though the project starts out late, everyone expects the project to finish on the original schedule. Ways to minimize this problem are the following:

- Reanalyze the priority for the project. If you feel overburdened with day-to-day priorities, communicate this fact to your manager to see if an adjustment is possible. If it really needs to be completed as scheduled, communicate the problem to management and get someone else to start the project or adjust your own work habits to make time for it.

- Communicate the new finish date to management and team players. If you need to keep the original date, complete a trade-off analysis of project changes as described in this chapter.

- Analyze your time management skills and determine if you are wasting time on less important activities. If you need time management training, get some. There are many good books that offer guidelines for identifying the time traps in day-to-day work—get one and implement its advice.

Too Much Work, Not Enough Time

Committing to more work than is possible is a common problem for project managers. Things always seem to take longer than we anticipate. In a search for solutions to this problem, look into the following alternatives:

- Delegate more of the activities and involve other people in the prioritization and assignment of work. Many times project management problems can be traced back to the delegation of the work on a project, either by the project manager or other team members.
- Eliminate work that is not really necessary. Accept that not everything can be done. Always question the necessity of each task and project. Skip projects that don't count.
- Change the priorities for the work, so some things get done later than originally planned.
- Work longer hours, when this is an option. But don't do it for too long; otherwise, you and your team will become less productive and less motivated. All work and no play is a prescription for disgruntled project teams and late or poorly executed projects.
- Analyze your work habits and improve your productivity. Learn to work smarter, not harder.
- Learn to say, "No!" when someone asks you to do something else.

Too Many Reports, Not Enough Communication

Reports are not a substitute for one-on-one communications with your project team. Too many reports also bog projects down in unnecessary paperwork—and this affects quality, schedules, and motivation. To assure that reports are not substituting for communication, do the following:

- Make a list of all the reports being produced for the project, the people responsible, and the content of each report. Then, critically review each report and make sure it is really necessary. Also, make sure that the reports are as simple as possible while still conveying the required information.
- Create a card file, or tickler file, reminding you to visit key team members on a regular basis. Note the last date you spoke with each person. Write a note to yourself in your calendar or organizer to talk to specific team members each week or day, as appropriate.

- Take people to lunch when you have time and ask them how things are going. Informal get-togethers often result in more open communications.

- Keep your door open. There is nothing more intimidating than a project manager locked behind a closed door. Let your administrative assistant or secretary, if you have one, know when it is okay to visit you without a scheduled meeting in your office.

- Regularly execute management by walking around as described in the last chapter.

We Need to Get It Done Faster

Changing the schedule is a necessary response to predictable business demands, especially competitive pressures to get products out faster or to generate the revenue anticipated from the completion of a project. It's always good to consider faster alternatives for completing a project. However, to implement a "crash" schedule, you must consider the trade-offs in terms of other business priorities, the use of resources, and the costs of getting things done faster. The ways to do this were explained earlier in the book.

"Ninety Percent Done Problem"

One of the most common phrases seen on the status reports for complex tasks is "90 percent done." Unfortunately, this can give a project manager a false sense of security. What is hiding behind that 10 percent that isn't done yet? Why does it seem that 90 percent of the effort only takes 30 percent of the time required to complete the task?

When people estimate the completion of their tasks in a status report, many people are optimistic or attempt to look good on paper. If you see that 90 percent or some other large percentage of a complex task is completed very quickly, but then work only inches up to 91 and 92 percent over the next couple of reports, you know you have some problems.

To determine the status of 90 percent tasks realistically, spend a little time to investigate the scope of the other 10 percent of the work. Are there technical difficulties that the team doesn't want anyone to know about? Should the task be broken down into smaller, more measurable tasks?

The "90 percent done problem" is usually based in creative tasks where the actual solution to the task remains unknown or indicates a task that is too broad in scope to be effectively monitored. In either case, the task needs to be more realistically assessed and the work that remains to be done should be clearly identified. You can help the team do this by encouraging open communication and pointing out the problems with being too optimistic about risky endeavors.

Too Many Milestones—or Too Few

In every project there are key milestones that are accomplished. The completion of a key milestone is an appropriate time to review the entire scope, schedule, and budget for a project. These milestones should be identified early in the project planning process, as we documented in earlier chapters. Unfortunately, time to review a project in its entirety may not be allocated until a major problem or setback occurs. This can be easily solved by implementing the controlled monitoring approaches we documented in the last chapter.

On the other hand, it is possible for project managers to be so overzealous in their monitoring of the project that every accomplishment and task is evaluated and reviewed in meetings and reports. As we've stated before, make sure your meetings and reports are necessary before you spend all your time documenting and reviewing, and none of your time managing. Keep the goals and end results of the project in mind and in perspective.

Moving Target Objectives

Changes in project objectives are valid for many reasons, as we've stated before. But sometimes the changes in project goals and work objectives seem to occur every day when your manager walks in asking for this change or that change to be made. There isn't time to plan and adjust for all these changes, so you just don't bother to update the current plan.

Well, this is about the easiest way to end up with a project disaster that we know of. When changes are requested frequently and arbitrarily on a project, it is an indication of a lack of consensus regarding the original plan or some other political problem between your manager, the project, and the organization. There are some ways to save yourself in this situation, however:

- Make sure the authority for making project changes is clearly documented in the project plan.
- Don't start a project until the plan is approved by all appropriate levels of management.
- Don't promise to implement changes in a project until you have time to analyze and document the impact of the changes, and follow all the other rules for making project changes that were discussed earlier.

The Key Person Quits

It is often the case in project work that one person has the special skills that are central to the success of a technical project. There are two basic ways to keep this from becoming a major problem: (1) Keep the key person happy in the first place. Listen. Be aware of problems in advance. Most people don't just walk out—it takes time for them to become disgruntled. There is a reason for the dissatisfaction, then try to find it and fix it. (2) Cross-train people as work is completed on the project so the impact of the key person will not be as severe as it would be otherwise. If the key person works in isolation, then the impact of this person's absence could be disastrous. Make sure the key person is also part of the team and try to have someone work with this person to document the accomplishments.

Costs Are Spiralling Out of Control

Budget and cost control problems occur for many reasons, including a lack of skill or discipline in estimating costs in the original plan, inadequate detail in the plan which results in vague or inaccurate budget allotments, schedule delays that cause more resources to be used than planned, unforeseen technical problems, changes in material or service costs that weren't anticipated, and changes in the scope of a project that are not reflected in the updates to the budgets, among myriad other "justifiable" reasons.

Cost control and budget problems are more often the result of controllable factors, however. Most cost overruns are centered on inadequate tracking methods as well as poor planning. Cost overruns don't just happen, they are the result of poor communications, lack of control, inaccurate reporting, or inadequate documentation of project changes. All these problems can be dealt with through direct confrontation when budget problems first become apparent through diligent monitoring of expenditures during the project. The key to controlling the costs is to keep on top of them through regular monitoring and appropriate accounting controls. There simply isn't any other way.

Staff with More Enthusiasm than Talent

You may have a great group of people working on the project, but they just don't seem to deliver the quality necessary to make the project a success. Unfortunately, the most likable people are not always the most competent. If you choose people for their personalities alone, and not their skills, you can end up in a situation where a congenial team just doesn't get the work done. An objective skills analysis used to select team members at the beginning of the project can help eliminate this problem. (You may remember that we covered ways to do this in Chapter Four.)

Sometimes there is no way to know that a person won't work out in advance. If the person is willing to be trained and has potential, this is sometimes a solution—if the schedule can absorb the time required for training. If training isn't an option, then someone else needs to be found. A consultant or outside vendor can sometimes make up the difference, allowing the person in question to remain on your team in a lesser capacity.

Other times, you just need to cut the ties and it's best to do this earlier than later. This is one of the tasks that all managers dread and put off. It's difficult to choose between people or the project. In business, if the goals for the project are important, the project must take priority—no matter how much you like the person.

The Impossible Remains Impossible

In the development of a new technology or in other high-risk situations, there may come a time when the breakthrough that is required to complete a project just doesn't happen. In other projects, the budget and schedule may be so unrealistic that there is no possibility for completing the work as specified.

It is difficult for project mangers to admit defeat, but for projects like these, the best solution is to realize that some things just won't happen as planned. Like walking on water, some projects are outside the realm of possibility for ordinary people.

The best way to deal with impossible situations is to document the risks in advance before the project is approved. If you still find yourself caught in an impossible trap, in spite of your planning efforts, the best way to get out is to get out as quickly as possible. Prolonging the agony makes the problem worse and has brought many a company (and project manager) down in the process.

Politics, Politics

Put two people in a room and there is instantly a political situation. Politics in human situations are unavoidable because people always have different opinions and motivations. If the political attitudes are only annoying, but don't affect the end results, ignore them. It's only when political agendas start undermining project goals that they pose a problem. When this happens, treat the politics as any other conflict—and resolve the situation by following the steps we've provided in this chapter.

At this point, you have a bag of tricks for dealing with project changes and problems. Using these, coupled with the reports and processes covered for managing the implementation of the project, you should be able to guide your project to a successful conclusion.

In the next chapter, we will explain how a project should be brought into the final project management phase—the termination phase. Though this sounds ominous, the termination phase is a time to acknowledge your team's accomplishment of completing the project on time and within budget.

Chapter Nine

TERMINATING THE PROJECT:
Applying What You Learn
to Improve Future Performance

The implementation phase is complete. The project is done at last. Plans are executed. Problems have been solved. Conflicts have been negotiated or ignored. The team is content, delighted, angry, or disappointed with the results—this depends on how well the project was executed—but at this point, the project is finished, whether people are happy with the results or not.

After any project is complete, a crucial component of project management methodology is to review the completed project so things can be learned to improve performance and techniques for next time. This involves meetings and written reports, but most important, it requires the willingness and ability to answer objectively critical questions on the results of the project.

Assuming your project was generally successful, before you start analyzing what you could do better next time, take time to congratulate yourself on what you have accomplished. Your project is complete. You and your team members need to take a moment and feel the sense of accomplishment. Then, after congratulating yourself on a job well done, complete the termination phase of the project. This chapter explains the steps for wrapping things up and ways to use what you learned from the completed project to improve your management skills for the next one.

THREE WAYS TO TERMINATE A PROJECT

There are three ways to terminate a project: by inclusion, integration, or extinction. (See Figure 9-1.)

A project is terminated by **inclusion** when a project is cyclic or is so successful that its organization and procedures become part of the ongoing business. Inclusion can involve the development of a separate, ongoing entity

Figure 9-1 The Project Termination Process

in an organization like a department or division. For example, a project team that developed a new product together may be permanently organized as a new product development division after the success of an initial project.

A project that is terminated by inclusion can also become part of the regular operating process of a company. The newsletter project is a simple example of a project that is terminated by inclusion, because it will become part of the monthly production of the marketing communications department. Most of the team will be regularly assigned to the same newsletter tasks each month.

The main problem for project managers when a project is terminated by inclusion is the routine aspect of the project and the standardization and routinization of tasks that were previously considered exciting or new. This sometimes leads to motivation problems and conflicts with project team members who were previously committed and creative. The transition from project orientation to routine assignments must be handled carefully by the project manager.

Integration of a project means reassigning people and resources to new activities after the project is complete—in other words, people are reintegrated into the parent organization. Some of the end results of the project may become part of the general operating procedures of the company, but the team and the procedures used to manage the project are no longer needed when a project is terminated by integration. Integration is the most common, and most complex, type of project termination.

Project Management Buzzword

☞ **Project Murder**—The sudden termination of a project without warning for reasons not related to the project's purpose. This is usually done because of environmental changes, such as economic downturns, new competitive situations, or changes in business strategies that are unplanned and unpredictable. Murdered projects are difficult to terminate because people resent not being able to complete something that is important to them personally or still has value. As a result, you may find people trying to revive the project whenever an opportunity presents itself.

The main problem with integrating projects involves the people and their developed commitments and relationships to the project and their perceptions regarding their new assignments and roles. Another problem with integration is centered on passing projects on to new organizations. For example, a complex technical product in a customer site requires ongoing maintenance, even though the engineers consider the project complete upon installation. Manufacturing may be handed the end results of a project that designed a new product, but there are still ongoing updates and enhancements that must be completed by the original project team. Sometimes, it is difficult for people to remain committed to these ongoing aspects of the project, especially when the main goals have already been accomplished. Again, it is the project manager's responsibility to see that the ongoing details are completed with the same fervor as the original project. Some of the monitoring and review techniques used for tracking the main project can be used in evaluating the ongoing support of the project after it is integrated.

Usually projects are terminated after the goals for a project are accomplished and the major tasks are complete. But there are times when projects are terminated before completion. When a project must be stopped or canceled because it becomes infeasible or inappropriate because of changes in business priorities or plans, it is called termination by **extinction**.

All the procedures for terminating a completed project that are documented later in this chapter apply to a project that is terminated through extinction. The reviews, reports, and other details must all be taken care of, even though your motivation to do this may be low because the project has been canceled.

The reasons projects are terminated through extinction include the following:

- There are better uses for the people, money, and time assigned to the project.
- The project is no longer economically viable. This may be a result of a project that is costing more than expected, because the money ran out due to changes in the company's financial situation, or based on the determination that the projected payback is no longer adequate after analyzing new data on the true costs (or anticipated benefits).
- A technical roadblock was encountered that made the project infeasible.
- The competition came out with a new product that makes the current project inappropriate or uncompetitive.
- The goals for the project are too broad to be achieved.
- The end results of the project became available elsewhere for less time and money.

The list could be extended ad infinitum. Some of the reasons for extinction can be minimized by adequate project selection and planning in the initial phases of a project. However, other reasons, including economic, competitive, or structural changes in the business environment that were not predictable or anticipated, may force a project into extinction.

How the execution or murder decision is made and who makes the final decision to terminate an incomplete project depends on the problem and the situation. In some cases, the project prioritization techniques described in Chapter One should be used to help make this determination. Sometimes the determination will be dictated by company management or other responsible sources. To the extent possible, the reasons for termination should be documented in the final report. In a large or complex project, it is helpful to use a project termination committee to write the final reports and termination plans and to diffuse the anger and frustration associated with a terminated project.

Terminating a project through extinction is difficult for people, because the sense of closure and completeness is lost. For this reason, they may resist the process. Be understanding, but be firm. If the decision has been made to murder a project, it must be done.

WHY IS A TERMINATION PHASE NECESSARY?

People need to be acknowledged for goals that are achieved and feel like the work is complete. Because project managers need to evolve their skills for managing projects, the techniques, processes, and procedures used on one project should be analyzed so they can be adapted and improved in the future. These are the most fundamental and underlying reasons to terminate a project formally. In addition, the following tasks are part of the termination process for most projects and are necessary to bring projects to final closure:

- **Finalize all contractual commitments to vendors, suppliers, and customers.** This may include reports or final payments. It may also include letters thanking vendors for a job well done, when appropriate.

- **Transfer responsibilities to other people, if required.** For example, the end results of some projects are inputs for new projects to be managed by other people. Consider a project to design a new product, for example. Once the product is designed, the responsibility for it is transferred to the manufacturing department, where the product will be produced and distributed. The development of the ongoing production system for the product becomes another project. In order to make this transfer, there are reports, drawings, and documentation that must be completed before manufacturing can begin. These activities are all part of the final termination of the product design project.

- **Reassign people in the project and redirect efforts to other priorities or projects.** People may be returned to their functional areas or assigned new projects, or both.

- **Release resources, such as equipment and materials, so they can be disposed of or used for other work.** Some construction and manufacturing projects also require cleanup tasks to prepare the facilities for new activities.

- **Complete the final accounting of the project.** This includes totaling the costs, paying all the bills, and closing the books on the project.

- **Document the results of the project and make recommendations for the future.** There is more information on the final reports and documentation required for a project later in the chapter. The amount and detail of final documentation will vary, based on the size, importance, and issues associated with each project.

TERMINATING A SMALL PROJECT

In small projects, the formal termination can be a simple matter of having a meeting with the team to acknowledge attainment of the project goals and writing a brief final report on the project.

When the copies of the newsletter (from the newsletter project) arrived from the printer, Joe sent out a letter of acknowledgment and appreciation with a copy of the newsletter attached for each team member and their managers. He also had a brief, informal meeting with the newsletter team to thank them for their efforts. He could have used this meeting to start work on the next newsletter, but he didn't. This is because it is important for people to "feel closure" on one project before they start the next one.

This sense of closure is important in projects of all sizes. It is better to have the brief meeting to acknowledge completion of the project separated from other activities. It's true that work on the next issue will begin right away, but another time should be scheduled to hammer out the goals, schedule, and budget for the next issue. The project termination meeting should focus only on the accomplishments of the completed project, so people feel satisfied with the work performed.

The Final Report for a Small Project

A final report on a small project can be simple, but it is still important to analyze the things that were done well and the things that require improvement or additional work. At a minimum, a final report for a simple project should cover the following general topics:

- Summary of Major Accomplishments
- Analysis of Achievements Compared to Original Goals for the Project
- Final Accounting and Explanation of Variances from Plan
- Administrative Performance
- Team Performance (This section should be confidential when it applies to specific individuals and their performance.)
- Issues or Tasks that Require Further Investigation
- Recommendations for Future Projects of This Type
- Special Acknowledgments to Team Members

A simple one- or two-page format can be used for completing the final report on small projects. You should have the team members in the project add their own comments or complete a report form of their own, if you feel the project has issues that make this process valuable. Any problems or conflicts that remain unresolved should be documented. Any opinions people have about better ways to do things next time should be considered. A copy of the project manager's final report is usually given to the project team and to functional managers who contributed staff to the project or otherwise have an interest in the end results. It is often appropriate to include a copy of the final time line and expenses, compared to the planned time line and budget, with the final report.

For the newsletter project, Joe's final report comes out a couple of days after the newsletter is printed. The report is used to kick off the discussion in the planning meeting for the next newsletter. The newsletter will become a cyclic project in the department, since it will be produced each month. The specifics learned about the schedule, plan, budget, and administrative procedures for the first newsletter, and the subsequent ones, are used to improve and streamline the production process and the content of the project over time.

Though the newsletter project is a true project with a beginning and an end, it is also a unique type of project, because a similar newsletter project will recur immediately after the first one is completed. Eventually, its production will become part of the organization's routine. With projects such as this, it is still important to go through the entire project management process for each issue: planning, monitoring, controlling the implementation, and finally terminating each iteration of the newsletter. The process will become easier each time, and managing the schedule and budget will become automatic. However, the process should not be routinized to the point that people no longer pay attention to the project management methods. Besides, every project can be improved—even ones that have been completed successfully a hundred times. It's important for people to continue to search for better ways to do things and suggest creative improvements to the overall goals and procedures of a cyclic project, just like it is for any other project.

Even in routine projects, things change. Inflation affects costs. People change jobs or roles in the project. New people may be added, or the scope of the project may be expanded to include new goals and outcomes. To continue to develop a quality product, the project plan, including goals, schedule, budget, team members, and administration, should be reviewed for each iteration of a recurring or routine project. It is when people start taking the routine aspects of projects for granted that projects begin to fail.

The project management process isn't something you do once—it is something that needs to be integrated with your way of doing business. If you hear project managers saying things like, "We know this is the way to do it, because it's always worked in the past," it's time to reread this book to remember why you adopted project management methods in the first place. Inspiration, innovative ideas, and new thinking are always required to optimize and refine your project management routine.

TERMINATING A LARGE PROJECT

For large projects, the termination phase can be a time of stress and anxiety. Team members may have friendships and a sense of family. Some team members will be going their separate ways, adding to the anxiety. Termination of a long project with a close-knit team is always difficult, and sometimes complicated. However, the frustrations can be reduced if the team members are acknowledged for their current accomplishments and then given new assignments and challenges as soon as possible.

In the sales office project, for example, working relationships with the contractors and leasing agents become less important, and some of the staff will miss the interactions with these people. Some people's roles will change significantly after the office is open. Jennifer, for example, becomes the office administrative assistant, a new assignment. She has less autonomy and more routine assignments. She will now have to start answering the same phones she spent so much time choosing. The project manager must be very cognizant of these feelings and frustrations—because many members of the project team continue to work for him with new functional responsibilities.

When the sales office project was complete, Roger and his boss, Ingrid, were so pleased with the new office, they decided to give a festive party for only the project team a few days before the official opening of the office. Like the informal meeting for the newsletter projects, the objective of this party was to acknowledge the work completed and come to closure on the project. The party was like a "rite of passage" into the next phase of operations for the Western Region—a time for friends to revel in their accomplishments and look forward to the challenges of the future. Roger made a special point to let people know of the challenges and new jobs ahead, now that the new office is open.

Because some people fear leaving the security of an established project team or changing roles after the project is complete, it is often difficult to get the final details of a large project completed. For example, Jennifer continued to work with the furniture company on insignificant changes in the installation. She spent time worrying about new plans for the front room and maintenance of the facilities in general. Many of these tasks were not required or were drawn out over a long period of time. Most of the tasks were now the responsibility of the maintenance crew, but working on tasks similar to the responsibilities she had on the project gave her a sense of continuity.

After a couple of weeks, Roger initiated an informal meeting with Jennifer. He noted his appreciation for her work and concern about the office environment, but explained that he would like her to work on administrative priorities. He worked with her to put a list of new goals together. With this support, she made the transition to the new role and gave up her project duties from the past.

As a project manager, it is your responsibility to see that the project ends. The project manager should help the people involved with the project move forward into new challenges and opportunities. To reduce the stress associated with project termination, remind your team members of the overall

Checklist for Terminating a Large Project

DESCRIPTION	NEEDED?		REQUIRED DATE	RESPONSIBLE PERSON	NOTES
	YES	NO			
Close-Out Meeting	☐	☐			
Termination Plan	☐	☐			
Personnel Evaluations	☐	☐			
Close-Out Work Orders	☐	☐			
Audit Final Changes	☐	☐			
Pay All Vendors	☐	☐			
Close-Out Books	☐	☐			
Final Delivery Instructions	☐	☐			
Customer Training	☐	☐			
Notify Purchasing of Completion	☐	☐			
Equipment Redeployed	☐	☐			
Materials Returned to Inventory	☐	☐			
Staff Reassigned	☐	☐			
Close-Down Procedures	☐	☐			
Engineering Documentation	☐	☐			
Final Staff Meeting	☐	☐			
Final Report	☐	☐			

Figure 9-2 Checklist for Termination of a Large Project

goals that have been achieved. Emphasize the importance of the project to the business and their contribution in meeting the project objectives. Then, remind them of the new goals and objectives they have yet to achieve on other projects and assignments.

In addition to having a formal meeting, or even a party, to acknowledge project completion, a large project involves other formal termination tasks, some of which we mentioned before, including reassigning personnel; auditing the final expenses and closing the books on the project, archiving any drawings or other project materials; passing the end results of the project on to another organization (for example, setting a product up for manufacturing or installing the final product at a customer's site); informing other departments, including purchasing, finance, manufacturing, or whoever needs to know, that the project is done; and completing other miscellaneous documentation of the project. And, of course, there will be an extensive final report.

The termination tasks for a large project are not always clear cut. When such a project is almost complete, there may be a number of small details that need to be brought to closure. The project manager must decide when a project is "finished"—so it can move into the termination phase. Don't drag the closeout phase and cleanup details to keep the project alive. This is a common problem in large projects. Get on with it, because there are always more projects—and the next one will offer new relationships and new challenges.

When major goals for a project are complete, begin the termination of the project. Because of loose ends, the termination of a large project may be a miniproject in its own right, demanding schedules, priorities, and budgets. Identify the major steps in the project closeout and implement them as quickly as possible. Follow all the steps and methods for managing any other project.

For a large project, a checklist is useful in determining the requirements for termination. (See Figure 9-2.) An example of a termination checklist for a complex product development project is provided to demonstrate the kinds of tasks that might be required to terminate a large project. Of course, the checklist may include entirely different elements for other kinds of projects, but this example should give you the basic idea of what to consider.

THE FINAL REPORT

The final report for a large, complex project is more formal than is one for a small project. The final report is both a history of the project and a final evaluation of performance. The report for a large project may be ten or twenty pages in length—or even more for a megaproject that spans a period of years. All key team members should contribute to the report.

All the topics covered in the project report for a simple project, described earlier, should be included in the final report for a large project, but they are covered in more detail. In addition, the following elements are appropriate to include in the final reports for most complex projects:

- A summary of performance, conflicts, resolutions, and results of each phase of the project
- Analysis of organizational structure used and recommendations for retention of structural format or changes required in the future
- In-depth analysis of reporting and administrative procedures and recommendations for improvements, if required
- Analysis of the project management process as a whole
- Description of any ongoing activities involving project team members that will continue after the formal project is terminated

In each section of a final report on a major project, the procedures used in the project should be analyzed. Things that worked should be acknowledged. Things that didn't work should be explained. Recommendations for improvements in future implementations of the project methodology should be made, with clear examples and rationales for the changes.

THE PROJECT DIARY

Experienced project managers often keep a day-by-day project diary to learn from projects and to document progress. A project diary is a simple daily log in a bound notebook (use something durable) where the results of key meetings, accomplishments, conflicts, and interactions are jotted down informally for permanent reference. The key is to put something in the diary each day.

This diary is not formalized and may or may not be shown to others—but it becomes the basis for writing status reports and, ultimately, the final project report. If a project is a long one, reviewing status reports may fail to reveal key conflicts or procedures that were significant. A review of your diary will help you recall significant aspects of the project that you may otherwise forget.

When you analyze the weaknesses in your project and write the final report, ask yourself two simple questions:

- How would you do it differently next time?
- What would you do exactly the same way?
- Then, put these answers in your report—and bring the report out when you start on the next project.

Archive the Plan and Final Report for Other Managers to Use

In addition to a final report, the key aspects of the project plan and progress reports should be archived for future reference—and other project managers in the company should have access to them. Good project management systems document the past so others can learn from it. As project management becomes integrated into an organization, the documentation of past projects can be used as input for new project plans, budgets, schedules, and administrative policies. Conflicts can be anticipated, because the problems with similar projects in the past are well understood. These archives make the project management process more efficient and significantly reduce the learning curve for new project managers.

Those who do not remember the past are condemned to relive it.
—George Santayana,
The Life of Reason

TEAM PERFORMANCE EVALUATIONS

In some projects, termination requires that formal performance evaluations be completed for each member of the project team. These will be completed by the project manager or the team member's project supervisor. Most companies that employ pure project organizational structure for managing their projects have an established formal personnel review process for use when projects are terminated. These reviews are then used as criteria for raises, promotions, bonuses, and new assignments.

In some companies, the project managers in a matrix organization will also complete performance evaluations of a team member's performance on a project. In a matrix organization, this review may be completed separately from the functional manager's regular performance evaluations or incorporated into it as a separate section of the regular performance review.

Each company has different forms and procedures for completing these performance evaluations. There are many books already available on the best way to implement review systems in companies. These vary, depending on the size of the company and objectives of the performance reviews. Regardless of the procedures and formats used by your company, here are some of the things you should be able to document as part of a team member's performance on a project:

- Quality of work
- Timeliness
- Administrative performance
- Attitude
- Technical ability

- Consistency in meeting deadlines
- Cost consciousness
- Creativity
- Teamwork
- Communication skills
- Recommendations for improvement

UNDERSTANDING WHY PROJECTS SUCCEED AND WHY THEY FAIL

> *Lots of folks confuse bad management with destiny.*
> —Ken Hubbard

Formal project evaluations are important in terminating a project. However, besides the formal review of a project, every project manager needs to do some personal soul-searching to understand why a particular project went well, or why it went poorly. After the project has been complete for a while and the emotion is gone, stand back and look at the project and your own management skills as objectively and dispassionately as possible. What did I do well? What could I have done better? What do I still need to learn? These are the observations, if acted on and taken seriously, that will help you prosper, develop, and improve as a project manager.

The reasons for successful projects vary by industry, project complexity, personalities involved, and the cultural environment of the company. In Chapter One, we listed several general factors that contribute to the success of projects and project managers alike. That list probably makes more sense now that you have gone through the entire process and methodology on your own.

By the way, a project that is terminated for unforeseen changes in the environment is not a failed project; it is just a project that was not brought to fruition. Projects that are extremely late, come in over budget, use up too many resources, or finish with angry participants, dissatisfied clients, or disgruntled customers are projects that were not managed successfully.

There are several basic reasons why projects do not meet their three goals relating to cost, performance, and schedules. In fact, the reasons projects fail to meet their goals are exactly the opposite of the reasons projects succeed. These reasons for projects with less than satisfactory results include the following:

- Plans are developed that are too simple, too complex, or unrealistic.
- Major conflicts are not negotiated to positive conclusions.
- The leadership of the project is unskilled or inappropriate in style.

- Disagreements over goals and objectives for the project are never resolved.
- Inadequate monitoring and controls keep problems from being anticipated and result in late schedules and budget overruns.
- The staffing is inappropriate, insufficient, or otherwise deficient.
- Requirements for equipment and facilities are not anticipated in advance.
- Communication about changes in project goals, schedules, or budgets is not adequate, honest, or complete.
- No use is being made of previous recommendations to improve project management procedures.

All these reasons for project failures, and any others you come up with on your own, can be reduced in magnitude or eliminated altogether by following the project management methodology consistently. The methodology we have covered emphasizes planning, monitoring, control, communication, documentation, and flexibility, but nothing is more important than being consistent in following through with the steps. Though things will never go perfectly, if you are dedicated to learning through past mistakes and diligent in mastering the technologies and methods we have outlined in this book, your risk of failure will be reduced significantly. Then, you can enjoy the benefits of predictably bringing your projects in on time and within budget.

At this point, you have been exposed to the complete process of project management. You have learned how to complete project management calculations and develop diagrams, reports, and communications that will help you plan, monitor, and control your project to a successful conclusion.

In the last chapter we explain the options and benefits in using project management software to help you implement the administrative aspects of project management with less effort and more consistency. You will learn that there is an easier and faster way to apply project management techniques by choosing the right kind of computerized project management software for your business and projects.

Chapter Ten

CHOOSING A COMPUTERIZED PROJECT MANAGEMENT PROGRAM:
Powerful Options for Projects of All Sizes

Creating a detailed project plan and keeping it up to date for a complex project can be very time-consuming if completed manually. The complexity of figuring in vacations, holidays, weekends, early starts, and other factors can be overwhelming to someone inexperienced in project management techniques or short on pencils. The details involved in producing networks and work breakdown structures seem daunting, and assembling a budget can be tedious.

Just producing the plan is a lot of work for a large project. And, as you've perhaps concluded by now, project management entails more than creating a good plan. Successful project management requires relevant information to be obtained, analyzed, reviewed, and communicated in a timely manner. Ongoing presentation and analysis of project data must be complete to provide advance warning of imminent problems. This information is then used to assess the impact of changes on other activities, resources, and schedules. Ultimately, alternate plans are developed to keep the project on track toward meeting its defined goals. Producing the reports, updating the charts, and incorporating changes to a project plan along the way adds complexity and more paperwork. Of course, if you need to manage multiple projects at the same time, the calculations, graphs, and reports can seem impossible.

Instead of taking on all this graphing, changing, and reporting, businesspeople may simply reject project management methods because of the work involved. Instead, they choose to manage projects with intuition and guesses. But the benefits of the methods are too important to be ignored because the charts and graphs take time to produce. Today, thanks to the rise of the personal computer, there is a better alternative.

Because of the wide range of programs available for computers and projects of all sizes, there are no longer any valid excuses to give up on project management. With the right project management program, you can concentrate on the management of the project, with more time for thinking and decision making, and let the computer provide tactical support, in the form of charts, graphs, schedules, and resource allocations.

This chapter covers the basics of selecting and using computerized project management programs. Brief descriptions of the most popular types of computer-based project management programs are provided, as are comparisons of desktop programs to larger systems on minicomputers and mainframes.

WHAT CAN PROJECT MANAGEMENT PROGRAMS DO?

Efficient and inexpensive alternatives for creating plans, schedules, reports, and updates by hand are now available for anyone with a desktop computer. And, when you start managing megaprojects, there are mainframe and minicomputer programs to help you handle thousands of people, myriad equipment, and a hundred thousand tasks—not to mention track the multimillion-dollar budgets involved.

Project management programs, or project management information systems (PMIS) as the software is often called in large corporations, range in capabilities from simple scheduling programs that produce Gantt charts to prodigious mainframe applications that are integrated with a corporation's budgeting, marketing, manufacturing, personnel, and other management information systems. (See Figure 10-1.)

The underlying methods supported by project management programs are similar to those presented in this book. Depending on the capabilities of the program, you enter task sequences, resources, dates, and costs, just as described in the last nine chapters, and the computer calculates or modifies the schedules, budget, or resource utilization for you. Most programs even draw the networks or can convert one network format into another.

In addition to assisting you calculate schedules and costs, project management programs produce a wide variety of reports—from simple to comprehensive. If you have a special project management requirement like a custom report or chart, there is probably a program out there with the capability of producing the output you require.

Today, project managers have a large array of software available to help in the difficult task of scheduling, graphing, tracking, and controlling projects. Though it is clear that even the most sophisticated software package is not a substitute for competent leadership and skilled decision making, and by itself does not correct any task-related problems or human-centered conflicts, project management software can be a terrific boon to the project manager

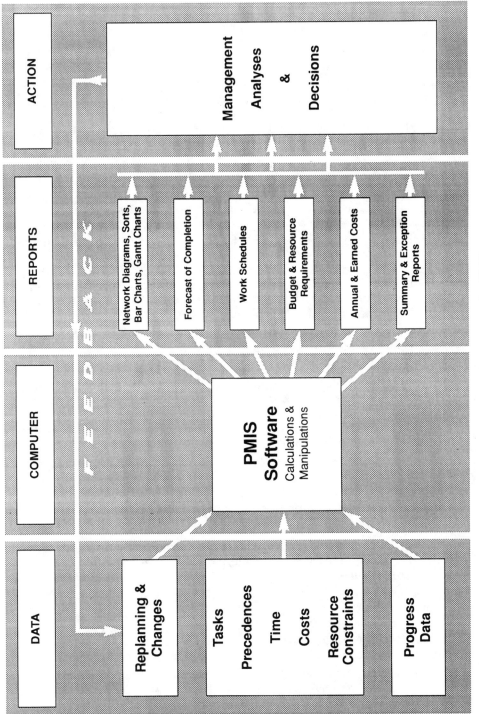

Figure 10-1 Conceptual Diagram of a PMIS

251

tracking interrelated variables, schedules, resources, costs, and tasks that come into play in project management.

Though not all programs do all the following things, common capabilities of project management programs include the ability to

- Graph costs, schedules, and resource utilization using Gantt charts, histograms, line diagrams, and a variety of other charts.
- Create standard and custom reports, including standard accounting and tracking, in addition to special report formats required by the government for projects with the Department of Defense (DOD), Department of Energy (DOE), and National Aeronautics and Space Administration (NASA), among others.
- Maintain resource and project calendars that record the availability of staff and equipment. These internal program calendars are used to determine optimum schedules. This feature allows the project manager to establish work weeks based on actual workdays and specify nonwork periods such as weekends, holidays, and vacation. The project calendar can be printed out in detail or in a summary format.
- Make schedule changes based on a variety of resource leveling parameters and priority scheduling attributes.
- Maintain skills inventories that match resources to task requirements.
- Track and schedule multiple projects at the same time. Some packages feature a single, comprehensive database which enables cross-project analysis and reporting. Cost and schedule modules share common data files which allow integration among projects and minimize problems of schedule inconsistencies and redundancies.
- Allow multiple people to access, input, and report on project data at the same time.
- Collapse the view of projects by work breakdown structure or organization structure subproject or milestone.
- Calculate and display the critical path for a network.
- Display alternative schedules, task assignments, and cost criteria, so the immediate impact of schedule, sequence, and resource changes can be evaluated.
- Assign early-warning parameters that let the program inform you of potential trouble, including schedule problems, resource conflicts with other projects, and cost overruns.
- Integrate with material management, purchasing, and accounting systems to assist in ordering materials, supplies, and equipment.
- Produce presentation-quality graphics for making reports to management and customers on the plans and status of a project.
- Display actual and planned data simultaneously.
- Summarize data in a variety of ways, including expenditures, timing, and activity data.

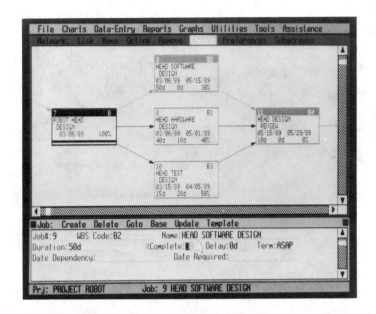

Figure 10-2 View a PERT or Gantt chart in various levels of detail. (Display from Project Scheduler 4. Reproduced courtesy of Scitor Corporation.)

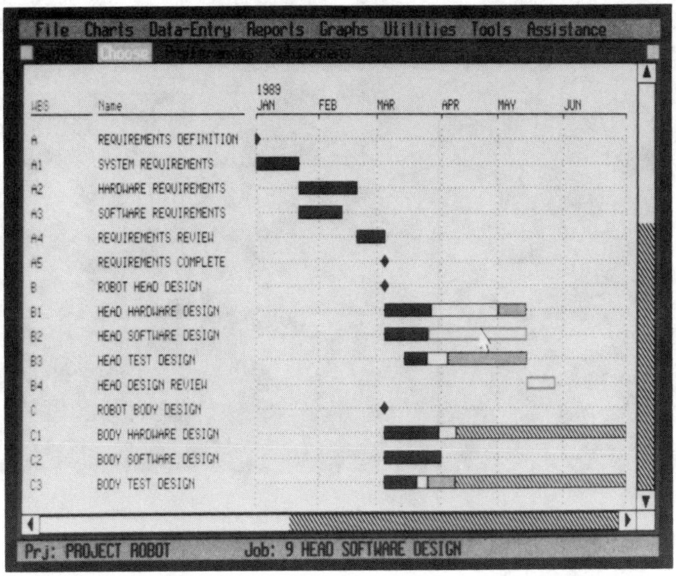

Figure 10-3 Flexible Gantt chart displays are available in most programs (Display from Project Scheduler 4. Reproduced courtesy of Scitor Corporation.)

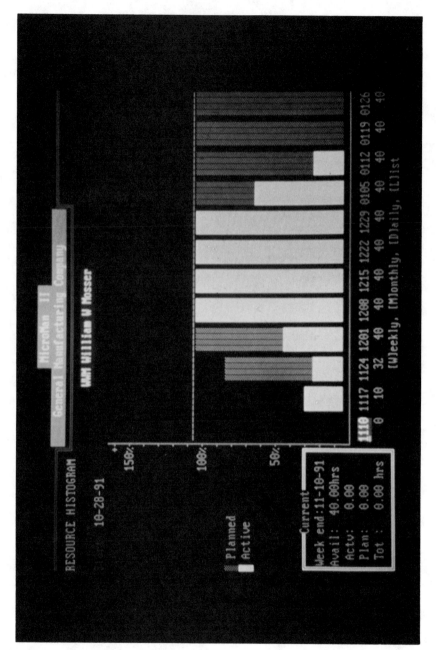

Figure 10-4 Resource leveling is simplified with easy-to-visualize resource histograms. (This chart from MicroMan II was reproduced courtesy of POC-IT Management Services, Inc.)

- Complete cost analyses, cost accounting, and variance analyses.
- Create free format reports with an integrated word processor or other report generator for incorporating personalized project annotations.

THE POWER OF "WHAT-IF" ANALYSIS

One of the most powerful benefits of using software to assist in the implementation project management methodology is the what-if analysis capabilities facilitated by interactive software products. Changes to the time estimates of individual tasks can be made and a new schedule is immediately displayed for review. The sequence in tasks can be changed and then put back the way they were, almost instantaneously. The same thing can be done with costs and resources. Imagine trying to do that with pencil and eraser. It would take hours. With a computer, it takes seconds.

To facilitate what-if analysis, many programs establish a separate, duplicate project database before changes are entered. The software then performs a comparative analysis and displays the new against the old project plan in tabular or graphical form. This makes it fast and easy for managers to review the impact of changes and come to better, more informed conclusions.

Trends in Modern Computerized Project Management

If you manage your projects using manual techniques, you will probably limit yourself to Gantt charts and simple precedence or PERT networks. Early project management programs were also limited to these simple displays, because they used "character-based" graphics. The imprecise resolution of character-based project management graphics makes it hard to build projects and more difficult to view results. For a project management software program to be considered for general business use today, it must facilitate interactive changes and support high-quality graphics.

Traditionally, project-driven organizations preferred mainframe software. Many of these mainframe programs offer desktop versions that can be integrated into a corporate-level project management system. Organizations that were less project driven, looked for less expensive, personal computer software that was either networked or not, depending on the size and consistency desired in project management procedures.

Mainframe and minicomputer programs, which are good at handling large databases and complex projects, tend to be more difficult to use and lack the interactive capabilities and graphic charts that are important in "what-if" analysis. Today, even for megaprojects, people are moving to desktop project management programs. The data from the desktop can often be sent to mainframe programs, if necessary, for integrating reports with other corporate information systems or for providing data on complex projects through networks to multiple locations.

Fueling the move to personal computer programs is the rapid improvement in personal computer graphics and user interfaces over the last few years. Color monitors are now standard in many offices, and not much more expensive than monochrome ones. The resolution of the monitors and the detail they display have also improved. And, with the improvements in printing technology, including high-quality laser printers and affordable high-resolution color printers and plotters, a project manager is no longer limited to grainy output on a dot matrix printer.

Modern project management software is graphic in nature. The best programs offer multiple reports, charts, graphs, colors, and printing options. Some programs allow you to display two or more charts at one time. This allows you to compare a time line and a resource utilization chart when optimizing a schedule, for example. The graphic interfaces employed by Apple's Macintosh, Microsoft's Windows, and other similar products are flexible and easy to use. Because modern personal computers are faster and more powerful, and continue to expand in processing capabilities, they offer many advantages to the majority of project managers in business.

THE TYPES OF PROJECT MANAGEMENT PROGRAMS

For purposes of easy classification, project management software products can be divided into four categories based on the functions and features they provide. These include scheduling programs, single-project programs, corporate-level programs, and megaproject programs.

Scheduling Programs

Scheduling programs are relatively simple software products, typically designed for people who manage small projects with only a few team members. These programs usually produce Gantt charts and work in a fashion similar to spreadsheet programs like Microsoft Excel or Lotus 1-2-3.

There are a large number of these programs available for both Macintosh and IBM PC and compatible computers. They typically cost less than $200 and offer little, if any, ability to report on resources or budgets. These programs are usually limited to producing a small number of charts and reports. Some of the programs allow you to enter actual data to be displayed simultaneously with planned data, others do not.

Choose a scheduling program if your projects are very schedule intensive but require minimal control of costs and resources. If your reporting requirements are simple, and your projects are small, one of these programs can be very useful. The good ones are easy to learn, provide color display capabilities, and offer a variety of Gantt charting symbols.

Single-Project Programs

A step up in sophistication from scheduling programs are full-featured software packages designed for managing single projects. These products are still relatively simple and easy to use, and their output is easy to understand. Most of them provide the ability to produce Gantt charts in a variety of formats, network diagrams (either PERT or precedence), and a number of standard reports. These programs sometimes offer simple resource management and cost control capabilities.

Single-project programs are best for projects with less than two hundred tasks. They provide only a limited analysis of the data, and since programs at this level often fail to provide automatic rescheduling based on specific resource changes, they are not useful for projects that require extensive staffing changes and "what-if" analyses. Programs in this category cost as little as $200 and are almost always less than $500.

Corporate-Level Programs

There are many programs in this category. Some of them are produced by well-known personal computer software companies like Microsoft, Computer Associates, Software Publishing, and Symantec. Others are produced by companies that specialize in project management programs like Primavera Systems, POC-IT Management Services, Lucas Management Systems, Scitor, and many others. (These and other companies and their products are listed in the sources section at the end of the book so you can contact them for information.)

These corporate-level programs extend the features already discussed for the other two categories of software and many run on personal computers. Others run on minicomputers or graphics workstations, and their manufacturers often provide a personal computer version for smaller projects. These programs typically allow sophisticated cost accounting, resource leveling, charting, and "what-if analyses." The specific features vary considerably—as do their ease of use, flexibility, and reporting capabilities.

If you intend regularly to manage projects with one hundred or more tasks, or coordinate multiple projects, you need to start looking at software in this category. Some corporate-level programs offer a beginner's and an expert's mode that allow you to start out simple and add functions and capabilities as your project management skills develop.

Corporate-level programs range in price from $400 to over $3,000 for a single user. Network, multiuser, or minicomputer versions, when available, can be considerably more expensive. The most sophisticated programs in this category may offer add-on modules for contract control or specialized reporting functions that rival the capabilities of the megaproject programs designed for mainframes.

Megaproject Programs

Megaproject programs, which may or may not have more features than the most sophisticated desktop programs, are typically designed for minicomputers and mainframes. There may be a personal computer version available that can share data with the mainframe program, but these PC-based versions are often difficult to use and lack the graphics sophistication of programs designed specifically for a personal computer. Some of the mainframe programs also lack the flexibility and interactive features of personal computer-based programs.

Megaproject programs can handle thousands of tasks and hundreds of resources. They almost always have sophisticated cost accounting modules and resource leveling functions. They are sometimes difficult to use and certainly difficult to install, but they offer advantages in processing speed and information exchange that are not available yet on personal computer networks. Most important, their success depends on a commitment from management to standardize on the program and use it consistently across projects. Mainframe packages (with sophisticated accounting and cost analysis modules) are priced from $50,000 to $150,000, and that doesn't count the equipment, training, and other implementation costs for a complex system.

If your project management requirements include the management of thousands of tasks or complex multiple projects with shared resources, adherence to government contract specifications, and integration with corporate accounting and information systems, then these programs may be necessary. These systems are designed for experienced project managers—and are not recommended unless they are absolutely required.

As features and functions continue to be added to the less sophisticated programs over time, the division between the types of programs is not as clear cut as presented. And with more than 200 different software packages available for project management, the evaluation and selection of software can become a tedious process. The requirements checklist provided here should be used to identify the kind of features you must have in a project management program—this will help you narrow the choices down to a specific category of software. (See Figure 10-5.)

For a more detailed report on project management software, write to the Project Management Institute. This organization produces a report that is updated regularly. (The address is provided in the listing of sources at the back of the book.) And you might want to join the institute at the same time so you can continue to learn about new project management techniques, conferences, and facilities. The organization is geared toward professional, full-time project managers, but there are many members who join for the general contacts and ideas the institute provides.

Other sources of information on project management programs are the computer magazines. *MacWorld, MacUser, PC World, ComputerWorld*, and many

Requirements Checklist for Project Management Software

Scheduling Programs

☐ Schedules

☐ Gantt Charts

☐ Presentation Graphics

Single-Project Programs

☐ Network Diagrams

☐ Simple Resource Tracking

☐ Actual versus Planned Reports

Corporate-Level Programs

☐ Tracks Multiple Projects

☐ Sub-Project Tracking

☐ Variance Reports

☐ More than 200 Tasks per Project

☐ More than 50 Resources per Project

☐ Resource Leveling

☐ Multiple Calendars

☐ Reporting by Milestone

☐ Reporting by Resource

Mega-Project Programs

☐ Integration with Corporate Mainframe Programs

☐ Over 2,000 Tasks to Be Coordinated

☐ Government Requirements for a Specific Program or Report

☐ Advanced Cost and Resource Accounting

If you check boxes at more than one level, choose a product in the highest category checked.

Figure 10-5 Requirements Checklist for Project Management Software

other computing magazines available in bookstores and on newsstands frequently run reviews of popular project management programs.

If you are looking for a mainframe or minicomputer program, or need a sophisticated corporate-level program for your division or company, you should look in your telephone book for consultants that specialize in project management systems. There are many consulting firms that can advise you in the selection of a program, help you install it, and train people after it is purchased.

SELECTION CRITERIA FOR PROJECT MANAGEMENT SOFTWARE

After you determine the category of software you need for your project management efforts, there are several critical factors for evaluating software you should consider before you make a purchase decision. As you complete the worksheet provided (see Figure 10-6), or one like it, consider the following factors:

Cost/Feature Analysis

Prices for project management software vary greatly. Depending on the kinds of projects you intend to manage, study the features of products under consideration to match your requirements. The most expensive products are not always the most capable. On the other hand, unless your budget is heavily constrained, rule out programs that skimp on features just to save a few dollars. A product that lacks basic functionality results in frustration, because it won't do what you need it to and after a couple of poorly managed projects, you'll once again be out shopping for software.

As you evaluate different products, add features to your requirements list that you hadn't considered before studying the software options. Don't make the mistake of selecting a package simply because it has more features at its price than any other package. Consider the other factors we discuss later in this section as well—but do make sure there are enough features for your current needs and those in the foreseeable future.

If you have the opportunity to evaluate products before purchase (either at a dealer's showroom or through a demo disk), try using the package to assemble a real project. That way you can test the package's reliability and see how it performs. Check also the program's speed when saving to disk, recalculating after new tasks are added, and printing efficiency. A program with a strong feature set that takes all day to print a network diagram is probably not the one for you.

Once you select what appears to be the right product, try to purchase it from a source that allows you a thirty-day money-back guarantee—that

Project Management Software Selection Worksheet

Product Name _____ Date _____

Price: List Price $____ Street Price $____ Dealer Name _____

Features 1 |—+—+—+—+—+—+—+—+—| 10

Ease of Use 1 |—+—+—+—+—+—+—+—+—| 10

Consistency of the Interface 1 |—+—+—+—+—+—+—+—+—| 10

Flexibility 1 |—+—+—+—+—+—+—+—+—| 10

Compatibility 1 |—+—+—+—+—+—+—+—+—| 10

Documentation 1 |—+—+—+—+—+—+—+—+—| 10

Reputation of the Manufacturer 1 |—+—+—+—+—+—+—+—+—| 10

Experience of Others with the Product 1 |—+—+—+—+—+—+—+—+—| 10

Technical Support 1 |—+—+—+—+—+—+—+—+—| 10

Training Availability 1 |—+—+—+—+—+—+—+—+—| 10

Distributor Knowledge (if applicable) 1 |—+—+—+—+—+—+—+—+—| 10

Overall Rating 1 |—+—+—+—+—+—+—+—+—| 10

Comments:
_____
_____
_____
_____
_____
_____

Figure 10-6 Project Management Software Selection Worksheet

way if the product performs poorly, or ultimately doesn't fill the bill, you can return it and try something else. If you purchase software through mail order, use a credit card. That way, you have more leverage returning the product because your credit card company may take your side.

When considering the cost of the software, don't forget the other system configuration requirements either. Will the program work on your existing computer or do you need to buy new hardware? What about the printer—is it compatible with the software you plan to use? Do you need to add memory to your personal computer or a new monitor to take advantage of the features? If you need to upgrade your system or buy a new one, add these costs together and put them in the evaluation sheet.

Ease of Use and Consistency of the Interface

All project management software takes time to be able to use it efficiently and effectively. One of the most important aspects of choosing software for managing projects is to select a package that's easy to use and responds consistently throughout its interface. For example, if you choose the most feature-laden package, you may acquire a product with a number of menus, commands, dialog boxes, and cryptic functions that not only get in your way, but actively interfere with laying out and managing projects. While, for the professional project manager, these are important functions, unless you have four months to learn the package, it may get shelved and never used. Such a package forces you into over managing even comparatively simple projects, thereby negating its usefulness.

Flexibility to Adapt to Projects of Various Sizes and Complexities

Because the projects in business vary from small to large, and from simple to complex, you want a package that's flexible in how it adapts to various project requirements. A package capable of handling the newsletter project should also have the power to manage the San Francisco sales office project with ease, and even more complicated projects involving more resources and longer time frames. You may find packages that easily handle the sales office project but are inefficient managing simple projects. Really simplistic products may have trouble handling anything more complex than the newsletter project.

Compatibility with Other Programs You Use in the Company

In many cases, you will want to take network diagrams and other project-oriented charts and combine them in other documents such as reports and presentation materials. If this is important to you, look for a package that can save or export images in a format compatible with the word processing, page layout, or presentation software you own or plan to acquire.

Documentation for the Program

Because your first point of refuge when looking for a solution to a problem in learning how to use a product is the manual, check the documentation carefully before purchase. Project management software may come with a user manual, reference manual, and a tutorial or a single all-purpose guide. You can usually tell how sophisticated the product is by the length and number of pieces of documentation that accompany it. Study the manuals. They should be well organized, have a detailed index, and provide plenty of screen shots showing how the product works; a lengthy troubleshooting section doesn't hurt either. Keyboard templates, quick reference cards, and disk-based sample projects are also useful. Complex products with skimpy manuals should be avoided at all costs.

Reputation of the Product Manufacturer

If you are purchasing an expensive product that will get considerable day-to-day use, check up on the company that designed the product. If the company discontinues the product or closes its doors, you will be on your own with the software. Look for a stable company with a strong track record of designing useful software and providing regular updates and bug fixes. Once a product becomes incompatible with the current version of your computer's operating system, project plans that could have been revamped for future use become unavailable if the software is not updated. Unlike spreadsheet, word processing, and graphics software, almost no project management packages can read files created by competing programs. In a company that produces a large number of project plans, the files may represent years of work and thousands of hours—so make sure the company will support what it sells over time. Also avoid Version 1.0 of project management packages whenever possible, unless you have the time to test the software before making the purchase. Software is notorious for being bug-laden and missing important features on first release.

Experience of Others with the Software

Talk to other users of a particular package to get feedback on how well the product performs with real-world projects. The users you query should use the package for projects similar in scope to the ones you plan to carry out. If calling references provided by the manufacturer, take anything less than a glowing tribute to mean that the product performs less adequately than expected.

Technical Support

When considering any software product, evaluate the technical support provided by the manufacturer. Find out if it's free or if you must pay an annual fee after ninety days. Does it provide a toll-free number, or must you listen to an automatic telephone system recite a long list of options before connecting you to a technician at your expense? Dial the number and see what happens. If you are fortunate enough to have other users to ask for recommendations, query them on the quality of technical support as well.

For sophisticated corporate-level and megaproject programs, the following factors must also be considered:

Availability of Training

To learn how to use a package capable of managing megaprojects, you will need training—even if you are already an experienced project manager. All packages work differently, and even an extended session spread over several weeks with the software manuals may not bring you up to speed. When considering such a package, find out if training is available, how much it costs, where it's held, and how often it's scheduled. Factor in installation, training, and travel costs to get a more realistic estimate of the total system cost before you decide to buy minicomputer or mainframe software.

Reputation and Knowledge of the Distributor

If you buy a program designed for a minicomputer or mainframe, you will likely buy it from a local distributor or private consulting company that represents the products. Make sure the distributor is accessible, knowledgeable, and reputable before you sign on the dotted line, as this will be your first line of defense when problems arise, and they always do with complex software.

So, which computerized tool is best for you? The one that meets your feature requirements, with the most flexibility, with an acceptable learning curve, from a reliable and supportive vendor, at a price you can afford. This is pretty much the standard formula for choosing any software or computer product, not just project management software, by the way.

THINGS COMPUTERIZED PROJECT MANAGEMENT PROGRAMS CAN'T DO

As powerful and efficient as project management programs are, many aspects of the project management process are not within the computer's realm. Using computer-assisted project management streamlines administration, reporting, and analysis, but the following are things the computer can't and shouldn't be allowed to do:

- **Project Management Software Can't Gather Data.** You will have to decide how much and what type of information you need to manage the project. You or members of your team will still need to gather data regarding the project status, as described in Chapter Seven. The computer only helps compute and display the information after it is gathered and entered.

- **Project Management Software Can't Make Decisions.** The computer can make it easier and faster to look at alternatives, but it is ultimately you and your project team who will have to make the choice between the alternatives and take responsibility for the decisions.

- **Project Management Software Can't Solve Problems that Require Subjective Judgments.** Sometimes human intuition is the most important ingredient in project management, especially when dealing with people. People require understanding. Software is programmed and not intuitive. It reports back only what you put into it. You still have to manage the conflicts and solve the problems and use your own judgment.

- **Project Management Software Can't Find the Errors in Your Input.** If you put biased, incomplete, or erroneous data into the project management program, it will output biased, incomplete, and erroneous project reports. Don't blame the computer for human error. The best way to eliminate this problem is to check the reports and entries multiple times before they are distributed.

- **Project Management Software Can't Do Your Communication for You.** Software is great at producing reports that look good and contain a wealth of detailed information, but there is more to reporting on a project than sending out the report. You still need to communicate with people face to face, building interfaces between people and departments, and listen to what is going on around you.

- **Project Management Software Won't Save Money by Reducing the Need for Project Personnel.** Automation almost never really reduces the personnel costs on a project. The software can make you more efficient and make decision making more effective because the information is better, but project management software will not significantly reduce the need for project management people.

Now you have been introduced to criteria for selecting project management software for your needs. Start talking to store personnel, reading computer magazines, and asking friends and colleagues about the programs they use. Then, go out, select a program, and get started in computer-assisted project management. Follow the step-by-step guidelines for implementing the project management process you have read about. As your projects come in on time and within budget, you will have achieved membership in the league of successful project managers—and the opportunities available to you and your company will take on new perspective. With each success, you will contribute to the business, the economy, and your own career—no mean feat for just learning a few project management skills. **Go for it!**

USEFUL RESOURCES

PROJECT MANAGEMENT ORGANIZATION

Project Management Institute
P.O Box 43
Drexel Hill, PA 19026

Project Management Institute (PMI) is an organization dedicated to the advancement of project management methodology and the training of project managers. The quarterly *Project Management Journal*, published by PMI, includes timely articles about project management procedures, experiences, and techniques. The institute holds regular seminars and meetings for members. As of this writing, the membership fee is $80 per year. A subscription to *Project Management Journal* is included for the membership fee.

PROJECT MANAGEMENT SOFTWARE SOURCES

The following companies sell or distribute project management software. This is by no means a comprehensive list. There are many other companies and products out there, and more being added every day. The ones here are either products we have worked with or ones that have been recently reviewed in the computer literature. Because companies are adding new products, the ones listed for a particular company may not be comprehensive. A listing in this book should not be considered a testimonial for the functionality or suitability of any of the products—it is only provided to get you started in your search for project management software. Most, but not all, of the products listed are corporate-level programs or above. Note that all product and company names are trademarks and registered trademarks of the respective companies.

Company	*Project Management Products*

Claris Corporation
P.O. Box 526
Santa Clara, CA 95052
Telephone: (408) 727-8227

MacProject II

Computer Associates International, Inc.
711 Stewart Avenue
Garden City, NY 11530
Telephone: (516) 227-3300
Fax: (516) 227-3913

CA-SuperProject
and others

Lucas Management Systems
12701 Fairlakes Circle
Suite 350
Fairfax, VA 22033
Telephone: (703) 222-1111
Fax: (703) 222-8203

Artemis Prestige,
Schedule Publisher, and others

Micro Planning International, Inc.
655 Redwood Highway, Suite 311
Mill Valley, CA 94941
Telephone: (415) 389-1420
Fax: (415) 389-8046

Micro Planner, Manager,
X-Pert

Microsoft Corporation
One Microsoft Way
Redmond, WA 98052-6399
Telephone: (206) 882-8080

Microsoft Project
Microsoft Schedule

POC-IT Management Services, Inc.
429 Santa Monica Blvd., Suite 460
Santa Monica, CA 90401
Telephone: (213) 393-4552
Fax: (213) 451-2888

MicroMan II and others

Primavera Systems, Inc.
Two Bala Plaza
Bala Cynwyd, PA 19004
Telephone (215) 667-8600
Fax (215) 667-7894

Primavera Project Planner,
Finest Hour, Parade,
Expedition, and others

Scitor Corporation
393 Vintage Park Drive
Suite 140
Foster City, CA 94404
Telephone: (415) 570-7700

Project Scheduler and others

Software Publishing Corporation
1901 Landings Dr.
Mountain View, CA 94039-7210
Telephone: (415) 335-2081

Harvard Project Manager

Strategic Software Planning Corporation
150 Cambridge Park Drive, 3rd Floor
Cambridge, MA 02140
Telephone (617) 354-1504
Fax (617) 354-8207

Promis, PromisLAN,
Project Outlook

Symantec Corporation
7200 Redwood Blvd.
Novato, CA 94945
Telephone (415) 898-1919
Fax (415) 898-1297

OnTarget, Time Line,
and others

Welcom Software Technologies
15995 N. Barker Landing, Suite 275
Houston, TX 77079
Telephone: (713) 558-0514
Fax: (713) 584-7828

Open Plan
and others

GLOSSARY

Action Plan A plan that describes what needs to be done and when it needs to be completed. Project plans are action plans.

Activity A specific project task that requires resources and time to complete.

Activity on arc (AOA) or Activity on node (AON) The two ways of documenting and drawing a network: placing the activities on the arcs or on the nodes.

Arc The line connecting two nodes or representing precedence in a PERT or CPM network.

Audit A formal inquiry into the progress, results, or some other aspecct of a project or system.

Baseline plan The initial approved plan to which deviations will be compared as the project proceeds.

Bills of materials The formal documentation of the complete set of physical elements required to build a product, which is used by the project manager or purchasing department to order any material or supplies that are required.

Budget decrement A reduction in the amount of money available for an activity.

Champion A person who takes on personal responsibility (though not usually day-to-day management) for the successful completion of "visionary project" or creative change in an organization. It may involve a product launch, an innovation in process, or any type of project.

Confidence level A level of confidence, stated as a percentage, for a budget or schedule estimate. The higher the confidence level, the lower the risk.

Contingency plan An alternative for action if things don't go as planned or if an expected result fails to materialize.

Control A process for assuring that reality or actual performance meets expectations or plans. Control often involves the process of keeping actions within limits by making adjustments to a plan to assure that certain outcomes will happen.

CPM Critical path method. A project management system described in Chapter Three of this book.

Cost-benefit analysis An analysis, often stated as a ratio, used to evaluate a proposed course of action.

Crash In project planning, an activity can be conducted at a normal pace or at an accelerated pace, known as crashing the activity of the project. Crashing is completed at a greater cost than a normal-paced project.

Critical An activity or event that, if delayed, will delay some other important event, commonly the completion of a project or a major milestone in a project.

Critical ratio A ratio that measures an important characteristic. This ratio is often plotted or tracked in some way to determine priorities among items or events.

Decision support system A sophisticated computer program to assist managers in making decisions. It may include simulation programs, mathematical programming routines, and decision rules.

Deliverables The physical items to be delivered for a project. This may include organization attributes, reports and plans, as well as physical products or objects.

Dependency diagram Another name for a network or precedence diagram that shows the dependencies (precedence) between tasks.

Early warning system A monitoring system that provides advance notification or indication of potential problems in a project. Many computerized project management systems incorporate early warning functions.

Effectiveness A measure of the quality of attainment in meeting objectives; to be distinguished from efficiency, which is measured by the volume of output achieved for the input used.

Evaluate To appraise or determine the value of information, resources, or options.

Event In CPM and PERT networks, the end state for one or more activities that occurs at a specific point in time.

Extinction The end of all activity on a project, usually before meeting its stated objectives. The end results of a project terminated by extinction are neither terminated by inclusion or integration.

Facilitator A person who makes it easier for other people to accomplish objectives by offering advice and assistance in solving problems, either with technical issues or with other people. Project managers are often referred to as facilitators.

Float The amount of time for a task to be freely scheduled without affecting other tasks in a project.

Functional management The standard departments of a business organization that represent individual disciplines such as engineering, marketing, purchasing, accounting, and so on.

Gantt chart A chart using time lines and other symbols that illustrates multiple, time-based activities or projects on a horizontal time scale.

Go/no-go Often a type of measurement that quickly tells a reviewer if an object's dimension is within certain limits. In the case of project management, this can be any monitoring or observation that allows a manager to decide whether to change, terminate, or continue an activity or a project.

Hierarchical planning A planning approach where each managerial level breaks planning tasks down into the activities that must be done at that level. Typically, upper-level planning establishes the objectives for the next lower-level manager's planning.

Inclusion A way of terminating a project by incorporating the project operations and team into the organization as a separate, ongoing entity.

Integration A way of terminating a project by bringing project team members back into the organization and distributing project results and outcomes among existing functions.

Interface management Managing the problems that often occur among people, departments, and disciplines rather than within the project team itself.

Interfaces The formal and informal boundaries and relationships among people, departments, organizations, or functions.

Lag The amount of time after one task is started or finished before the next task can be started or finished.

Lateral communication Communication across lines of equivalent authority or between managers at the same level in an organization's hierarchy.

Material Requirements Planning (MRP) An approach for material planning and ordering based on known or forecast demand requirements, lead times for obtaining each item, and existing inventories of all items.

Matrix organization An organizational structure that uses functional supervisors as well as project supervisors to manage the same people, depending on the assignment. A strong matrix is similar to a pure project organization, while a weak matrix operates more like a functional organization.

Milestone A clearly identifiable point in a project or set of activities that commonly denotes a reporting requirement or completion of a key component of a project.

Mixed organization This organizational structure includes functional groups, pure project groups, and perhaps a matrixed group, in its hierarachy. It is similar to a matrix organization.

Model A way of looking at reality, usually for the purpose of abstracting and simplifying it to make it understandable in a particular context.

Network A representation of project tasks connected by two or more lines or arrows, commonly used for depicting the sequence of tasks in a project.

Path A sequence of lines and nodes in a project network.

PERT (project evaluation and review technique) A project management system described in Chapter Three of this book.

Portfolio A group of projects or other items that are being worked on at the same time or have been completed and are used as an indicator of ability.

Pro forma Projected or anticipated, usually applied to financial data such as balance sheets and income statements.

Project Management Information System (PMIS) A system used to chart activities and data and used to track progress and information flow in a project that is most frequently computerized, but not always.

Risk analysis An evaluation of the feasibility or probability that outcomes of a project or policy will be favorable. Usually conducted to compare two or more alternative scenarios, action plans, or policies.

Slack See *Float*.

Split Dividing a task into two sequences or tasks.

Subcontract Delegating tasks or subprojects to smaller contractors or to other organizations.

Suboptimization The optimization of a component of a system or project, such as task sequence or schedule, perhaps to the detriment of the overall plan or project.

Systems approach A wide-ranging method for addressing problems that considers multiple and interacting relationships. This approach is often contrasted with the analytic approach. Project management is a systems approach to managing projects.

Termination team A project team responsible for wrapping up the administrative details of a project.

Trade-off Allowing one aspect to change, usually for the worse, in return for another aspect of a project getting better.

Win-win When both parties are better off in the outcome after a negotiation has been completed.

Work breakdown structure (WBS) A basic project diagram that documents and describes all the work that must be done to complete the project. The WBS forms the basis for costing, scheduling, and work responsibility.

BIBLIOGRAPHY

Aburdene, Patricia, and John Naisbitt, *Re-inventing the Corporation*. New York: Megatrends Ltd., 1985.

Belasco, James A., Ph.D. *Teaching the Elephant to Dance*. New York: Crown Publishers, 1990.

Collins, Eliza G. C. and Mary Anne Devanna. *The Portable MBA*. New York: John Wiley & Sons, 1990.

Dinsmore, Paul C. *Human Factors in Project Management*. New York: AMACOM, 1990.

Gray, Clifford F. *Essentials of Project Management*. Petrocelli Books, 1981.

Kerzner, Harold, Ph.D. *Project Management: A Systems Approach to Planning, Scheduling, and Controlling*. New York: Van Nostrand Reinhold, 1989.

Kotter, John. *The Leadership Factor*. New York: Macmillan. 1988.

Mantel, Samuel J., Jr., and Jack R. Meredith. *Project Management: A Managerial Approach*. New York: John Wiley & Sons, 1989.

Posner, Barry A., and W. Alan Randolph. *Effective Project Planning & Management: Getting the Job Done*. Englewood Cliffs, N.J.: Prentice Hall, 1988.

Pournelle, Jerry, "Do Computers Save Time?" *Byte Magazine*, Vol. 16, No. 17, July 1991.

Thomsett, Michael C., *The Little Black Book of Project Management*. New York: AMACOM, 1990.

Winston, Stephanie. *The Organized Executive*. New York: Warner Books, 1983.

Worksheet for Listing Current and Planned Projects

Completed by _____

Date _____

Projects in Progress

PROJECT NAME	PROJECT PLAN YES OR NO?	SIZE OF PROJECT S/M/L	PROJECT MANAGER	DATE STARTED	TARGET COMPLETE DATE

Projects Planned

Project Selection Worksheet

Completed by _____

Date _____

PROJECT	NEED	TARGET DATE	ROUGH BUDGET	FEASIBILITY SCALE 1-10	RISK H/M/L	PRIORITY

Prioritized Project List

Completed by_____

Date _____

PROJECTS IN ORDER OF PRIORITY	NEED	TARGET DATE	ROUGH BUDGET	FEASIBILITY SCALE 1-10	RISK H/M/L	CURRENT STATUS

Goal Setting Worksheet

Your Name_____ Date _____

Project Name _____

Initial Goal Statement _____

	Names	Titles
Who should be involved in goal setting?		
Who needs to approve the goals?		
Who should be responsible for achieving the goals?		

Are their any hidden agendas to consider?	
How will attainment of the goals be measured?	
When should the project start and finish for maximum success?	Start: Finish:
Are the goals feasible?	
What are the constraints on the goals?	Time _____ Budget _____ Resources _____

Worksheet for Determining Skills Required for Project Tasks

Project _____ Date _____

Completed By _____ _____

TASK	SKILLS REQUIRED	POSSIBILITIES

Skills Inventory

Group _____ Date _____

Completed By _____

NAME	EDUCATION	PRIMARY SKILLS	RATING	SECONDARY SKILLS	RATING

Equipment and Supply Worksheet

Project _____ Date _____

Completed By _____

REQUIRED	RESPONSIBLE PERSON OR VENDOR	HOW MUCH IS NEEDED?	WHEN IS IT NEEDED?	CHECK IF AVAILABLE
MATERIALS:				☐ ☐ ☐ ☐ ☐ ☐
EQUIPMENT:				☐ ☐ ☐ ☐ ☐
SUPPLIES:				☐ ☐ ☐ ☐ ☐
SPECIAL SERVICES:				☐ ☐ ☐
OTHER:				☐ ☐ ☐ ☐ ☐ ☐

Scheduling Assumptions Worksheet

Project Name _____ Date _____

1. **Are all the resources currently available for this project?**

   If no, list the resources required that are not available:

   People
   _____

   _____

   Equipment
   _____

   _____

   ☐ YES

   ☐ NO

2. **Is there a due date when the project absolutely must be complete?**

   If yes, enter date:
   _____

   Reason:
   _____

   ☐ YES

   ☐ NO

3. **Will overtime be allowed?**

   If yes, how much?
   _____

   ☐ YES

   ☐ NO

4. **Are there any holidays or other breaks during this project?**

   If yes, list dates:
   _____

   ☐ YES

   ☐ NO

5. **Have additional resources and people been approved for this project?**

   ☐ YES

   ☐ NO

6. **Have the work schedules and availabilities of all resources been documented?**

   ☐ YES

   ☐ NO

   Notes: _____

   _____

Master Schedule Worksheet

Project Name_____ Date_____

Scheduled Start_____ Scheduled Finish_____

Prepared by_____ Date_____

Approved by_____ Date_____

TASK	RESPONSIBLE PEOPLE	START DATE	FINISH DATE	ACTUAL START	ACTUAL FINISH

* Critical path tasks are marked with an asterisk.

Critical Path Worksheet

Project Name_____ Date_____

TASK	DURATION	EARLIEST START	EARLIEST FINISH	LATEST START	LATEST START	TOTAL FLOAT

All tasks with zero float are on the critical path.

Ideal Schedule Worksheet

Project Name_____

Scheduled Start _____ Calculated Finish _____

TASK	RESPONSIBLE PEOPLE	DURATION	EARLIEST START	EARLIEST FINISH	LATEST START	LATEST FINISH

Budgeting Assumptions Worksheet

Project _____ Date _____

Completed By _____

1. What has priority—schedule or cost control?   ☐ Schedule

                                                    ☐ Cost Control

2. Is there a fixed overhead rate for this project?   ☐ Yes

                                                    Amount _____

                                                    ☐ No

3. Is there another similar project that can be used for budgeting comparisons?

                                                    ☐ Yes

                                                    Name _____

                                                    ☐ No

4. Has a general budget amount been allocated to the project?

When ?_____ By Whom? _____

How Much? _____ When is the money available? _____

Is it adequate to meet current project goals?   ☐ Yes

                                                    ☐ No

5. What financial and economic assumptions are being made that affect the budget?

_____

_____

_____

_____

_____

_____

Budgeting Worksheet

Project _____ Date _____

Completed By _____

TASK	DURATION	STAFF OR VENDOR REQUIRED	SPECIAL EQUIPMENT & SUPPLIES	ESTIMATES

Sample Budget Form

Project _____

Date _____   Completed By _____

| TASK NUMBER | RESPONSIBLE PERSON OR VENDOR | DATES | | ESTIMATED COSTS | | | | ACTUAL |
		START	END	EQUIPMENT	MATERIALS	LABOR	TOTAL	

Worksheet Identifying Management Approaches for Team Members				
WHO	RELATIONSHIP WITH YOU	REASONS TO COOPERATE	REASONS TO RESIST	MANAGEMENT STRATEGY

Requirements Checklist for Project Management Software

Scheduling Programs

- ☐ Schedules
- ☐ Gantt Charts
- ☐ Presentation Graphics

Single-Project Programs

- ☐ Network Diagrams
- ☐ Simple Resource Tracking
- ☐ Actual versus Planned Reports

Corporate-Level Programs

- ☐ Tracks Multiple Projects
- ☐ Sub-Project Tracking
- ☐ Variance Reports
- ☐ More than 200 Tasks per Project
- ☐ More than 50 Resources per Project
- ☐ Resource Leveling
- ☐ Multiple Calendars
- ☐ Reporting by Milestone
- ☐ Reporting by Resource

Mega-Project Programs

- ☐ Integration with Corporate Mainframe Programs
- ☐ Over 2,000 Tasks to Be Coordinated
- ☐ Government Requirements for a Specific Program or Report
- ☐ Advanced Cost and Resource Accounting

If you check boxes at more than one level, choose a product in the highest category checked.

Project Management Software Selection Worksheet

Product Name _____ Date _____

Price: List Price $_____ Street Price $_____ Dealer Name _____

Category	Rating
Features	1 ———————————— 10
Ease of Use	1 ———————————— 10
Consistency of the Interface	1 ———————————— 10
Flexibility	1 ———————————— 10
Compatibility	1 ———————————— 10
Documentation	1 ———————————— 10
Reputation of the Manufacturer	1 ———————————— 10
Experience of Others with the Product	1 ———————————— 10
Technical Support	1 ———————————— 10
Training Availability	1 ———————————— 10
Distributor Knowledge (if applicable)	1 ———————————— 10
Overall Rating	1 ———————————— 10

Comments:

_____
_____
_____
_____
_____
_____

INDEX

X

Z